A Lynching at
Port Jervis

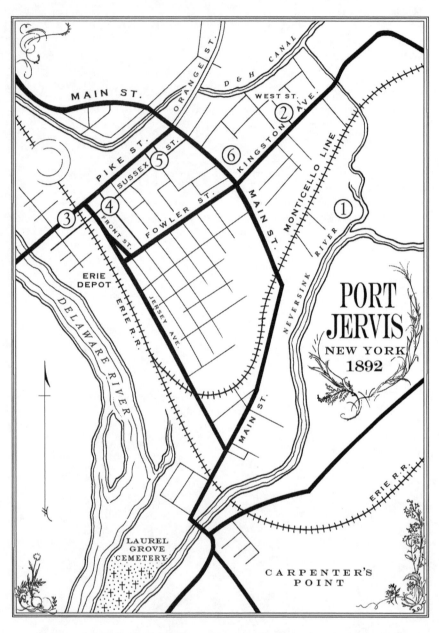

1. *Lena McMahon allegedly assaulted* 2. *McMahon home, 3 West St.*
3. *Delaware House* 4. *Village lockup, Ball and Sussex* 5. *Orange Square*
6. *Robert Lewis was lynched here.*

A Lynching at

Port Jervis

RACE AND RECKONING
IN THE GILDED AGE

———◆◇◆———

Philip Dray

Farrar, Straus and Giroux
New York

Farrar, Straus and Giroux
120 Broadway, New York 10271

Illustration credits can be found on pages 259–260.

Library of Congress Cataloging-in-Publication Data
Names: Dray, Philip, author.
Title: A lynching at Port Jervis : race and reckoning in the Gilded Age / Philip Dray.
Description: First edition. | New York : Farrar, Straus and Giroux, [2022] |
    Includes bibliographical references.
Identifiers: LCCN 2021059700 | ISBN 9780374194413 (hardcover)
Subjects: LCSH: Lynching—New York (State)—Port Jervis—History—19th century. |
    African Americans—New York (State)—Port Jervis—History—19th century. |
    Racism—New York (State)—History—19th century. | Port Jervis (N. Y.)—
    Race relations—History—19th century.
Classification: LCC HV6462.N7 D73 2022 | DDC 364.1/34—dc23/eng/20220114
LC record available at https://lccn.loc.gov/2021059700

Designed by Gretchen Achilles

Our books may be purchased in bulk for promotional, educational,
or business use. Please contact your local bookseller or the Macmillan Corporate
and Premium Sales Department at 1-800-221-7945, extension 5442, or by email at
MacmillanSpecialMarkets@macmillan.com.

www.fsgbooks.com
www.twitter.com/fsgbooks • www.facebook.com/fsgbooks

1   3   5   7   9   10   8   6   4   2

Nations reel and stagger on their way; they make hideous mistakes; they commit frightful wrongs; they do great and beautiful things. And shall we not best guide humanity by telling the truth about all this, so far as the truth is ascertainable?

—W.E.B. Du Bois, *Black Reconstruction in America*, 1935

CONTENTS

A Lynching at
Port Jervis

INTRODUCTION

————◦◦◦◦———

One morning in the spring of 1985, I drove along a country road in Alabama to the Tuskegee Institute, one of America's oldest and most venerated Black colleges. I was researching a book about the 1964 murder of the civil rights workers James Chaney, Andrew Goodman, and Mickey Schwerner in Mississippi and had heard there was a folder on the case in a collection at Tuskegee, then known as "the lynching archives." When a librarian led me to the room where the materials were kept, I was surprised to see not a solitary cabinet, as I'd expected, but dozens of containers and cardboard boxes, sixty-three in number. She explained these held a century's worth of newspaper clippings and other published accounts of the many thousands of lynchings in the United States, most of African Americans.

This substantial repository, overseen by the pioneering Black sociologist Monroe Nathan Work in the years 1912–1935 and maintained for decades by students and staff, had defied lynching's code of impunity and silence. It had done this by refusing to allow the stories of what the crusading Black journalist Ida B. Wells called "America's national crime" to be forgotten and die along with its victims. Notably, I was told this archive held only the known cases, those recorded by the press or civil rights groups, but that an immeasurable number still remained unknown or unsubstantiated.

It was my encounter with the Tuskegee collection and its unavoidable truth—that lynching was not a series of random, aberrational incidents but an institutionalized form of white terror—that led me to write the book *At the Hands of Persons Unknown: The Lynching of Black America*, which was published in 2002.

The chronological accounts in the Tuskegee collection, although drawn from all over the country, chiefly concerned the Southern states, where historically most lynchings took place. But incidents of racialized mob violence occurred in the North as well. There, given their infrequency, and because they tended to reveal the hypocrisy of the region's vaunted superiority as a place of assured civic authority and respect for the rule of law, they often attracted greater notoriety.

Several years ago, I was drawn to examine one such case. It occurred in Port Jervis, New York, on June 2, 1892, and claimed the life of a young Black man named Robert Lewis. It was infamous at once, for it was seen as a portent that lynching, then surging uncontrollably below the Mason-Dixon Line, was about to extend its tendrils northward. There had been a sharp rise in the reported number of Black people killed in this manner in recent years—74 in 1885; 94 in 1889; 113 in 1891. The year 1892 would see the greatest number, 161, almost one every other day. The nation's newspapers were rarely without news of a lynching somewhere, a crime that emerging Black activists described as driven by the impulse to thwart African Americans' social and economic advance toward equality and full citizenship, by the presumption that Black people were inherently criminal, and by white men's insecurity about Black male sexuality and threats to male hierarchy generally.

What perplexed white Port Jervians and other New Yorkers was why a lynching had occurred in a village just northwest of New York City with a modest African American population of roughly two hundred men, women, and children, or 2 percent of its approximately nine thousand residents. Although the town was hardly free from the common social and economic inequities of the era, and its normalized racism, it had no flagrant history of racist mob violence.

The man put to death by the Port Jervis mob, Robert Lewis, was a twenty-eight-year-old teamster, or bus driver, for the town's leading hotel, the Delaware House, who had allegedly beaten and sexually assaulted Lena McMahon, a young white woman. Lewis, before being killed, was reputed to have confessed to the crime but had also named McMahon's white boyfriend as an accomplice.

Sensational news stories of violent crime in the streets of large cities like Boston, Philadelphia, and Chicago might have been consumed by readers and as quickly forgotten. Not so with the troubling bulletin of a lynching at Port Jervis. Because such incidents reported then occurred almost exclusively in the South, the fact that a lynching had taken place in a community only sixty-five miles and a two-hour train ride from Manhattan, and had been witnessed by two thousand people, brought immediate national condemnation. Situated at the confluence of the Delaware and Neversink Rivers, where the states of New York, New Jersey, and Pennsylvania meet, Port Jervis was a largely peaceful, orderly burg, surrounded by water and mountains, attractive to city folk who came in summer to fish for trout, canoe in the scenic Delaware, or enjoy a breeze on the verandas of the local boardinghouses.

(Collection of the Minisink Valley Historical Society)

In recent years, due to the efforts of a small group of current and former residents, and the influence of the Black Lives Matter movement, there has been new interest in the lynching of Robert Lewis at Port Jervis, arguably the most troubling incident in the city's past. But decades of aversion to the subject have left many residents, Black and white, substantially unfamiliar with it. This collective lack of remembering (or remembrance) has been determined and willful, a result of the town's profound shame over the lynching itself, as well as the ensuing humiliation when, after vowing to punish those responsible, the community failed to do so. Lingering resentment at being singled out for censure and the lack of overt efforts by whites to mend relations with fellow Black citizens have been exacerbated by a far more slow-motion calamity—the loss by the middle of the twentieth century of Port Jervis's prominence as a Northeast rail, industrial, and commercial hub.

The yellowing pages in the Tuskegee archive derive their authority from the irony that the very aims of lynching—the denial of due process, the oblivion of the act itself, and the lasting anonymity of participants—were undone by the reality that such crimes made for scandalous newspaper copy. A white woman violated, a Black man accused, a gallant posse in pursuit, the "people's" righteous vengeance attained—such elements fed multiple days of headlined coverage wherever lynching occurred, from initial alarm and outcry to the ultimate barbaric spectacle.

White-reported and -published newspapers are often the chief historical sources of these incidents. Contemporary Black newspapers, such as the *New York Age*, *Washington Bee*, and *Richmond Planet*, never failed to register their severe condemnation of lynching but usually offered little in the way of locally sourced information. The killing of Robert Lewis at Port Jervis occurred a generation prior to the development of thorough methods of inquiry by anti-lynching crusaders or organizations such as the National Association for the Advancement of Colored People (NAACP); as a result, there are no known accounts of what occurred at Port Jervis from the vantage point of the local Black community, except what can be discerned from public actions. A public coroner's inquest was held, involving numerous witnesses, but a copy of the original transcript, if one ever existed, has vanished. It is helpful that it was the practice of contemporary reporters to copy down such legal proceedings verbatim, although different published versions can vary slightly in tone and nuance.

This, then, will be the story the book attempts to tell—an alleged crime, a lynching, a misbegotten attempt at an official inquiry, a past unresolved. What factors prompted such a spasm of racial violence in a relatively prosperous, industrious small New York town? What meaning did the country assign to it? And what did the incident portend?

The commercial district of Port Jervis today retains its low-rise, storefront appearance, with eaves and cornices out of the Victorian era. A twenty-minute walk will take one by many of the places involved in the Robert Lewis lynching, from the home of Lena McMahon to the banks of the nearby Neversink, where she was allegedly attacked; to the now-abandoned Delaware & Hudson Canal, along which Lewis was pursued and captured; and to the lynching site on East Main Street, where merchants, railway workers, lawyers, doctors, hoteliers, and factory workers, most of whom knew one another, and many of whom knew Robert Lewis, saw him repeatedly beaten and then hoisted by a rope until he was dead. On a quiet summer morning, when no cars are about, it can seem that a portal to the past might open for a moment and beckon one through.

I believe it is necessary that we take that step and revisit this place and time, to consider the event's not insignificant legacy and weigh how it reflected, and in turn influenced, late nineteenth-century American ideas about race, gender, and justice. Some details of the story remain elusive; nonetheless, my aim is to help place it, even with its lingering mysteries, in our communal history.

————·•·————

The books on civil rights history I have written since the 1980s have been to a great extent guided by a confidence in the forward advance of racial progress, a faith never unanimous among citizens of the United States but for many years broadly assumed. While no one seriously believed Barack Obama's presidency would usher in a post-racial nation, there was a sense that the successes of the modern civil rights movement and the laws and policies it inspired, though not comprehensive and not attained without suffering and immense struggle, had at least moved the country to a place of enlarged racial understanding and opportunity.

Today, instead of guarded optimism, there is a weary pessimism that, as the Port Jervis lynching signaled in *its* time, the assault on and devaluing of the lives of Black Americans are neither a regional nor a temporary feature but a national crisis and, for the foreseeable future, a permanent one. Much like at the end of Reconstruction in the 1870s, when post–Civil War idealism was supplanted by Southern whites' bare-knuckle tactics of exclusion and intimidation, so now do we find ourselves confronting the abandonment of hard-won gains from the New Deal, the civil rights and environmental movements, and other progressive causes. Voting rights, gained courthouse to courthouse by Black Southerners and civil rights workers, have been gutted by the Supreme Court, and conservative forces continue to seek creative new ways to curtail and impede them, targeting Black people and other minorities, as one North Carolina judicial opinion noted, "with surgical precision." Each fortnight brings a new report of the killing of a Black person by police. "Jim Crow," a term once seemingly relegated to the nation's past, has found new purpose in expressing the harsh conditions of post-prison life for those formerly incarcerated, as well as large-scale efforts by states to make voting inaccessible to Blacks and other minority citizens, while seizing ever-greater control of whose votes are counted. These elements of racism and white supremacy that refuse to die have for decades contributed to the perversion of our politics. It is essential they be challenged and addressed in the name of moral decency, and to preserve the future of American democracy.

Nor can we look away from the connection between the nation's lynching legacy and the recent resurgence of armed vigilantism in America. The crowds of whites who once amassed outside Southern courthouses demanding that sheriffs relinquish Black prisoners, or who forced their way inside to abduct them, have as their twenty-first-century counterparts the open-carry white militiamen, the Oath Keepers, Three Percenters, and Proud Boys, who invade statehouses and the Capitol in Washington, plot the kidnapping of elected officials, and seek to intimidate voters, legislators, and peaceful protesters. This "mobocratic spirit," a phrase Abraham Lincoln used as early as 1838 to describe vigilantism's corrosive effect on America, frightfully insinuates that mob violence is a legitimate means of effecting political change.

These issues remain as deserving of our concern as they did 130 years ago, when America turned its gaze to Port Jervis.

Nothing illustrates the need to revisit this unfortunate history more than the opening in 2018 of the National Memorial for Peace and Justice in Montgomery, Alabama, which honors the memory of more than four thousand African Americans killed by lynch mobs between 1877 and 1950. Lynching has for too long been associated exclusively with the South, of which Montgomery is a historic capital, and with images of Ku Klux Klan night riders and angry white crowds gathered outside rural courthouses. While the Southern lynching epidemic did not replicate itself fully in the North, as some feared, Port Jervis proved an augury of early twentieth-century white-on-Black terroristic violence in places as diverse as New York City, rural Pennsylvania, Chicago, southern Illinois, and Duluth, Minnesota. And it is impossible not to see lynching's vestiges in the biases of our own times: racial profiling and police brutality, the continuing presumption of Black criminality, and a willingness to subject Black people to summary justice, as well as prejudice in the courts and in the nation's penal system, including the use of the death penalty.

Today parts of the country are engaged in an effort to redefine the nature of policing, with the particular goal of stopping the far-too-numerous instances of deadly force used against African Americans by officers of the law as well as vigilantes. We say the names of George Floyd, Breonna Taylor, Eric Garner, Tamir Rice, Sandra Bland, Ahmaud Arbery, Trayvon Martin, Michael Brown, Philando Castile, and many others because it is long past time white America educated itself about the methods and presumptions responsible for their deaths. We must also acknowledge the traumatic and terroristic toll such murders and their endless online video repetition have on Black citizens. Accordingly, this book will, as it narrates the story of a great injustice and provides historical context, seek to be at all times respectful in quoting words of intolerance or depicting scenes of graphic violence.

On June 10, 2020, in the immediate aftermath of the police killing of George Floyd, a peaceful, locally organized Black Lives Matter march took place in Port Jervis, attended by hundreds of Black and white residents and protected by local police. At the same event, members of a committee called the Friends of Robert Lewis spoke with marchers about the effort to establish in Port Jervis a memorial plaque and signage bearing details about the 1892 Robert Lewis lynching, as one step in an ongoing commemorative and educational effort.

"There is no hero in this story," Ralph Drake, the group's white founder, who grew up in Port Jervis, observed of the long-ago tragedy. "The town must become the hero, in confronting its legacy."

The Black Lives Matter march through the streets of Port Jervis, the work of the Friends of Robert Lewis group, and the Montgomery memorial itself, like the Tuskegee archives, remind us that it is a national reckoning that is due, and that the historic confidence of any section of the United States in some immunity to racial injustice remains, as it was in Robert Lewis's time, a false faith indeed.

ONE

JUNE 2, 1892

———————◦◦◦◦———————

Beneath a chestnut tree along the banks of the Neversink River, the two lovers awoke to the familiar cry of train 97 as it came down the valley from Otisville and crossed the trestle, where it entered Port Jervis. It was the morning of June 2, 1892, so early the village behind them had barely stirred, yet the sun was already warm—a portent of summer.

Philip Foley and Lena McMahon had chosen this remote spot because they were avoiding the world just now, particularly Lena's parents. Lena, twenty-two, had become smitten the previous fall with the dapper Foley, a decade her senior, who was new to Port Jervis and sold insurance for a New York firm. He was a highly presentable man, undeniably handsome, a "ready talker" who dressed well and kept his mustache neatly groomed. Initially, Lena's parents had welcomed him as a likely suitor for their daughter, a striving young man of business who shared their Irish American heritage. But all that had changed in January after he was arrested for trying to duck out on a hotel bill and other unflattering accounts of his behavior came to light.

The McMahons, John and Theresa, lived in a modest house on the north side of town. John was a glassblower, a skilled job in what was a prominent local industry. The family also maintained a confectionery, where Theresa had once made fudge, licorice, and other treats; although by 1892 it appears to have been operated as a shop. Lena had recently assumed its management and, as a local paper noted, added several flavors of ice cream to the menu. Raven-haired with large brown eyes, Lena was taller than other young women her age, had an imposing presence, and was well-spoken and considered bright. "Her mental traits are in keeping with her personal appearance," one local newspaper would relate, for "she is a girl of considerable beauty [who] received an excellent education in the public schools of Port Jervis." Although she still lived with her parents, she handled her own and the shop's finances and traveled independently—mainly to Middletown, a larger city twenty miles

MISS LENA McMAHON.

away, or to Goshen, the county seat, but also occasionally to Boston or New York.

There was a sense of fragility and secretiveness about Lena, however, possibly a consequence of her having lived her first five years in a New York orphanage. She was known to sometimes lose track of her surroundings and even claim a loss of her short-term memory. Walking home along Fowler Street from Sunday school in May 1878, she lost her footing and tumbled into a creek. Discovered unconscious in the shallow water a few minutes later, she was carried to the home of David Swinton on Barcelow Street, whose family co-owned a hardware emporium. The Swintons revived her, exchanged her wet, muddy clothes for dry ones, then sent her home in a wagon. Lena told her anxious parents she did not know exactly what had happened; one moment she was walking along looking in a book she had with her, and then she recalled nothing except waking up in another family's house. As she had no head wound, it appeared she had lost consciousness before entering the water. "It is thought she may have had a fit," the *Gazette* reported. As a result of such episodes, the McMahons tended to be overprotective of her health and well-being, and, as she grew up and came to be regarded as one of the more attractive and popular local young women, of her reputation.

Lena had mixed thoughts about playing it safe, it would appear. She seemed wary of the too-comfortable fate of becoming just another Port Jervis wife, a "Goddess of the Household" with a recipe box and an herb garden. Her waking dreams, when she indulged them, tended to carry her well beyond the surrounding hills.

That greater world announced itself with frequent intrusions—the piercing blasts of train whistles and the churning of steam locomotives near and far—for Port Jervis was a busy railroad town. Residents knew intimately the comings and goings of the day's numerous trains—the Three, the Milk, the Extra 10, the 620 Westbound—and often each train's assigned conductor and engineer. Children who grew up in the village were accustomed to seeing passengers from New York and other cities disembark from the trains, to watching maneuvered along the platforms the towering carts of luggage and the trunks of "the summer people" who came each May to the resorts and boardinghouses. Traveling salesmen passed through town— "drummers," as they were known—with their cases that opened into displays of costume jewelry or household goods, as did a continual stream of touring vaudevillians, violin prodigies, and revivalists. There appeared also the pool hustlers, card sharps, and con men. Last night's new acquaintance might, by sunup, be a hundred miles away, for the railroad was as much about the discreet getaway as the grand arrival.

Monday, May 30, had been Decoration Day, a military holiday of considerable importance in Port Jervis, home to about 125 Civil War veterans, including Lena's father. Scores of veterans from the surrounding area were also in attendance. It had been a somber occasion of mourning and patriotic speeches, beginning at the village's own forty-five-foot-tall memorial to the war in Orange Square and continuing with a march to several local cemeteries to honor the Union soldiers who had died during or since the war. But it was also a day of reunion, renewed comradeship, fraternal toasting, and staggering quantities of beer. The following morning found the municipal benches occupied by dozens of spent celebrants, fast asleep.

That same Tuesday morning, Foley had come calling for Lena at her home on West Street, only to be met by a decidedly inhospitable Theresa McMahon. She'd earlier tried unsuccessfully to have him arrested for vagrancy, a charge particularly insulting in Port Jervis, where it was commonly leveled at "depot loafers," tramps, and Black men of no apparent means. Now she refused to let Lena come downstairs to see him and ordered Foley to leave at once. "Well, I'll get square with you yet," he muttered while walking away. The mother then turned on Lena, whose infatuation with the older man she could no longer abide. Mother and daughter argued about the matter until Theresa's frustration erupted, and she struck Lena hard enough in the face to draw blood. Stunned and humiliated, the young woman quickly threw some items into a bag and fled the house, vowing never to return.

———•—•———

Port Jervis was an ideal setting for glass manufacturing given its proximity to the Pennsylvania anthracite fields; coal, transported by canal to the village, provided the fuel for the fires needed to anneal and mold glass's raw materials into finished products. The opening of a new glass factory on the northeast side of town, owned and managed by William Pountney and Charles Brox, had drawn John and Theresa Reddy McMahon there from Boston in the late 1860s, along with two of Theresa's relations, Thomas and Edward Reddy. Thomas, aged nineteen in 1870, was likely Theresa's younger brother; Edward, ten, is listed in both 1870 and 1880 census records as Theresa's nephew, although a later news article from 1886 refers to him as her son. If the latter is true, she would have given birth to him in 1861, when she was only sixteen, which may account for the alternative identification the family twice provided to the census taker. In a small, everybody-knows-your-business place like Port Jervis, where, the joke went, it was harder keeping your name out of the paper than getting it in, she may have thought it prudent to safeguard their true relationship. The McMahons in 1870 resided in a house near the canal with several other men employed at Pountney-Brox. By 1880,

Thomas had departed and Eddie, then nineteen, and ten-year-old Lena, who had been adopted in 1874, were, along with their parents, its sole occupants.

The factory thrived. Employing seventy to one hundred skilled workmen and boys at forty to fifty cents an hour and three dollars a week, respectively, the plant filled dozens of freight cars per month with tableware, lamps, and other glass products, which were shipped all over the country. So good was business that in 1873, Charles Brox left to start another glass manufacturing facility, known as Brox-Buckley, on the opposite end of town closer to the railroad.

The McMahons, like many other families of men employed at Pountney, were part of the village's residential expansion, as workers' homes filled in the former cornfields north of Main Street. By the mid-1880s, Edward, now a young man, had returned to Boston to work as a horse car conductor, and John, Theresa, and Lena moved to an attractive house at 3 West Street, just off Kingston Avenue.

Friends in the neighborhood were aware the couple had their hands full with the headstrong Lena. Theresa McMahon later told a reporter that one source of tension was Lena's conviction that she might be reunited someday with her birth father, a man named Gallagher whom she had never met but had reason to believe was well-to-do. Lena's "great expectations," and perhaps some vestigial recollections of her early life in Manhattan, had given her a sense of destiny. Managing the shop and selling penny candy and ice cream to neighborhood children put cash in Lena's pocket and granted her some financial independence, but she still lived with her parents and, at twenty-two years old, could not be blamed for dreaming of something different.

A much-talked-about 1891 event involving a fellow Port Jervian would certainly have encouraged her. Sarah Cassidy had emigrated from Ireland in the 1860s, thinking to rejoin her older brother Robert, who had come to America a decade before. Not finding him, she settled in Port Jervis, where she found work as a servant. In 1871, at a friend's suggestion, she placed an ad requesting information about him in the *Boston Pilot*, a Catholic newspaper read by many Irish Americans. A few months later a letter arrived from Robert, now residing in Portland, Oregon, where he said he had done well and acquired property. A correspondence ensued, but after two years it mysteriously ceased and by 1891, twenty years later, Sarah assumed her brother had died. Then, one day, a letter came from a West Coast lawyer bearing the stunning news that Robert had passed away only recently, and not before designating his sister his sole heir. Accompanied by the esteemed Port Jervis attorney William Crane, who served as her legal adviser in the matter, she traveled to Oregon to claim her fortune.

Growing up, Lena appears to have had a typical small-town American childhood at a time when small towns were viewed sentimentally, as thriving, ideal communities, patriotic, devout, and neighborly. She earned high marks and maintained an exemplary attendance record at the Mountain House School, which was located in a converted hotel on the near west side of town. John and Theresa, according to a local news item, were "good people," and Lena "was greatly loved by her parents and no wish of hers, that was within the limit of their means, remained ungratified."

The town's several newspapers served as an all-knowing grapevine and social bulletin board, reporting children's school attendance records and the salaries of policemen (fifty dollars a month), and providing a daily recitation of gossipy local news, such as "Mabel Jones left yesterday on Train Number Two for Paterson," and "a colored boy named Landis hooked a 12" trout at Shohola," and even "Mr. R. Puff's rash is much improved." The town knew what color you planned to paint your house and when your cat had its kittens. Lena's name appears often in connection with school activities; musically inclined, she appeared in several class recitals, including one in which she sang an a cappella version of the children's hymn "How Lovely Are the Flowers."

State and national political news, as well as brief reports from distant lands, were often condensed in a single column. More popular items included reports of remarkable individual feats of endurance—shooting five hundred clay pigeons without a miss, spending forty-eight hours on roller skates, walking to Montreal—as well as fascinating yet macabre incidents, like a sleepwalker who "strolled" out of a hotel window or an exhumed corpse found to have hair grown down to its feet. Life's comical mishaps made for diverting filler: a freight car collapsing under the weight of a circus elephant; wedding guests splashed with mud from a passing wagon.

More seriously, the past, as viewed through Port Jervis headlines, begins to look like a treacherous place. Young women died in childbirth because of the lack of sterilized medical instruments; people suffered from respiratory ailments from the indoor burning of coal; men lost fingers or legs or were crushed to death in the train yards. On June 2, the morning Lena and Foley woke together beside the Neversink, Port Jervis readers learned that a Callicoon boy had killed his sister while cleaning a shotgun and that Charles P. Weeks, commodore of the Brooklyn Canoe Club, who'd been leading a group of rowing enthusiasts on a ninety-mile journey down the Delaware to Port Jervis, had washed up drowned at his destination.

———•◦•———

Philip Foley was introduced to the McMahon family in the fall of 1891 by A. M. Rich, one of his fellow salesmen with the Guaranty Alliance Insurance Company of New York. The two men, and Rich's wife, were staying at the Delaware House, the venerable Port Jervis hotel whose columned portico fronted on the railroad tracks at Pike Street and where rooms cost two dollars a day. Foley was new to the area but, like the firm that had sent him, recognized the town's potential. It had a decidedly up-and-coming feel. The town's architectural pride, the elegant Erie Depot on Jersey Avenue, had recently opened, an aesthetic counterpoint to the majestic St. Mary's Church, whose towers had risen a dozen years before, as well as the commodious Farnum Building, offering prime office and ground-floor shop space on Pike Street. Surely, in keeping with such evident progress, residents might allow a young gentleman from the city to sell them on the advantages of life insurance.

(Collection of the Minisink Valley Historical Society)

How Mr. Rich came to be on friendly terms with the McMahons is unclear, although it's possible the conduit was George Lea, owner of the Delaware House. Raised in England, Lea had appeared in the village shortly after the Civil War, opened a successful pharmacy, eventually bought and operated two hotels as well as the opera house, and accrued a small fortune organizing popular day trips by rail to New York City and Coney Island (well before the Erie Railroad thought to do so). "Cast ashore on a desert island with a single companion, he would make money swapping jackknives," offered a local paper in appraisal of his business acumen.

Phil Foley, a bachelor only recently arrived in Port Jervis, may have been asked to accompany the Riches on their visit to the McMahons expressly to meet their eligible daughter. Lena was intrigued at once; he was urbane, well-spoken, and as handsome as a leading man in a play. Foley, for his part, would have found appealing those attributes for which Lena was known: that she was a modern girl, frank in her manner, and stylishly attractive. "Miss McMahon took a violent fancy to him," the *Gazette* said of the encounter, "and they were constantly together." Her parents approved, and once he and Lena began seeing each other in October, he was welcome at the house.

According to the author Bruce Jay Friedman, who in 1955 went to Port Jervis on a magazine assignment to interview residents with living memories of the Robert Lewis lynching (one of the few outsiders to do so in the twentieth century), Foley was

> a trim, foppishly handsome little man, whose pockets were alternately bone dry and flushed with money [who] soon became known as a rascally lady-killer . . . [He] had just about exhausted the supply of available girls when his eyes alighted one day on a tall, well-formed, black-haired miss named Lena McMahon. He got himself introduced by a friend as a high-type man about town and displayed to Lena his big-city mannerisms that had been so effective in weakening various other Port Jervis girls.

This depiction, though based on firsthand recollections, seems unduly caricatured, as it slights Lena's own agency in the matter and suggests the unlikely possibility that Foley, conspicuously new to town, could have already courted and abandoned numerous young ladies without such boorishness coming to the attention of the community.

P. J. FOLEY.

Foley's real troubles began just after the Christmas holidays of 1891, when George Lea accused him of submitting a worthless payment order from the insurance company for part of his rent and had him arrested. But Foley apparently managed to explain the mix-up satisfactorily to his new girlfriend and her family. John McMahon paid his bond, and Lena gave him money to hire a lawyer. He was judged guilty, however, and sentenced to four months in the county lockup at Goshen. Lena traveled there at least once to visit him.

Such a minor financial irregularity might have been forgiven, but Lea, a man not to be trifled with, and likely upset that he could be thought to have vouched for Foley to the McMahons, hastened to impart other disturbing news: Lena's young man had been accused of trying to force the door of a chambermaid's bedroom, had nicked liquor from the hotel bar, and had even departed for jail wearing cuff links another guest had reported missing. It also seemed Foley gambled and, as a newspaper reported, "manifested a strange preference for the society of colored people." His colleague A. M. Rich was unable to put in a good word for him, because he, too, had been denounced as a fraud by Lea and sent packing from the hotel.

Lea's inclination to warn the McMahons may have sprung from a protective impulse toward Lena, for he was a prominent donor and guardian to the children of the orphanage at St. Mary's, the church where the McMahons worshipped and where Lena, who had been adopted from a Catholic orphanage in New York City, attended Sunday school. It would have been second nature for him to show a godfatherly interest in her well-being.

Foley and Rich were not the only individuals cast out that season from the Delaware House. Also dismissed was Robert Lewis, a lightskinned Black man who had worked as a teamster, or bus driver, for the hotel. Lea had fired Lewis for "impudence," likely a failure to defer sufficiently to the hotel's white guests, staff, or possibly Lea himself. Although technically Lewis was no longer employed there, he'd become such a familiar figure in his highly visible role—meeting guests as they detrained at the Erie station, hoisting their luggage into the back of a wagon, and driving them safely across the tracks to the hotel—Port Jervis had trouble thinking of him otherwise.

Born in 1863 in Sussex County, New Jersey, Lewis was the stepson of Henry Jackson, a Black Civil War veteran widely known as "Happy Hank" for his inexhaustible good cheer. Hank, who alternately introduced himself as "Exuberant Henry," was a local celebrity, mentioned frequently in press accounts of public events of the 1870s

(Collection of the Minisink Valley Historical Society)

and 1880s, whether a masquerade ball or a home game of the Red Stockings, the local Black baseball squad. Once, a newspaper sought out his preferences in an upcoming election. An 1885 feature in the *Gazette*, AT THE CAKE WALK, depicts easygoing relations between the races that Hank himself seemed by his very presence to further:

> Our colored population had a jolly time Thursday evening at the Opera House. Every man was dressed in his best and every woman had on her best holiday attire. The music seemed to imbue new life into the limbs of the dancers and it is safe to say no such dancing was ever witnessed in the Opera House since its dedication. "Happy Hank" was late in arriving and seemed hurt he was not asked to be one of the judges. But everything passed off quietly and no trouble ensued, although one of the managers remarked that "the white trash" were drinking too much beer. There were 200 persons present and the races were equally divided.

Hank was one of about a hundred Black men from Orange County to serve in the Civil War, although they were excluded from joining the county's namesake regiment, the Orange Blossoms, and forced to enlist in other New York units or those from Massachusetts or Rhode Island. When he died of consumption in July 1891 at age forty-seven, however, Hank was interred with full military honors in a veterans' section at Laurel Grove, the town's scenic memorial park, located on a peninsula between the Delaware and Neversink Rivers. It's tempting to speculate that had he been alive when his stepson Robert Lewis got into the worst kind of trouble, things might have turned out differently.

At age twenty-eight, Robert was still close with his mother, and although he had lived and worked for several years in Port Jervis, he often visited Paterson, New Jersey, where she had gone to live. When in Port Jervis, his maternal grandmother and her husband, Henry Sampson, who worked at a grocery on Front Street, reputedly "kept an eye on him." An apparent relation, Frank Sampson, known as "African Sampson," was the celebrated leader of a "Negro fire brigade."

"BOB" LEWIS.

That Robert Lewis held the job he did at the Delaware House suggests he impressed Lea as both reliable and personable. Assisting arriving guests at the depot, he was the first representative of the hotel one would encounter; in addition to seeing their luggage safely transferred to his wagon, he might respond to questions about local landmarks or advise where particular services could be obtained. He was about five feet seven in height, stocky, with a muscular build. The most important part of his job was getting his bus, loaded with new arrivals and their belongings, safely across the eight very active railroad tracks that separated Front Street from Railroad Avenue. It would have been considered good work for a Black man in Port Jervis, where many toiled in more menial jobs.

In a town of such a modest size, many Black and white people certainly knew one another casually, or as employer and employee, but as the newspapers that inform our knowledge of the period were all white owned and edited, it's not clear that many African Americans figured prominently in public life. Other than Happy Hank, there was the gambler and ballplayer Robert "Bob" Brodhead, who had also worked at the Delaware House; and Adam Piggory, the patriarch of a large clan who seems to have been respected as a wise man and dispute-settler among his peers in the Black settlement north of town, called "N***** Hollow," later rechristened Reservoir View. There, he may have even acted as a kind of liaison to the white community.

Like Bob Brodhead and Adam Piggory, Robert Lewis, given his prominent and highly visible job, may have been a familiar character; certainly, in the wake of his death, many white people said they had known him and recalled him favorably. But if local newspapers are any guide, whites viewed the village's Black population mostly with condescension. Except for the occasional press notice encouraging townspeople to catch a Red Stockings game or take in a musical presentation by "our colored talent" at the opera house, the papers more often cast the town's Black residents as harmless, humorous characters, and used offensive white stereotypes of "Negro dialect" to depict a community given over to childish disputes, the sale of moonshine liquor, and individuals' absurd schemes for self-enrichment.

In this the Port Jervis papers were hardly unique. As Rayford Logan, a prominent Black historian of the era, would record, leading newspapers and publications in the North and South routinely presented African Americans as speaking in poorly rendered dialect and as outlandish comic characters with ridiculous-sounding names, like Abraham Lincum, Apollo Belvedere, Prince Orang Outang, Nutin' Tal, Wanna-Mo, and Piddlekins. Port Jervis papers entertained readers with stories about the enclave north of town, lively tales of "dusky denizens" and their "colony of vice and misery," where "romance in ebony" led invariably to disappointment, quarreling, and minor injury. One battle at a taffy-eating party resulted in a young woman being kicked in the shins; in another incident George Jefferson, "a great masher among the dusky damsels," aimed stones at the dwelling of "Rufe" Miller. Jefferson was ordered to lockup for ninety days, an exile so harsh it was said to have brought several of the Hollow's marriageable females to tears as he was led away. A popular story involved a Black shop assistant who was handed a ten-dollar bill by his employer, a local merchant, and told to go to the bank to get change; instead, the young man disappeared with the money. When caught in a neighboring town and brought back before a judge, he explained that on his way to change the bill, he overheard a white man say there were "too many [Blacks] in town and they ought to get out," and so he had. Unamused, the magistrate ordered him to jail.

The effect of this type of coverage was doubly offensive: it reinforced the false notion that stealing, cheating, and fighting were common among Black people, while reassuring whites that, even at their most larcenous or diabolical, Blacks lacked the courage and imagination to seriously disrupt public order. Where real inconvenience or injury did result, of course, a firm white hand was ready to judge and punish.

TWO

CITY IN PROGRESS

———————◦◦◦◦———————

The village took its name from John B. Jervis, the chief engineer of the 108-mile-long Delaware & Hudson Canal, a technological marvel of the 1820s, dug to carry anthracite coal from Pennsylvania through Port Jervis to Rondout, south of Kingston, New York, from where it went by Hudson River barge to New York City. The canal's importance to the town's early life is reflected in the fact that the "Port" in its name alluded not to the two major rivers that met there, which were too shallow for commercial navigation, but rather to the manmade D&H. Some 1,600 boats passed through the canal each year, mostly coal barges, but some carrying lumber or other materials. There were occasional pleasure cruises; one converted barge, the *Fashion*, boasted a dining room, carpeted floors, and room to accommodate a hundred passengers. We can assume the ride was leisurely, as the canal vessels were drawn by mules led along the towpath and rarely exceeded three miles per hour. Known locally as "the Ditch," the canal wound directly through

Port Jervis and featured prominently in village life. Children swam there in summer and skated on its frozen surface in winter; lovers strolled along its towpath. Once in a while an inebriate fell in and required rescue.

(Collection of the Minisink Valley Historical Society)

The Erie Railroad arrived in 1848 and soon located its extensive machine shops in Port Jervis, creating what eventually became one of the largest industrial complexes in lower New York State. By 1892, there were two railroad stations: the Erie, on Jersey Avenue, parallel to the Delaware, and a smaller depot on East Main Street for the Port Jervis, New York, and Monticello Railroad. The latter was commonly known as the Monticello Line for its service to neighboring Sullivan County. With the Erie's twenty daily through trains between New

York City and Chicago, Port Jervis was an important regional station stop and something of a final west-looking outpost of the Atlantic Seaboard, the point after which rail travelers entered the wild beauty of the upper Delaware, then the quilted farms of Western New York and Ohio, and eventually the Midwestern plains.

In a community of just over 9,000 people, more than 2,500 men worked on the rails as engineers, brakemen, firemen, or flagmen, or in the Erie shops. Railroad work, though relatively well paid, was frequently dangerous, at a time when individual workers, not their employers, largely assumed responsibility for their own safety. Headlines of railway misfortunes—CRUSHED BY THE WHEELS; STEPPED IN FRONT OF A TRAIN; A MISPLACED SWITCH—ran almost daily in the newspapers' inner pages. "The men themselves appear not to appreciate the chances of death and injury incurred by entering the train service," commented the local *Tri-States Union* in an 1892 article titled SLAUGHTER OF RAILROAD MEN. The coupling, uncoupling, and braking of trains were the cause of most accidents, although men also tumbled fatally onto the tracks while shoveling coal or walking atop cars. Death might be the cost of a bad footing or a single moment's inattention.

Lacking adequate warning systems or sufficient separation from public thoroughfares, trains often took the lives of civilians as well—pedestrians cutting through a rail yard or walking along the tracks, and occupants thrown from their carriages by a spooked horse at a grade crossing. One elderly Port Jervis woman was sought by anxious parents almost daily for her skill at plucking the hot cinders that flew from locomotive smokestacks out of children's eyes. And while no one used the term "noise pollution" in 1892, a strongly worded petition was delivered that year to the Erie Railroad by residents demanding that it "abate the ear-splitting serenades of the railroad and shops" heard at all hours of the day and night.

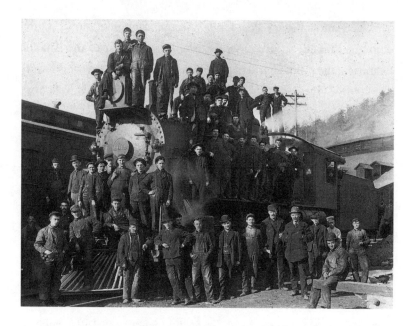

(Collection of the Minisink Valley Historical Society)

Six days a week the village was all tumultuous industry, home to a silk mill, five bottling works, a tannery, a brewery, and no fewer than eighty-two large and small factories turning out finished products such as lamps, gloves, windows, and stoves. The residential streets were largely unpaved dirt or gravel, but the chief business blocks were laid with cobblestones, and many sidewalks were raised as wooden "board walks," some partially protected by shop awnings. Culture was not neglected: along with the opera house, the village boasted a music conservatory, a vaudeville theater, and a lending library. Theatrical touring companies played almost nightly. At the opera house, managed by the pharmacist-turned-hotelier George Lea, one could witness a juggling demonstration, a lecture on reptiles, and the peculiar Victorian entertainment known as a "broom drill," in which sturdy young women armed with brooms instead of rifles performed synchronized military exercises to piano accompaniment. Determined not to be taken for rubes, youthful Port Jervians filled the house in March 1891 to hiss at and catcall a pretender named Professor Archer, who, claiming spiritualistic powers to summon the dead, brought forth from the spectral world the biblical Adam, Longfellow's "Hiawatha," and the recently deceased British actress Adelaide Neilson.

Directly to the east of Port Jervis, in the lower half of Orange County, was an area once covered by a glacial ice sheet that, upon its prehistoric retreat, left behind what locals called the Drowned Lands, or the Black Dirt Country—twenty-six thousand acres of wetlands and moist, dark, extremely fertile soil in which almost any crop would thrive. The results included a flavorful species of regional onion as well as grassy pasturelands so lush that Orange County's dairy products became renowned, its fresh milk a staple for generations of New York and Philadelphia children. The Erie Railroad was said to have made a considerable part of its initial profits in the 1840s transporting Orange County milk to New York City, an enterprise that helped give original meaning to the term "milk train," as the transports were obliged to make frequent stops at scattered dairy farms.

In the early eighteenth century those who worked the county's land began to unearth large, mysterious objects from deep in the rich soil. The Boston cleric Cotton Mather pronounced them relics of a race of prediluvian giants; Benjamin Franklin suggested a fossilized molar (of a similar creature found in Ohio) may have belonged to an elephantine creature, now extinct. An 1801 dig in a farmer's field outside Newburgh, overseen by the Philadelphia artist Charles Willson Peale, resulted in his iconic painting *The Exhumation of the Mastodon*, and the fossilized skeletal remains of the creature were later exhibited in Peale's Philadelphia museum. "We think of his majestic tread as he strode these valleys and hill-tops," mused the Orange

County historian Samuel W. Eager of the mastodon, "snuffing the wind with disdain, and uttering his wrath in tones of thunder." Over the centuries, these megafauna had waded into the bogs of the Drowned Lands to feed on vegetation and had become entrapped in the muck (perhaps, some experts believe, with the connivance of human hunters). So numerous and continual have been the discoveries that many modern paleobiologists consider New York's Orange County "the Mastodon Capital of the United States."

Where the retreating glacier did not leave bountiful farmland, it sculpted a brutish landscape of boulder-strewn hillsides, steep escarpments, and the narrow ravine-like valleys the Dutch called "cloves." These untamable precincts made the region, in colonial times, a kind of early version of the Wild West, with outlaws, highwaymen, and deadly warfare between settlers and Indigenous peoples. "Every lonely road has its tale of tragedy, and every mountain pass its story of encounter with wild beast or savage Indian," noted one historian. Legends were born of this unrest, such as that of Tom Quick, "the Indian Slayer," a genocidal murderer who devoted his life to avenging the death of his father at Native hands. And Claudius Smith, a loyalist outlaw hanged at Goshen during the American Revolution, whose skull is said to have later been placed in the facade of the town's 1841 courthouse. Within present-day Port Jervis lies the scene of the area's most infamous Indian raid, at a settlement known as Machackemech, where in July 1779 Joseph Brant, or Tyendinaga, a Mohawk military leader and an ally of the British, swept into the Minisink Valley at the head of his band of Tories and Native warriors. After extensive pillaging, Brant and his 90 men retreated to the heights above the Delaware River, where a failed ambush laid by 120 local minutemen resulted in a devastating defeat for the Americans, a massacre that remains sacred regional lore.

On July 5, 1886, Lena McMahon would have gone with her parents and the rest of the village to witness the unveiling of the large monument commemorating the area's Civil War veterans. Some ten thousand people, slightly more than the village's population, were said to have joined a three-mile-long parade to Orange Square. There, to the ringing oratory of Lewis Eleazer Carr, the county's most eminent jurist, the town saluted the local veterans of the 124th New York Regiment, known as the Orange Blossoms, many of whom were on hand. John McMahon had served in a different unit, the 16th Massachusetts Volunteers, a regiment organized at Cambridge, but the 16th and the 124th had shared a role in two major battles—Chancellorsville and Gettysburg.

The town's rise to importance as a rail and manufacturing center was hailed, at least by itself, a year later, when in 1887 it installed electric streetlamps. It was the first municipality in Orange County to do so, ahead of both Goshen, the county seat, and Newburgh, its largest city—places that one Port Jervis paper had the cheek to dismiss as "backward examples of towns hostile to nineteenth century ideas." Port Jervis was better able to see its own devotion to progress reflected in its closest neighbor, Middletown, whose State Homeopathic Hospital was one of the country's most advanced healing centers for mental disabilities, featuring innovations like occupational therapy, an art studio, a patient-edited newsletter, and an athletic program. The Middletown Asylums, a baseball team made up of hospital employees, a recovering patient or two, and numerous ringers, played against competing professional squads. Enthusiastic local fans packed the bleachers on Asylum game days, and the Middletown papers printed box scores and sidebars about the team's heroes, a few of whom graduated to the major leagues.

That it was considered unsurprising for a psychiatric hospital to field a baseball squad speaks to the broad popularity of the sport during the 1880s and 1890s. "Baseball is the hurrah game of the republic!" cheered the poet Walt Whitman. "[It] has the snap, go, fling of the American atmosphere." Port Jervis had its own crack teams, although the most renowned were the Red Stockings, African American players who on the Main Street field regularly trounced other local and visiting teams, white and Black. Coverage of their games was laudatory and evinced much local pride. "The whites outnumbered the [Black people] ten to one, but swarms of youngsters of all ages, sexes and color, poured in rapidly, and the crowd mingled freely together, everyone talking and carrying-on, making a perfect Babel of voices," read the 1885 *Gazette* article FUN ON THE BALL FIELD: BLACK AND WHITE CLUBS MEET. "[The Red Stockings] are a strong nine, and we will pit them against any colored club in this section. In fact, they are more than a match for a majority of 'de white clubs.'"

There had long been a modest Black population in the village, due to New York's long history of slavery. The first eleven Africans to arrive in New Amsterdam landed at the foot of Manhattan Island in 1626. An estimated 42 percent of New York City households counted enslaved persons in 1703, and by 1790, the time of the first United States federal census, twenty-one thousand in New York State—the largest such population in the North, New York City itself having more enslaved people than any other American city except Charleston, South Carolina. The Hudson Valley alone was home to fifteen thousand people in bondage, most laboring as teamsters or diggers, or in some type of river commerce, while others were skilled smiths, coopers, or carpenters. Large numbers of house servants and gardeners were needed to maintain the great Hudson River estates of families such as the Livingstons, the Van Rensselaers, and the Van Cortlandts.

"The two biggest slave markets in the country before the American Revolution were in New York City and Albany," notes A. J. Williams-Myers, a scholar of regional Black history. "New York was not a society *with* slaves, it was a *slave society*, dependent on enslaved Africans."

While slavery in the Northeast was reputed to be less brutal than in the cotton South, its laws were no less strict, and the British, who took possession of the colony in 1664, were thought far less lenient than their Dutch predecessors. A slave revolt over harsh conditions in New York in April 1712 took the lives of nine white colonists. As a result, twenty-one Black people were put to death. When, in 1741, the mysterious destruction by fire of a fort at the Battery led to rumors of a planned insurrection by enslaved persons allied with poor whites, two hundred people of both races, but most Black, were swept up in arrests. Following a sensational trial, eighteen people were hanged, including a white man and his wife, a second white woman, and an English priest; fourteen others were immolated; and seventy Black people were deported.

Lethal measures were enforced upriver as well. "In 1735 an African slave who resided in Dutchess County named Quacko was sentenced to thirty-nine lashes at Poughkeepsie and an additional forty-eight at Rhinebeck for attempted rape," recounts Williams-Myers. "Another African, 'Negro Jack,' was burned alive in Ulster County in October 1732 for 'burning a barne and a barrack of wheat.' And in the town of Kingston, a slave known only as Tom was executed for the attempted rape and the murder of a white woman." White suspicions about incidents of arson in Albany in 1793 fell on two teenage Black girls, Bett and Deena, who were convicted and executed the following March on the "Hanging Elm Tree," a local emblem of terror at the corner of State and Pearl Streets that literally loomed over the town's Black population. An alleged fellow conspirator, a young man named Pomp, was hanged a month later on Pinkster Hill, later the site of the state capitol.

Because they held value in enslaved persons as property, whites were frequently willing to intervene on their behalf when Blacks were accused of petit lawbreaking such as stealing a chicken, gambling, or violating curfew. No such intercession was made, however, to rescue Quacko or Tom for alleged sexual crimes, suggesting that as early as the eighteenth century these offenses were held in special regard. Adulterous white men, accustomed to taking predacious advantage of subjugated Black women, became, in their massive guilt and hypocrisy, fiercely defensive of what they then projected as the flawlessness and purity of white womanhood. Knowing their relations with Black women to be inherently nonconsensual, they chose to believe relations between Black men and white women must be so as well. Black male lust for a white female became in this calculus a vengeful act, a defiance of white male dominance, and a transgression warranting punishment so severe as to blot out the horrible deed itself as well as the perpetrator. In this latter determination, Southern apologists were always quick to point out, red-blooded white men were much alike, regardless of section.

The New York Manumission Society, founded in 1785, had as its members prominent whites such as John Jay and Alexander Hamilton, as well as numerous Quakers. A gradual law of emancipation was enacted by the state, freeing all children born to enslaved women after July 4, 1799, on the condition that they would be retained by the white families who "owned" their mothers and serve as indentured servants, the men until the age of twenty-eight and the women until twenty-five. Unrestricted emancipation in New York arrived by official decree on July 4, 1827. By the early decades of the American republic, however, Northeast textile mill towns such as Lowell and Lawrence, Massachusetts, and Woonsocket, Rhode Island, as well as cities like New York, Boston, and Philadelphia, were part of a global cotton economy supported by enslaved labor, its overseers the Yankee "lords of the loom" and their Southern counterparts, the "lords of the lash." Partly due to these economic bonds, Northern sympathy for and complicity with the plantation South would persist throughout the antebellum era and into the Civil War.

The Underground Railroad was active in eastern Orange County during the 1840s and 1850s, chiefly in Goshen and the river town of Newburgh. New York City was a center of intense pro- and anti-abolitionist fervor, the scene of confrontations between the Kidnapping Club, corrupt police and judges who conspired to abduct and sell free Negroes, as well as those who escaped from bondage, into Southern hands; and the Committee of Vigilance, led by the Black journalist David Ruggles. Worse trials lay ahead, for with the passage of the Fugitive Slave Act of 1850, a white man who swore under oath that a Black person was his runaway "property" was entitled to the assistance of federal marshals and U.S. commissioners in returning him or her to bondage. Northern citizens were required to not interfere with the law and, in some instances, to abet its enforcement, and persons caught shielding or transporting a runaway could be fined one thousand dollars. Suspected Black men and women taken into custody had no right to a jury trial, nor were they permitted to testify on their own behalf. Rather, after a cursory hearing before a federal commissioner, they were to be removed to a waiting boat or train and hustled directly "home" to the landowner who claimed them.

Although legend contends that sympathetic Erie Railroad conductors conveniently looked the other way when runaways rode the rails west to Lake Erie, where passengers could cross by ferry to Canada and freedom, there is scant evidence Port Jervis played a significant role. At the time, it likely would not have been safe for a man or woman following the North Star to linger in the village, as amid its small Black population a stranger would not long remain anonymous.

A signal event was the 1857 U.S. Supreme Court ruling in *Dred Scott v. Sandford*. The case involved an enslaved man, Dred Scott, who had been brought from Missouri, a slave state, into Northern territories in which slavery was not allowed. Upon his return to Missouri he sued for his freedom on the grounds that, having set foot in a free territory, he could legally no longer be held in bondage. Rebuffed by Missouri judges, his appeal reached the U.S. Supreme Court, which ruled that Black people, in the opinion of Chief Justice Roger Taney, "are not included, and were not intended to be included, under the word 'citizens' in the Constitution, and can therefore claim none of the rights and privileges which that instrument provides for and secures to citizens of the United States." The Constitution, he said, established that "a perpetual and impassable barrier was intended to be erected between the white race and the one which they had reduced to slavery." In the same ruling the Taney court undermined the premise of the Missouri Compromise of 1820, in which Congress had set limits on the extension of slavery into the western territories. As Abraham Lincoln would argue the following year in his debates with Senator Stephen Douglas from Illinois, Taney's disastrous ruling laid the groundwork for slavery (as well as the non-personhood of Black people) to become a national reality, in spirit and in fact, not limited to the South or any other distinct region.

The Dutch families of the Lower Hudson Valley, including western Orange County, had been among the white New Yorkers most reluctant to relinquish "ownership" of enslaved people. Some, disdainful of having to lose their "property" without compensation, arranged quietly (and illegally) to send the enslaved south to be sold. Perhaps it was due to this obstinacy, as well as the region's violent years of settlement and a later territorial dispute with neighboring

New Jersey, that Port Jervis long retained a conservative bent. The *Tri-States Union* editorialized during the 1856 presidential election in favor of maintaining the institution of slavery, and Deerpark, the town in which the village was then formally situated, voted in 1860 by a staggering margin of 664–17 against a state ballot initiative to enfranchise non-property-owning Black men. That same year, it narrowly backed Abraham Lincoln for president, and in 1864, at the height of the Civil War, it voted to deny him a second term, apparently no longer sharing the faith, so eloquently voiced in his first inaugural, that "the mystic chords of memory, stretching from every battlefield and patriot grave, to every living heart and hearth-stone, all over this broad land, will yet swell the chorus of the Union, when again touched, as surely they will be, by the better angels of our nature."

───◦──

Lynching has existed since the earliest days of the republic. The term derived from the name of a Virginia magistrate, Charles Lynch, the original "Judge Lynch," known for ordering, on dubious authority, the flogging of Tories during the American Revolution. For many years after, it referred to incidents of nonlethal shaming punishments such as tarring and feathering, or the hauling of an undesirable from a community tied to a fence pole (the origin of the expression "ridden out of town on a rail").

In summer 1835 there were mob killings of gamblers in Vicksburg, Mississippi, as well as summary executions of Black people alleged to be fomenting a revolt elsewhere in the state. In St. Louis the following year, a free Black man, a steamboat porter named Francis L. McIntosh, fatally stabbed one constable and wounded another while resisting a wrongful arrest; pursued by a white mob, he was seized and put to death by immolation. The local abolitionist editor Elijah P.

Lovejoy wrote critically of the lynching of McIntosh and of the inaction of Judge Luke E. Lawless, who, concerned that with abolition "the free Negro has been turned into a deadly enemy," refused to indict those responsible. Enraged by Lovejoy's published words, whites sacked his St. Louis office and destroyed his printing press. In November 1837, after he had relocated twenty-five miles upriver in Alton, Illinois, vigilantes again besieged him and his publishing operation, setting his warehouse on fire and shooting Lovejoy dead when he emerged from the building.

What had stirred this intense paranoia and reaction was the filtering from North to South of fierce antislavery sentiment in the form of periodicals, broadsides, and the intensifying of agitation in Congress, making Southern whites fear the destabilization of their society and economy. A singular provocation had been the 1829 publication of David Walker's *Appeal to the Colored Citizens of the World*. This seventy-six-page assault against slavery, written by a young Black Bostonian, ran through several printings and was disseminated widely in the South, unsettling many a slave owner with its alarming caution: "Remember Americans, that we must and shall be free . . . Will you wait until we shall, under God, obtain our liberty by the crushing arm of power? Will it not be dreadful for you? I speak Americans for your own good."

This call for freedom was followed in August 1831 by Nat Turner's rebellion, in which the visionary preacher and field hand in Southampton, Virginia, having "seen" God's commands written in the sky, launched an insurrection that killed sixty white men, women, and children, most of whom were dragged from their homes and hacked to death. Turner and his band were captured and executed, but the planter aristocracy slept badly ever after, fearful of a righteously vengeful uprising from the slave quarters and the sound of barefoot intruders on the stairs. An added source of consternation was the appearance that year of *The Liberator*, published in Boston and soon to become the nation's leading abolitionist newspaper, in which the printer and Bible-read reformer William Lloyd Garrison committed his life to a frontal assault on the American slave empire and to its utter and final collapse.

It was the murder of Elijah Lovejoy that moved Abraham Lincoln, then a twenty-eight-year-old lawyer, to address the Young Men's Lyceum of Springfield, Illinois, on January 27, 1838. In his talk, "The Perpetuation of Our Political Institutions," Lincoln decried "this mobocratic spirit, which all must admit, is now abroad in the land." He told listeners who had gathered to hear him that winter evening:

> When men take it in their heads today to hang gamblers, or burn murderers, they should recollect that in the confusion usually attending such transactions, they will be as likely to hang or burn someone who is neither a gambler nor a murderer as one who is, and that, acting upon the example they set, the mob of tomorrow may, and probably will, hang or burn some of them by the very same mistake. And not only so; the innocent, those who ever have set their faces against violations of law in every shape, alike with the guilty, fall victim to the ravages of mob law; and thus, it goes on, step by step, till all the walls erected for the defense of the persons and property of individuals, are trodden down and disregarded.

Lincoln warned of the sure descent of mob law into anarchism, when the "perpetrators of such acts going unpunished . . . having ever regarded Government as their deadliest bane," will "make a jubilee of the suspension of its operations." He was prescient in noting that mobs taking the law into their own hands are neither peculiar to the eternal snows of [New England], nor the burning suns of the [South]; they are not the creature of climate; neither are they confined to the slave-holding, or the non-slave-holding states. Alike, they spring up among the pleasure hunting masters of Southern slaves, and the order loving citizens of the land of steady habits. Whatever, then, their cause may be, it is common to the whole country.

Mobs and the extrajudicial punishments they meted out in the antebellum South brought an eloquent rebuke from a future president. However, it was after Lincoln's death, in the crucible of the untidy postwar years, that lynching became both institutionalized and more consistently lethal. The depravity of the practice was such that while some lynchings were carried out in secret, many were staged spectacles—public executions with dramatic and ritualistic features that in part resembled both a picnic and an outdoor religious revival. Announced beforehand by local newspapers, the incidents drew thousands of white onlookers, some arriving from larger nearby cities such as Atlanta and Charleston aboard special excursion trains, joining the multitude that had come by horse, by buggy, or on foot. The lynching itself typically involved torture, mutilation, and the shooting, hanging, or immolation of a living human being—frequently all three. It was followed by a frenzied competition for relics of the event—a piece of charred tree trunk or link from a chain with which the victim had been bound.

Nor were lynch mobs necessarily sated by the consummation of their goal, but they frequently turned their fury on adjacent Black neighborhoods, looting and torching stores and houses while visiting hellish violence on any Black person unfortunate enough to fall into their path. The impact of such terrorizing scenes on African Americans, whether one mile or one thousand miles away, was profound, enough so to inspire, where feasible, out-migrations to safer precincts and to linger permanently in the psychology of the Black family. It is no exaggeration to suggest that in the dread horror of lynching, of whites' capricious assaults that might inexplicably leave a son, husband, or brother dead, lies the origins of "the talk," the necessity for Black parents throughout U.S. history and to our present day to alert their children to the dangers inherent in encounters with white people, especially police, from whom no hope of protection or safe passage is guaranteed.

Today one can drive in minutes from the center of Port Jervis to the historic site of the village's Black settlement, still a piney grove on a crystal reservoir north of town, but to imagine its residents walking that distance, perhaps twice a day, as they reported to and returned from domestic work in the village, speaks to a literal and substantial separation by race.

Such habitations, set apart from white residential areas and peopled by manumitted slaves and their descendants, were common elsewhere in the Lower Hudson Valley. "Skunk Hollow" was in Rockland County; the town of Chester had "Honey Pot," later called "Guinea," while a Black village near Harrison in Westchester County was known simply as "the Hills." The Black population on the northern outskirts of Port Jervis was referred to as "N***** Hollow" by white Port Jervians as recently as the 1960s, long after it had been forced from its original site amid a pine and birch forest, although beginning in 1877, white town boosters and the local press, conscious of the term's offensiveness, used the name "Reservoir View." After 1883, when the community was forcibly relocated from its original location to an area at the top of North Orange Street, it became known as Farnumville, likely a gentle dig at the memory of Henry H. Farnum, a wealthy D&H Canal superintendent whose widow, Diana, had financed the construction of the town's Civil War memorial and whose zeal for civic uplift was frequently, if quietly, derided.

"The town reaped little in labor from these curious suburbs," the novelist Stephen Crane, who grew up in Port Jervis, would recall in a lightly fictionalized account, written from his perspective as a privileged white youth. "In the main the colony loafed in high spirits, and the industrious minority gained no direct honor from their fellows, unless they spent their earnings on raiment, in which case they were naturally treated with distinction. On the whole, the hardships of these people were the wind, the rain, the snow, and any other physical difficulties which they could cultivate. About twice a year the lady philanthropists . . . went up against them, and came away poorer in goods but rich in complacence."

A critical juncture for the community came in 1883, when the local water utility forcibly removed 150 people from the original settlement, citing concern that "all the waste of this cesspool, whenever it rains, is carried into the reservoir and then drank by many [white residents] who do not realize what this water contains." But the alleged "pollution" extended beyond concern for drinking water safety to what many white Port Jervians perceived as the encampment's immorality and shantytown-like poverty. "This resort of the negroes and the very low whites is becoming notoriously bad," the *Gazette* complained.

The Hollow eventually met the judgment suffered by other African American settlements in New York, including Seneca Village, the Black town uprooted from Manhattan's west side in the 1850s to make way for the building of Central Park. Deemed by whites to be unhygienic, or simply in the way, the Hollow was declared uninhabitable and ordered cleared. When the forced exodus commenced in

48

October 1883, the paper offered half-hearted condolences: "There is weeping and wailing in [Reservoir View] today . . . [It] was where many of their children were born and raised, where many a wedding took place, where many a festive night was spent, and where many [an inhabitant] closely followed by officers of the law, found a safe retreat."

In summer 1892, a full decade after relocating the Black settlement to an area at the end of North Orange Street, thus safeguarding the town's drinking water, white Port Jervis could look ahead to bettering circumstances. The national financial crisis known as the Panic of 1893 was still nine months away, and for now the town's diverse industry was creating decent wages and supporting commerce. Architects came from New York City and Philadelphia to design large homes along the village's treed avenues. From Point Peter, a noted sightseeing peak high above town (once visited and praised by Washington Irving), one could gaze out on what might be a panorama of burgeoning America—intersecting rivers and nearby mountains framing a low-rise grid of church steeples, hotels, parks, and ballfields, constituting what village promoters liked to call the "Scenic Queen of the Shawangunk Range."

"Remote but prosperous, small-sized but grand-minded in its aspirations for modernity and sophistication," as the scholar Jacqueline Goldsby has described it, 1890s Port Jervis "saw itself as an adjunct to the big city 65 miles away."

—•—

The abolitionist minister and author Jonathan Townley Crane and his wife, Mary Peck Crane, had come to Port Jervis from New Jersey in 1878, when he was appointed minister of the Drew Methodist Church on Orange Square. They lost little time in establishing themselves as spiritual and reform leaders, devoted to religious as well as industrial education, temperance, and efforts to improve the lives of Black residents. Of the family's fourteen children (nine of whom survived into adulthood), several would become fixtures in local affairs: Agnes, a teacher; William, a lawyer and civic leader who had served one year as a special judge for Orange County and was thereafter known as Judge Crane; Edmund and Luther, who both held positions with the railroad; and the youngest, Stephen, who was born in 1871 and would attain worldwide fame in the mid-1890s upon the publication of his Civil War novel *The Red Badge of Courage*.

(Collection of the Minisink Valley Historical Society)

The Reverend Crane wrote extensively on temperance and the evils of frivolity, especially dancing. "Young lady," he warned in one treatise, "by imbibing a love for the dance, you will almost necessarily acquire a distaste for the duties of everyday life. The dancing master is the Devil's drill sergeant." Temperance was an especial cause in Port Jervis, with its dozens of saloons serving railroad workers and travelers, and Mary Peck Crane was an ardent foot soldier in the movement, fighting liquor sales with prayers and petitions urging young men to keep their bodies a fit temple for their souls. The Reverend Crane's book *Arts of Intoxication* was hailed nationally as a cautionary work on the subject.

The elder Cranes also set out at once to address the village's racial inequities, especially as they impacted education. Their Drew Mission Sunday School, open to all, eventually attracted forty-eight Black adult students and twenty-one children, with a sizable number attending the school's first-anniversary party on May 30, 1879. The Reverend Crane, who like many white reformers had an unrealistic and overly optimistic impression of the cause he wished to serve, stressed to Black parents that education for their children must be secured at all costs, as "only by industry, sobriety, economy and piety, [can] the people of any race rise from an inferior to a higher position."

Mary Peck Crane helped found an industrial school for Black women, with the dual aim of compensating for their lack of schooling and teaching useful household skills. To enable participation, the classes were often held in Reservoir View, with local teamsters contributing wagon transport for the white instructors and their equipment. To the African American residents, a caravan of determined white ladies bouncing over a final hill, their wagons laden with sewing machines and mounds of fabric, must have been a memorable sight. The finished clothes and shoes produced by this endeavor were given at no cost to the residents, with the suggestion that they wear them to Sunday school.

The Cranes' anti-liquor fervor was far from trivial. Temperance was arguably the leading American reform movement of the final decades of the nineteenth century, along with labor organizing and the effort to alleviate the suffering of the urban poor. Under the national guidance of Frances E. Willard, the Woman's Christian Temperance Union, founded in 1873, built a large membership confident in the superior character of women and their essential role in the salvation of mankind. In so well-watered a locale as Port Jervis, the crusade had special resonance, particularly in the capable hands of Mary Peck Crane and her husband. It was the temperance crusaders of Port Jervis who established a reading room in the Farnum Building and campaigned successfully to bring a Carnegie library to the village, in the hope that books would offer an alternative to drink.

As a small boy, Stephen sometimes accompanied the Reverend Crane on buggy rides to minister to hardship cases. "Once we got mixed up in an Irish funeral near a place named Slate Hill," he later recalled. "Everybody was drunk and father was scandalized. He was so simple and good that I often think he didn't know much of anything about humanity." Neither William Crane, the jurist, nor his younger brother Stephen, the author, would adopt their parents' religiosity, straitlaced causes, or methods of reform. But as sons of Port Jervis, they were called upon to respond to the community's supreme moral crisis, the lynching of Robert Lewis, parsing right from wrong and restoring meaning to ideals of justice and tolerance. Each would have an outsize role in reckoning with the event's legacy.

THREE

A Shadow Cast Over
My Sunshade

━━━━◦◦◦━━━━

After Philip Foley's ouster from the Delaware House, it was reported, he "was frequently seen about the shanties of some negroes along the Erie tracks . . . [and] lived with a colored family when he was broke, [for] he was usually in that condition." While many of the town's African Americans remained north of the village, others resided in the area between Kingston Avenue and the Neversink River, or in the far west end of the Acre, the low-lying land between the rail yards and the Delaware, where, it appears, Foley had found at least a temporary home. Sometimes called "the Bully Acre," the strip of land was dominated by Irish and Italian gangs, which brawled in defense of territory, while the small Black population did its best to stay out of the way.

The absorption of white men like Foley into what temperance crusaders saw as a Black demimonde of gambling, vice, and whiskey stills was the very issue that often alarmed the town's church leaders and editorialists. Local press clippings of the era, however, suggest that many whites were drawn to join Blacks in their places of entertainment not solely because they viewed them as exotic or risqué but for the pleasure of listening to Black music and dance, much as George Gershwin, Tallulah Bankhead, Charlie Chaplin, and Theodore Dreiser flocked to Harlem nightclubs a generation later. The newspaper coverage could cut both ways, as the *Gazette* did in telling of a white man named Jacob Lane who visited Reservoir View frequently, "for he loves to listen to the dulcet tones of the dark-skinned maids of that locality, and lavishes his money upon them for beer, etc.," but having blissfully dozed off, he awoke to find his wallet missing. Elsewhere the paper cautioned readers of the lure of Black resorts to white youngsters and "low whites," explaining:

> The places are resorted to by young white boys, sons of well-to-do and respectable parents, who would be refused beer or liquor in any respectable drinking house in the village, and who go there simply because they can do so without meeting parents or relatives or acquaintances, who would be likely to inform on them. It is the means of sowing seeds of everlasting degradation that no right-minded person can calmly contemplate without a shudder.

There was considerable hypocrisy in this, for some very grown-up white people might be seen on occasion making their way clandestinely to the town's illicit establishments. Since the mid-nineteenth century, nightlife in Port Jervis had been centered on the diagonal intersection of Front Street and Jersey Avenue. Some of the place's rougher edges had been smoothed away by the opening of the new train depot and the related arrival of a better class of hotels, but on railroad paydays the district still took on the feel of a Wild West boomtown, where even the most transient railroad hand could cash a paycheck at Bauer's Hotel before hitting the saloons. For the presence of its "houses of assignation," second-story rooms behind lace curtains that could be rented by the hour, the area had become known as "Grab Point." This was a riff on that other well-known local landmark, Carpenter's Point, the jut of land where the Neversink merges with the Delaware, the inference being that here one might "grab" whatever one wished—a bottle, a game, or a woman. In a belated effort at respectability, the name, after about 1920, was occasionally given as *Graeb* Point, on the improbable fiction that an immigrant by that name had once kept a shop nearby.

The railroad was Port Jervis's lifeline, but the sense of impermanence it created and the mass of newcomers it delivered almost hourly lent this part of town a slack character that was, depending on one's perspective, either joyfully riotous or woefully debased. Due to the nature of its attractions, it could not afford the pretense of exclusivity; men and women of all races met and mingled there. More moderate citizens held the perceived depravity at arm's length with school honor rolls, church picnics, and temperance meetings, while the police kept rowdy drunks in line with reminders to move along and, if necessary, a meaningful tap with their batons. It was the era of the nation's great labor convulsions—Haymarket, Homestead, the Pullman Strike—and while Port Jervis saw relatively little of it, the sense of upheaval, even anarchy, was in the air and rarely skipped a station stop entirely. The police were expected to be vigilant at keeping hooligans and troublemakers in line, whatever their political or professional calling.

How deeply Foley was immersed in this milieu is unclear, but for Theresa and John McMahon it was enough to know that their only daughter was seeing a man who, however refined in manner and attire, upon his release from Goshen jail after two months served had found work at Barber's, a billiards hall at the corner of Jersey and

Front, the very heart of Grab Point. While the McMahons declared Foley an unsuitable companion and forbade further contact, their vivacious daughter was no longer a child. With her intellect and fashionable Gibson Girl figure, Lena might have had her pick of local boys, but she seemed indifferent to the options of dairy farmer or railroad man. Yet, because her own family was working-class, the sons of the town's professionals and elites were likely inaccessible; neither she nor her parents moved in those circles.

The pet name Foley gave her was "Little Girl," which may have been a private joke, as she was likely the taller of the two, though he was far more worldly. For him she felt a compelling attraction, an appeal undiminished, perhaps even sharpened, by his recklessness and the vehemence of his pursuit. In his dress, in his charming confidence, he had brought the city to their small-town courtship. Where her friends and family thought him overly slick, she sought to protect him from their gossip and suspicions.

He cared for her, she knew that. Norman V. Mulley, the judge who had presided over Foley's case at Goshen, likely knew of George Lea's many objections to this particular young man, as well as the McMahons' mounting concern for Lena's involvement with him; yet it would have been natural for Mulley to have compassion for a fellow in a strange town far from home whose actual crimes, all told, had been fairly innocuous. Mulley had devised a judicious compromise, agreeing to set Foley at liberty two months early if he would promise to leave Port Jervis and not return. Foley, in order to gain his freedom, had readily consented. But he then defied the judge's order and did not leave town; he remained for Lena. He would defy her parents too, if he must.

With the judge's conditional release hanging over his head, as well as George Lea's and the McMahons' disapproval, he and Lena had extra reason to be discreet. To avoid attention, he "introduced her to a back-alley kind of romance," Bruce Jay Friedman recorded, "and the two were soon meeting behind barns, in cemeteries, and along the banks of the Neversink."

———•◦•———

On Tuesday, May 31, after ordering Foley away, Theresa had struck her daughter across the mouth with such force that, upon leaving the house and walking blindly toward the Erie Depot, Lena had to stop at Luckey's Pharmacy, on the corner of Front and Fowler, to have her lip dressed. Subsequent events suggest she looked for Foley and, not finding him, left a message for him, perhaps at the pool hall where he worked. She then boarded the 2:28 p.m. train for New York, and from its windows watched the only real home she'd ever known recede from view as the train rumbled over the planks of the Neversink bridge and began its broad left turn toward Otisville.

Lena later described to reporters a most curious journey to New York City, where she would have arrived just after five o'clock. There existed no Hudson River bridges or tunnels at the time, so passengers arriving from Port Jervis detrained at Jersey City and rode an Erie-operated ferry to Lower Manhattan. Once there, Lena recounted, she went up the west side of Manhattan to a friend's place on Eighty-Sixth Street (by some sort of conveyance, no doubt, as it was a considerable distance) and, failing to find them at home, began walking back downtown in the early evening twilight. The last thing she recalled was entering a dive bar, a "sort of a rough place I noticed after I got inside," where she asked for and was given a glass of water. Drinking it was her final recollection, for she had no memory of where she spent Tuesday night—"where I was or what I did." The *Gazette* concluded that Lena's "description of her flight to New York City, and her actions while there, would lead one to suppose that the girl had either been temporarily deranged, or that she had been drugged."

The robbery or abduction of individuals with the use of knockout drops was an infamous New York street crime of the period, so it was not surprising that a reporter trying to deconstruct Lena's story would suggest it, but there is no evidence that this is what befell Lena. As for where she spent the night, likely it was in Lower Manhattan near the ferry that had initially deposited her there, as she was up early Wednesday morning to recross the Hudson and board Train Number 1 to Port Jervis, arriving there at 12:20 p.m. She had been away less than twenty-four hours.

This rather surreal adventure, as she related it, was reminiscent of her childhood "fit" of 1878, when she mysteriously lost consciousness, fell headlong into a stream, and nearly drowned. If she had not been drugged, or been made temporarily insane by her traumatic departure from her mother's violence and Port Jervis, why was she unwilling subsequently to reveal her actual movements? Where had she gone, and whom had she seen? Much was inexplicable, yet her curious narrative, as she later told it, became no less clear upon her arrival back in Port Jervis. Here, she claimed to have walked alone to Laurel Grove, where she spent the night among the headstones, before coming to her senses the following morning (Thursday) on the steps of Grace Episcopal Church on East Main Street, close to her parents' home and a mile from the cemetery.

Foley later shared with newsmen a more believable account of Lena's return. By prior arrangement, they had met at Fowler and Front about 12:30 p.m. on Wednesday, shortly after her train from New York pulled in. She appeared exhausted and somewhat tearful, but with great relief assured him she'd left home for good. "Her mother had abused her terribly," Foley related, "and [Lena said] that she would not stand it any longer." Glancing around, they saw there were a lot of people on the street and, thinking it best that they not be seen together, separated after agreeing to meet up again at Carpenter's Point, the hamlet named for the landmark peninsula and located on the far side of the Neversink. Lena took the more visible route down Main Street while Foley walked along the Erie tracks. The two reunited at the far side of the bridge, then ascended a hill along an old turnpike road into a wooded area where they wouldn't be disturbed. In this secluded place, Foley later said, they were "as husband and wife, and Lena proved her love to me."

They remained there until after midnight, then walked back into town. By habit, it seems, they went in the direction of Kingston Avenue, until Lena halted suddenly to remind him she had no intention of going home. Here a crisis presented itself: they had nowhere to go. It's not clear Foley had any fixed abode that would afford them privacy, and they'd be far too noticeable at a Front Street hotel, and certainly knew it would only cause more trouble if her parents learned he'd brought her somewhere disreputable.

All day they had discussed what to do, but without arriving at any firm resolution. Was Lena really leaving town, breaking from her parents to strike out on her own? Should he go with her? Some of his later statements suggest that Foley had begun to have realistic doubts about their future together, given her parents' hostility to their relationship and his lack of prospects. Lena, firm in her conviction there was no hope of reconciliation with her mother, continued to insist on her plan. "[Lena] had fully made up her mind by this time to leave home and not have anything more to do with the old people," Foley recalled, although she now said that, instead of New York, she would go to Boston, where she had relatives.

Just before two o'clock in the morning they paused to rest on the steps of Grace Episcopal Church (here Foley's version of the story rejoined Lena's). When Lena complained of feeling faint, Foley went to Bauer's Hotel on Jersey Avenue, where the café stayed open all night, and returned with two bottles of lemon soda. They sat on the church steps for a half hour longer, then walked across the tracks of the Monticello Line and followed a dirt path to a secluded area along the Neversink where there was a deserted fairgrounds, a harness factory, and a meadow that sloped down to the shore.

Using what extra garments they had and Lena's meager luggage, the two bedded down to spend the night beneath a chestnut tree, just to the north of where a stream called Cold Brook enters the river. It was the kind of place Stephen Crane would describe as being "well-known and well-traveled by the young people of the village . . . and cherished . . . as refuge from the prying supervisory eyes of the adult world." Since they found so isolated a spot with confidence in the dark, it seems likely they had been there before. Sheltered by a few large trees, the place's most ideal feature was that just at the edge of the water the land dipped down several feet, creating a smooth grassy ledge that shielded anyone there from view. Secluded, many hundred yards from the nearest dwellings, it was a vagabond lovers' idyll.

When the sun woke them Thursday morning, Lena wasted no time. She dictated a note for Foley to take to the Erie Depot, authorizing the expressman there to retrieve her belongings from West Street. "Mrs. McMahon," the message read, "give the bearer my trunk, valise, and package, as they have the articles I need. Unless you will deliver them to the bearer, I will send the sheriff with him. You are nothing more to me. Will write you later. Lena McMahon."

Foley walked to the Erie and delivered the note to the expressman on duty, Charles Mesler, insisting that under no circumstance was he to reveal to Theresa McMahon that Lena was still in Port Jervis; nor was he to let on that Foley had given him the note, or, as Foley later said, "the jig would be up." Mesler expressed solidarity with their situation and agreed to help, but said he could not leave his post to go to the McMahons' until 10:30 a.m. Foley then returned to Lena at the riverfront with some sandwiches and drinks he purchased at Kirk's, the café at the depot.

The *Middletown Daily Times* paints a bucolic picture of Lena and Foley passing the morning by the riverside, Foley dozing, Lena reading a book, while children played nearby and a few boys waded in the shallow water to fish. The comforting mix of sun and water, the seductive location, and the laughter of the swimmers upriver surely promoted a sense of well-being, even of possibility. Despite their enormously tangled predicament, the confining strictures of the adult world might, through their own earnest and insistent efforts, yet fall away. They ate and then both drifted back to sleep and did not awaken until well after eleven o'clock. It was about 11:20 a.m., Foley later recalled, when he stood and stretched and announced he would return to the depot to see if Mesler had obtained the trunk. He left Lena alone beneath the chestnut tree, her umbrella lying on its edge nearby to shield her from the sun's glare.

At the depot Mesler reported that he had gone to West Street as requested and shown Lena's message to Theresa, but that she refused to hand over the trunk without her husband's approval. The frosty tone of the note Lena had dictated, with its stiff salutation to "Mrs. McMahon" and the contradictory closing phrases ("You are nothing more to me. Will write you later") no doubt only further convinced Theresa that her daughter was confused and in turmoil, and precluded her from doing anything rash that would abet Lena's flight. The expressman advised Foley that if Lena really required the trunk today, the only option was "to go and get the sheriff and take him there and demand the goods."

"It was left in this way," Foley remembered. "I was to go back and see the girl and tell her, and we would come down in the afternoon and see about it. As it was a warm day, and as the Monticello train had just backed down, I got into the smoking car and rode up to the depot near the fair grounds."

———•◦•———

A short time after Foley had left the riverside to check in with Mesler, Lena had returned to her book when, she later recounted, "I noticed a shadow cast over my sunshade." Sitting up abruptly and squinting into the sun, she dimly saw the face of a Black man looming above her in an intrusive manner. He was heavyset, she would remember, and of a light complexion. He spoke before she could: "Why, your mother thinks you are in Middletown." She later claimed to have never seen the man before, and so the familiarity of his statement was perplexing. It may have occurred to her that he was someone she *should* know, perhaps one of her customers, but he seemed slightly off, as though he was drunk, or maybe a tramp. "I was terribly frightened," she said. "He had such an evil look in his eyes." In an attempt to discourage his lingering any longer, she scoffed at his remark and turned away, but he reacted badly to being dismissed and angrily grabbed her by the shoulders. She screamed, which infuriated him; he clutched her by the neck and covered her mouth with his hand, and "savagely said, 'Shut up!'"

Hearing her cry of distress and coming on the run was a twelve-year-old white boy named Clarence McKetchnie, who was a neighbor of the McMahons' and, like all the children in the area, knew Lena as the proprietor of the sweets shop. With his pals Will Miller and Ira Brown, a white and Black boy, respectively, McKetchnie had been heading along Cold Brook toward the river when the man he would later identify as Robert Lewis appeared:

[He was] about a hundred yards ahead of us going toward the bank of the brook where it is the highest. We couldn't see if there was anyone there, and I don't believe [he] could either, but he went straight ahead as if he was aiming for something. When he disappeared behind the bank, we heard a woman scream. The other boys ran for help, and I ran toward the place.

When McKetchnie came to the top of the knoll above the chestnut tree, he saw Lewis and Lena struggling near the edge of the water. "Her clothing was torn and the ground was trampled about the place," he later said. Seeing the boy, Lena implored him, "Help me! Help me!" But, McKetchnie reported, Lewis gestured menacingly toward his pistol pocket and warned him not to come near. Then, abruptly, the attacker stood up, gathered some fishing gear he had with him, and went away, while Lena lay perfectly still on the ground. "I thought she was dead," McKetchnie said.

It is not clear whether Lena was sexually molested or how long she and her attacker tussled before help arrived. In later remarks she was demure about the matter, as she would have been expected to be, but did not dispute the assertion made by others, including her physician, that the assault she had endured was sexual in intent. Numerous witnesses who saw her in the immediate aftermath of the incident said her face was bleeding and her clothes were torn, the condition McKetchnie said he found Lena in as he assisted her to her feet and led her to the top of the bank. "Then I called [to] some factory girls and left her with them, while I went and got her mother."

The young women, teenage harness-factory workers who had been taking their lunch in a nearby grove, later testified that a light-skinned Black man had passed them as he headed to where Lena was sitting, and that he had glanced them over and commented, "You look like a lot of chippies." The recollection of the young women—

Katie Burke, Katie and Ida Balmos, Mary Jane Clark, Nellie Stines, Jennie Banigan, and Katie Judge—as summarized by Burke at the coroner's inquest, was that the man had actually been in the company of McKetchnie, Miller, and Brown when he'd passed. Subsequent testimony would suggest it was plausible the boys had shown Lewis where Lena was seated by the river.

The factory girls also said that when they first heard Lena's screams from the direction of the water, they assumed they were the sounds of those same three boys swimming and frolicking; they grew concerned, however, when it became apparent they were hearing a woman plead for help. "We found her leaning against a tree and looking exhausted," Burke stated. "We fixed up her hair and dress which were disarranged." Lena told them a Black man had jumped her and had "tried to tear her tongue out."

Foley, meanwhile, who had hitched a ride back to the riverside aboard the Monticello train, had just reached the brow of a hill and started to walk down when he caught sight of Lena standing with a group of young women he did not know. Lena saw him and beckoned for him to come down, but he hesitated, fearful, he explained later, that the scene had something to do with her mother, so Lena walked up the hill to where he was. "He seemed unsurprised by her condition," according to the factory girls. "He took her aside and whispered to her." Lena told him of the assault, although, in Foley's recollection, she did not act as though the incident was anything serious and, out of modesty, forbade him from asking for details. When Foley inquired if she knew who had attacked her, she replied, "No, I do not; but I am sure I could identify him if he were here." Lena never suggested, as did the factory girls, that the Black stranger had been with McKetchnie and his friends, but she told Foley she believed the boys knew who he was.

"We then went to the river," Foley recounted, "where I washed her face with her handkerchief. I did not think there were many scratches on her face."

To the factory girls Lena seemed "very much excited," but refused their suggestion that she go home. According to Burke, Foley was calm about the situation and instructed them, "Well, girls, you go, and keep this secret and don't tell anyone, and I'll try to find out who the negro was." She later testified: "We did not know Foley, but we saw that Lena did, and supposing that it was right, came away."

McKetchnie's companions, however, Miller and Brown, had already roused the neighborhood. One of the first people to arrive on the scene was Sol Carley, a twenty-four-year-old railroad flagman who was the McMahons' neighbor and friend—and in the view of at least one newspaper, "an admirer of Miss McMahon." He found Foley holding Lena's umbrella over her. She appeared much distressed and was crying, while one of the young women tried to soothe her by brushing and braiding her hair. In Carley's wake came several older women from the neighborhood, who remonstrated with Lena to return home. Foley, knowing Lena's determination to leave Port Jervis, argued against it, but "soon after I saw her mother coming," he recalled. "Not wishing to meet her, for I knew it would not be a pleasant one, I withdrew. [Lena] seemed to be all right then and walked about with apparent ease." Hanging back and making himself as invisible as possible, he went with the group as far as the Monticello track, then quietly split off and followed the rails back to the village.

After Carley, Theresa, and the others had walked Lena to her house and a doctor was summoned, Carley returned alone to the riverside to look for Lena's assailant. Known as "Cool-Headed Carley" for his prowess on the baseball diamond, the young man was himself no stranger to life-or-death crises: nine summers earlier he had accidentally shot himself in the breast while cleaning a revolver on the back stoop of his father's house. The bullet had missed his heart by a centimeter, and his survival was ever after recalled in the neighborhood as a kind of miracle.

Like Lena, Carley suspected the light-skinned man was a tramp who might have come off the nearby railroad or was living in the woods. He devoted much of the afternoon to searching the area, but failing to find the man or learn anything about him, he retreated to Gilbert's Store, a popular gathering spot on the corner of Kingston and Spruce. There he found a group of men and boys gossiping about the incident. Among them was the boy Miller, who was in the midst of recounting a particularly interesting detail: just before the attack, he and Brown had been hanging out at the small Monticello Depot on East Main with several neighborhood boys, as well as Robert Lewis. Miller had mentioned then that he'd seen Mrs. McMahon earlier that morning substituting for Lena at the store, and that when he'd idly asked after Lena, the mother explained she had gone to Middletown. Right then, someone else in the group of boys had spoken up to say that was unlikely, as they'd seen Lena only a short time before, down by the shore where Cold Brook entered the Neversink. Upon hearing this news, claimed Miller to the group at Gilbert's, Lewis had stood up and, looking perturbed, gone off in that direction.

The gathering at the store was shortly joined by John Doty, a carpenter and neighborhood regular. After greeting everyone, he sought out Carley. "Do you want to catch the n*****?" he asked. Carley assured him that he did. Doty said a light-skinned Black man had been spotted on the towpath of the D&H Canal, heading north.

FOUR

"I Am Not the Man"

———⊸∘⊶——

So Carley and John Doty left Gilbert's Store together and headed on foot in the direction of the canal, which was only a few blocks from Kingston Avenue. Along the way, they encountered and enlisted the help of two friends, Seward "Duke" Horton, a house painter, and Walter Coleman, a confectioner, who were in Horton's horse-drawn wagon. After they'd ridden a considerable distance, Carley asked Coleman and Horton to drive on to the village of Huguenot by road in order to cut off a possible escape route, while he and Doty walked along the towpath in the hope of overtaking Robert Lewis.

They soon caught sight of him, although to their surprise, rather than hurrying along the path, Lewis was hitching a ride on a slow-moving coal barge. At five feet seven and 170 pounds, he was a powerfully built man, and caution would be needed to safely apprehend him, particularly as Clarence McKetchnie had reported he was armed.

The white men walked alongside the barge, chatting amiably with Lewis so as not to startle him into flight. After several minutes, they, too, climbed aboard.

The Black man's decision to flee Port Jervis by canal boat, if that was what he was doing, and the fact that he did not spring to his feet and immediately run from the white men, sits rather incongruously with the allegation made against him, as did the fact that he had with him the same gear he'd been toting earlier in the day—a minnow pail, a lantern, and a reel of wire for making setlines, often used to hook catfish. He also knew Carley well enough to associate him with Lena's Kingston Avenue neighborhood, and perhaps to suspect why he and Doty had appeared on the towpath. Either he had not committed a sexual assault on a white woman and was just a simple fisherman with his bucket and tackle, or he was displaying remarkable sangfroid.

Lewis asked Carley, the amateur baseball player, if he was on his way to a game, to which Carley shook his head and replied, "We are going to Huguenot; there is a ball there tonight and I intend to shake my foot." Lewis, in turn, related that he was headed to Port Clinton to spend the night fishing, and that in the coming days he wanted to visit his mother in Paterson and go to New York to see if he could hire on to an ocean freighter.

Carley had no way of knowing if the man with whom he was conversing had a gun; though McKetchnie had said that Lewis had threatened him with one, the fact that the boy hadn't actually seen a weapon would have suggested to Carley that the Black man had been bluffing. Carley focused on relieving Lewis of the knives he would be certain to have in his fishing gear. He mentioned casually that he had something stuck between his teeth and asked Lewis if he had a knife he could use to whittle a toothpick. Lewis handed over a pocketknife, but Carley tried it and said it was too dull and asked if Lewis had an-

other. He hesitated a moment, then reached into his tackle and produced a sharper knife.

Carley then rose suddenly and said, "Bob, we'll have to take you
in." Lewis jumped to his feet but was restrained by the two white men,
as Carley gestured to the boat's driver to pull it to shore. Ascertaining
that Lewis did not, after all, have a gun, they tied his hands and
marched him to the road, where they found Horton and Coleman.
The whites lashed Lewis's feet together and made him lie down on the
floor of Horton's wagon behind the driver's bench, where he would
not be easily discovered. Subsequent testimony would reveal that Carley and others in his posse, as well as a captive Lewis, understood the
urgency of getting him into the hands of the law as soon as possible,
before, as Lewis himself warned his captors, "a gang gets around."

SOL CARLEY, WHO CAPTURED LEWIS.

By now, word that a Black man had assaulted a white woman in
Port Jervis had reached Huguenot, and a small crowd of men gath-

ered menacingly around the wagon. Nervously eyeing them, Carley urged Horton to leave at once. With a click of the reins, the wagon shot forward, a few startled citizens jogging along after it, demanding it halt while abusing Lewis with curses.

Carley and the others later told of an unusual conversation with their prisoner. By his account, Carley asked Lewis if he had assaulted Lena; Lewis confessed that he had, but swore that the white man, Foley, had urged him to commit the act. Lewis said he had been going to the river to fish when he ran into Foley, who told him where Lena was sitting, and said, "It's all right, go down and do it. She'll do it." Duke Horton remembered the directive attributed by Lewis to Foley as being more sinister, that "Foley told him that if he wanted 'a piece' to go down and get it . . . she would 'kick a little but never mind that.'" After a pause, Lewis allegedly confided to the men in the wagon, "My God, what a mess Foley has got me into."

Later told of these remarks, Foley vehemently denied them, insisting that he had no more than a nodding acquaintance with Lewis, having seen him a couple of times at the pool hall, and that he had not seen or spoken with him that day. If the boy Will Miller's story is to be believed, it is possible that Lewis learned from the group at the Monticello Depot, and not from Foley, that Lena was alone by the river. But Foley's claim that he barely knew Lewis is questionable. He had lived at the Delaware House for several months while Lewis was employed there, and they had both been banished from the place at about the same time. George Lea would later vow that the two men did in fact know each other.

Having confessed his crime to Carley and the others in the wagon, Lewis then allegedly made an unexpected suggestion: if he were only allowed to "see Johnny" (Lena's father, John McMahon), or if Carley would do so on his behalf, the whole matter might be cleared up. In the context of the day's events, this was a startling offer, not only for the degree of familiarity it implied existed between Robert Lewis and John McMahon, but more significantly for Lewis's faith that a report of a violent sexual assault by a Black man against a white woman, one that ended with her bleeding and screaming for help, could be explained in reasonable terms to anyone, let alone her father, and by the very man suspected of the act.

Many of the questions that would come to haunt the story of the lynching of Robert Lewis, and befuddle those trying to understand it, hinge on these several unusual statements by the accused, attributed to him by white men who had him bound hand and foot in the bottom of a wagon. Lewis's confession to accusations of the worst transgression a Black man could commit was novel in its implication that a white man had been the true instigator. It made the relationship between Lewis and Foley as central to the story as the encounter between Lewis and Lena, and would ultimately raise the question of whether a Black person might be excused for a crime a white man had instructed him to commit. If Lewis is to be believed, or rather, his captors' account of his confession, there seems a strong likelihood that a relationship existed among Lena, Lewis, and Foley; one that, at least in Lewis's mind, was more innocent than it appeared—if only he'd be given a chance to explain it.

While Carley was pursuing Lewis, authorities in Port Jervis had been telegraphing and telephoning the description of a light-skinned Black man to nearby towns, and members of the village's police force had been dispatched to check out various local leads. A break finally came when authorities at Otisville, thirteen miles northeast of Port Jervis, sent word they had arrested someone fitting the description and had put him aboard the Orange County Express under guard to be brought to Port Jervis. White men drawn from the rail yards and the stores and saloons along Front Street quickly gathered between the railroad and the city lockup on Ball Street, just off Sussex. The suspect, Charles Mahan of Middletown, would likely have been mobbed at once had he been delivered there, but Benjamin Ryall, the general manager of the Monticello railroad, ordered the Express to make an unscheduled stop at Carpenter's Point. There, Ryall personally escorted Mahan from the train and installed him in a room at Drake's Hotel.

The actions of Ryall in intercepting Charles Mahan and of Carley in hurrying Robert Lewis swiftly away from Huguenot suggest that both white men were alert to the risk of a lynching. Surely they both knew intuitively that an accusation that a Black man had outraged a white woman would arouse great indignation among whites, but that awareness had been charged in recent years by the almost daily news reports emanating from the South of lynching carried out in response to such allegations. They may even have noticed recently in local newspapers that two days before, May 31, had been proclaimed the "Colored People's Day of Prayer," a national day of fasting and reverential protest of this most egregious form of racial violence, with endorsements from dignitaries including New York governor Roswell P. Flower and U.S. president Benjamin Harrison.

As Horton's wagon bearing Lewis approached the outskirts of Port Jervis, Carley asked Doty and Coleman to run ahead and discreetly warn village authorities that they had the man everyone was looking for, and to prepare to get him quickly and safely behind bars. They found Officer Patrick Salley standing in front of Cohen's Dry Goods at the corner of Sussex and Front and confided to him that they would be delivering the suspect in the McMahon case to the jail in about ten minutes, and to prepare. Salley, only six weeks on the job, nodded and, making no reply, hurried away.

———•·•———

By the end of the nineteenth century, most major U.S. cities had large, publicly funded police forces. The New York City Police Department, though burdened with its share of corruption, was nonetheless a leader in modernizing efforts aimed at improving crime detection and the interrogation of suspects. It also broke up prostitution rings, used mounted cops to harass workers' gatherings, struggled to disentangle the secretive plots of the Italian Black Hand, and battled the city's numerous street gangs. One police inspector, Alexander "Clubber" Williams, earned his legendary nickname for his novel method of clearing a neighborhood of suspected gang members by bludgeoning them preemptively, before they'd had a chance to commit a crime.

By and large, Black people were viewed unjustly by the law as second-class citizens, habitually inclined to crime and immorality. Such attitudes had been enshrined in some of the country's first police forces, such as the Charleston City Watch and Guard, formed in the 1790s to control the enslaved population in the busy Southern port. Many historians of law enforcement in the United States draw a direct line from the modern police to the antebellum slave patrollers who regulated Black lives on Southern plantations.

Port Jervis, where Irish Americans were prevalent in the police ranks, was not immune to such prejudices. The Irish had been the largest group of immigrants to enter the Northeast beginning in the 1840s, at which time they and free African Americans were forced to compete for housing and low-skilled jobs, and the new arrivals had come of age with an inherent resentment of draconian English laws and a respect for the use of violence to combat authority and settle scores. Only a day's train ride distant were the anthracite fields of Pennsylvania, where in the 1870s a band of Irish American vigilantes, the Molly Maguires, waged a guerrilla war of terror and assassination against the bosses of mine and railroad. Many coal-mine-region Irish in the 1860s had been draft resisters, refusing military service in protest of the fact that too many of their countrymen had been conscripted to fight, and die, in "the Negro's War."

Of course, in contrast to a big city like New York, the village on the Delaware presented a relatively placid scene, and the Port Jervis constabulary were relatively few in number. They were occasionally given the unpleasant chore of fishing the remains of someone ignorant of the Delaware's strong current out of the river, but their work chiefly consisted of keeping the peace, scolding misbehaving drunks, and watching for petty acts of theft or vandalism.

Tramps—itinerant, jobless, hungry—were a notorious social problem of the age, the bane of many rural American communities for their neediness and suspected criminality; because they often moved along rail lines they were an especial threat to Port Jervis. A sentimental image has survived of a hungry tramp stealing a freshly made pie left cooling on a farmhouse windowsill, but their presence was viewed as an annoyance and a civic burden. If there was a distinction in the minds of local cops between harmless and harmful characters, it likely had less to do with who was Black or white and more to do with who was unfamiliar, homeless, and without local connection—a tramp.

No doubt a cop might be inclined to bring his baton down on a Black head quicker than a white one, for it's probable he viewed Black people much as the local press did, with a mix of patronage and suspicion. A survey of local newspapers of the period, however, which tended to unsparingly scrutinize police conduct, fails to show evidence of a pattern of Black people disappearing into the local jail or emerging with wounds sustained in police custody. Of course, it's conceivable there is no mention of police brutality toward Black people not because it was rare, but because it was too common to warrant mentioning.

74

If there was an inevitable weakness in Port Jervis's approach to law enforcement, it was its relaxed approach to police hiring. Turnover on the force was frequent, and in a community with substantial Irish and German constituencies, many officers owed their hiring to political or ethnic allegiances. Not that there was an abundance of qualified candidates. With few exceptions new recruits had no prior experience wearing a badge, the work was relatively easy, and many were moonlighting for the extra few dollars per week. Most chiefs of police in the 1890s had other primary occupations: Thad Mead was a dentist, Dave McCombs was a butcher, Abram Kirkman worked in the railroad machine shops, and Simon Yaple was a blacksmith.

The lack of professionalism was often apparent even among local law enforcement's best. Officer Yaple had once literally fallen down on the job in a disturbance on May 17, 1890, when, intoxicated in the middle of the day, he began harassing shop owners up and down Front Street for a drink or money to buy one. Chief McCombs hurried to the scene, but when he tried to quiet his subordinate, Yaple cursed at him and shoved him violently aside. With help, McCombs finally got his officer under control and convinced him to come along peacefully, although the village president, Obadiah Howell, confiscated Yaple's badge temporarily and suspended him. "Such an outrageous violation of decency, law and decorum as the one described cannot be tolerated in a public officer, without bringing the administration of the law into contempt," observed the *Tri-States Union*, although the paper did note that, aside from this incident, Yaple enjoyed a good reputation.

Two months later it was McCombs's turn to be chastised, after he unjustly pummeled a German American man who had repeatedly demanded, in broken English, to know why he was being arrested. In

THE COWARDLY CLUBBING CASE, the *Gazette* warned, "McCombs has an evil temper which exceeds his power of control," and in words anticipating the town's moral failure at the time of the Lewis lynching, counseled: "Both McCombs and the German should receive perfect justice under the law. It is due to law and order and to the peace and welfare of the community that justice should be impartially meted out. If there be any deviations from public duty and justice, they will be quickly detected and denounced by the press and people of the village."

The perception of police laxity, and the reassuring likelihood that the cop one encountered on the streets of Port Jervis was your neighbor, friend, or cousin, could in turn inspire white citizens to brazenly defy the law. This weakness was exposed in a chaotic episode later that year involving two policemen, E. G. Loreaux and Patrick "Patsy" Collier, the latter of whom was off duty. On December 28, 1890, a former Port Jervis saloon owner named James Atkins was holding court at the Fowler House, a four-story hotel on Jersey Avenue. Atkins had lost his business in Port Jervis several months before on suspicion of maintaining a brothel and had moved across the state line to New Jersey. He had also recently been named as a defendant in a civil suit, and because police were prohibited from serving civil warrants on the sabbath, he dared return only on Sundays to fraternize with his Port Jervis friends. However, Officer Loreaux arrived to announce he'd come to arrest Atkins on an outstanding criminal warrant, which, unlike a civil warrant, was enforceable seven days a week. It involved a complaint from a man named Louis Schick, who said his son had been bilked in a gambling racket at Atkins's saloon.

Loreaux was a capable officer (his arrest of two violent tramps the previous summer had been written up in the local papers), but at the Fowler House his adversary was backed by a large group of rough-looking associates. Realizing he wouldn't be able to take Atkins without help, Loreaux called on some bystanders to assist, including his colleague in blue, the off-duty Collier. Instead of honoring the request, Patsy sent word to his brother Billy, who ran a livery stable and undertaking establishment, to quickly bring around a horse-drawn sleigh to enable Atkins's escape. As the sleigh, driven by Billy, heaved into view, Atkins bolted out a side door and began running along Front Street toward the bridge leading to the state line, with Loreaux in pursuit. Collier was in the street too, not assisting his fellow officer but directing his brother how best to aid Atkins's getaway. Loreaux, unable to catch up with the sleigh, drew his gun and took aim at the fugitive, but the weapon jammed and wouldn't fire, and he was left to watch helplessly as the sleigh whipped around the corner, carrying Atkins safely across the state line. The entire drama was witnessed by Atkins's amused cohort from the porch of the Fowler House, where they'd gathered, drinks in hand, to cheer his dash for freedom.

"A disgraceful farce," the *Union* judged it, "one of the saddest commentaries that it has ever been our duty to record against the people of Port Jervis." The idea of saloon riffraff doubled over with laughter at the plight of a lone policeman trying to enforce the law was an uncomfortable reminder of the town's perpetual struggle to contain the vice and immorality of its rougher elements. "Who from other parts will care to visit us, or to make this town their home?" the paper asked. "The whole town is responsible. The openhanded mob sway Sunday was worthy of a town in the wild West, and it cannot be looked on with indifference by a town that has the pretensions of civilized life."

———•·•———

An official inquest into the lynching of Robert Lewis would ascertain not only that Officer Patrick Salley failed to act on the warning he'd received from John Doty and Walter Coleman but also that he was little more than a spectator to the disaster that ensued. One of only eight officers who composed the Port Jervis police force, Salley was a part-time "special" or auxiliary officer; at this critical moment some of his colleagues had been dispatched to deal with other leads connected to the assault on Lena McMahon, and with his nonparticipation, this left only three officers to get Robert Lewis into the Port Jervis jail in one piece—Simon Yaple, William Bonar, and Ed Carrigan. This task was made more challenging by the fact that the jail, surrounded by other structures, tucked behind a fire hose station, and likely windowless, offered no direct access on either Bank or Sussex Streets but was reachable only via a narrow alleyway. With the continued swelling of the crowd, the trio of policemen was outnumbered by at least a hundred to one, and nothing in their experience had prepared them for so intense a crisis of crowd management and riot control. Even the batons they were issued were shorter than those used by their big-city counterparts, which could if necessary be held crosswise in both hands and used to push back against throngs of strikers or protesters.

As Duke Horton later testified, a pack of men fell in behind and surrounded his wagon the moment it stopped before the jail. Climbing down from the buckboard, Horton recalled, "I couldn't get to my horse, the crowd was so thick." According to an account in a Poughkeepsie paper:

> Every man in that crowd was for a time nothing more than a mad man, made insane by the thirst for the blood of the Negro who had so brutally assaulted one of the best girls in the place, a girl loved by everybody.
>
> When the Negro arrived, the pent-up fury vented itself in one long, loud howl, and a wild break was made for the wagon. Lewis

looked for a moment about him, arose and tried to jump. A hundred
men stood like so many panthers, ready for him.

Yaple, whose walking beat had taken him regularly by the Delaware House and who was acquainted with Robert Lewis, now heard
his beseeching words: "Officer, lock me up. They're tearing my
clothes off. I am not the man." Yaple tried to keep the prisoner from
being pulled away, but his efforts and those of his colleagues Bonar
and Carrigan were useless. The police became, the *New York Sun* reported, "like children in the hands of the mob . . . A dozen times Yaple was thrown to his knees, and once down on his side." When he
tried to strike back at his assailants, he found the crowd so dense
he could not raise his club.

In the melee, neighbor confronted neighbor. William T. Doty, editor of the *Orange County Farmer*, claimed he saw the hotelier James
Monaghan urging the mob on. When Doty scolded Monaghan that
he "should be in a better business," Monaghan turned, his face unrecognizable with rage. "Keep your goddam n****** off the street,
then!"

Exhilarated at having wrested control of the accused from the police, the mob began pushing and dragging Lewis up Sussex Street.
"Gentlemen, you have the wrong man," Lewis pleaded. "I didn't do
it. I am the wrong man." In reply came the vilest obscenities, along
with the exhortations: "Lynch him!" "Hang him!" "Kill him!" "String
him up!" The intensity of the physical assault on the captive was
shocking in its violence—a blinding flurry of blows and kicks and the
slashing with knives of Lewis's clothes and ultimately his flesh.

Lewis's plea to be brought inside the jail had been his appeal for
due process of law; his statement "I am the wrong man," his desperate
cry of innocence. But the witness Dr. Halsey Hunt recalled, "No one
really listened. You might as well have talked to the ocean."

The police were still reeling from the shock of forfeiting their prisoner when a rope appeared, likely from a nearby business, and within seconds was slipped over Lewis's head. The sight emboldened Yaple and Bonar, who with renewed effort pushed back against the onslaught. Yet as often as they pulled the noose off Lewis's head, as many times the mob replaced it, and in turn tossed it mockingly over the heads of the officers. Several other policemen now arrived, but there was little they could do. They either withdrew or allowed themselves to be shoved to the fringes of the crowd. Even the former police chief Dave McCombs appeared uncharacteristically passive; several witnesses, including Yaple, looked to him for assistance but did not see him in any way resist the lynching. Patrick Collier, reinstated to the force after having been fired over the James Atkins fiasco two years earlier, was again seen seriously shirking his duties, even siding with the mob.

The village president, Obadiah Howell, tried to restore order. An attorney known for defending the legal rights of children and incompetents, and, as a special judge, for upbraiding poorly prepared lawyers, now let loose his temper on the police. He fired one officer, William H. Altemeyer, on the spot. Then, seeing the mob tie the rope that was looped around Lewis's neck to an electric light pole, he cut it down with a pocketknife and ran with it to the closest store, where he ordered the proprietor to hide it. The crowd howled with outrage at the interference.

Yaple later said that he recognized several faces in the group—John Kinsella, a railroad engineer who had been in the news himself two months earlier when his westbound milk train 17 struck and killed a man walking on the tracks; the Front Street grocer John B. Eagan; and the depot worker John Henley, who kept insisting, "Shoot Yaple! Get Yaple out of the way!" One man present—possibly Henley—was speaking through a tube hidden by a kerchief around his throat, apparently as the result of an operation, and his croaking, mechanically altered utterances added greatly to the sense of disorder.

The prisoner, when possible, appealed to people he knew in the crowd. Recognizing Dr. Hunt, he implored him to save his life, and the physician briefly joined President Howell in trying to convince others to stop and allow the law to take its course. Others were also urging calm—the Reverend William Hudnut of the Presbyterian Church; Volkert V. Van Patten, a Civil War veteran who ran a local tailoring business; and Ben Ryall, the railroad manager—but all were cursed at and warned away. A reporter saw Chief Abram Kirkman being "roughly handled by some of the ruffians, a minister of the Gospel [Hudnut] struck with a stick," and several other notable citizens assaulted. Howell was surrounded by a group of red-faced men who shoved and screeched at him, then, for added insult and emphasis, yanked his hat down over his eyes. As the crowd advanced up Sussex Hill toward Main, sending up cries and catcalls, it paused momentarily beneath every electric streetlight, ironically the very symbol of Port Jervis's most progressive aspirations, weighing whether it was suitably sturdy to support a hanging.

The crowd meanwhile grew in size and length. Sussex Street was a commercial and residential artery that climbed a substantial hill, and the press of bodies ascending this narrow passage, with the loud exhortations of the crowd and the victim's shrill cries of pain and protest, would have created an unimaginable din and commotion.

Lewis continued to protest that he was "the wrong man," but his fate only grew more perilous when, as the mob made the right turn from Sussex onto Main, Clarence McKetchnie appeared, the boy who had confronted Lewis on the riverbank. "This is the right man, Mr. Ryall," McKetchnie announced. "I saw him commit the act." The Reverend Hudnut, for one, was unconvinced. "The mob had no proof of the victim's guilt," he would later say. "There was merely the

evidence of one man [Sol Carley] who said that the negro had confessed, and of one small boy, a boy so bad that at 12 years of age he
is beyond his parents' control, who cried 'that is the man!'" But Hudnut understood the multitude was by now deaf to any information of
a potentially exonerating nature. "Port Jervis people say a regiment
of soldiers could not have stopped the mob," the *Gazette* would
comment.

Lynch mobs had their own hierarchies of participation. One
could be both present and yet at a considerable remove from what
was happening. As the throng moved and surged, a person might find
it hard to maintain his footing, let alone a clear view of what was taking place. The merely curious, hovering at the edge of the crowd,
craning for a view, had to be content with speculating about what was
occurring at the center. Those closer in might shout insults or encouragement or dart in opportunistically to verbally or physically
torment the captive. The leaders tended to be individuals who held
some special grudge against the victim or, more likely, were men who
took pride in exhibiting their physical strength and powers of intimidation. Intoxicated, if not by liquor then by their own sudden importance, having banished all possibility of retreat, these figures now
guided the whole in a loose yet determined improvisation, heading
toward some dimly perceived objective—a tree, a fence, a field—
where the mob's work would become final.

Officer Bonar suddenly offered an inspired suggestion. Citing a
feature common to some Southern lynchings, he proposed that Lena
McMahon be allowed to see and positively identify her attacker. President Howell, recognizing its potential as a stalling tactic, endorsed
the idea at once, as did others nearby, but rather to savor its potential
melodrama. "Take him to see the girl!" someone shouted, to broad
assent, and the crowd moved forward with this new purpose in mind.

Such encounters belonged to the grotesque theatrics of Southern

lynchings known as lynchcraft, the aesthetic by which the "performance" of a summary execution, and the conduct of its participants,
were judged. "Lynchcraft" might refer to rituals such as bringing an
assault victim face-to-face with her alleged attacker or having her
"sentence" him to his fate. These feeble simulations of due process
might make for gripping theater but had little to do with ascertaining
innocence or guilt. Only a few months before, on February 20 in Tex-
arkana, Arkansas, a Black man named Edward Coy had been lynched
before a thousand onlookers after his affair with a white woman
named Julia Jewell was made public. Coy, moments before his immolation, had asked plaintively of Julia, who was given the "honor"
of setting the pyre alight, "How can you burn me after we've been
sweet-hearting for so long?"

Of course, these measures were also understood to potentially
retraumatize women in Lena McMahon's position, forcing them to
relive the original outrage they'd suffered as well as to become complicit in condemning the lynching victim to a horrific death. The view
that the female victim of an assault should at all costs be spared meeting her "ravisher" was a concern invoked frequently as a rationale for
lynching itself, since hurrying an alleged assailant to his death elimi-
nated the possibility a vanquished woman would ever be made to sit
opposite him in open court, or be questioned and cross-examined
about what she'd endured.

Grateful for the delay Bonar's idea had won, Howell went by a
back route to the McMahons' house on West Street to ask that, in order to avoid further violence, Lena *not* identify Robert Lewis as her
attacker, even if he was in fact the man she thought responsible. The
family, still huddled around their recuperating daughter, was stunned
to learn a crowd of hundreds was heading toward their door, but reassured Howell not only that Lena would deny recognizing him if she
saw him but also that neither she nor they considered the bus driver

from the Delaware House to be the perpetrator. Lena, recovering under the gentle influence of laudanum given to her by her physician, Dr. Solomon Van Etten, maintained that she was unsure who her attacker had been, other than to say she thought he was a stranger, perhaps a tramp who'd been living in the woods.

Regardless of what reassurances Howell had obtained at West Street, the plan to carry Lewis there was short-lived, made obsolete by the arrival of the bizarre and incendiary news that Lena had already died of her wounds. The rumor was attributed to the unimpeachable authority of Dr. Van Etten—a Civil War surgeon, commander of a local war veterans' lodge, and descendant of some of the region's original Dutch settlers. The effect was to bring instantly from the crowd a full-throated cry for vengeance.

Van Etten would strongly denounce the notion he would be so reckless as to spread such a falsehood. At the inquest he testified that he was called to attend to Lena early in the afternoon and that later, as he walked down the street, as many as twenty people had stopped him to ask after her. He said that at City Hall he had "pictured the crime in strong terms to impress on the Chief [Abram Kirkman] the necessity of a diligent search" for the perpetrator, who was then still at large. Van Etten's depiction of Lena's condition, like his urgings to Kirkman, repeated by numerous others, had likely grown in force with each repetition, until one reprinted version had him saying, "If they could know what I knew and could see what I've seen, they would not hesitate to lynch the negro."

Now there was no longer any call for delay. The crowd settled on a substantial maple tree at East Main near Ferguson Avenue, feet away from a house owned by Edwin G. Fowler, in view of the looming steeple of the Dutch Reformed Church. Fowler, an accomplished horticulturalist who grew fruit trees on his property (and also gave singing lessons), was likely not at home.

A rope was rigged to an upper limb and, with a gasp from onlookers, Lewis, bloody and bare-chested, was hoisted high into the sky, as if, one witness remembered, "the negro was going like a kite." In the deep twilight his distorted features were made garishly visible by an electric streetlight, and as it was a warm evening and the town's windows and many of its doors were wide open, his cries entered every home.

———•·•———

Judge William Howe Crane was in his study at 19 East Main Street, the site of some of the town's most stately homes, when a maid entered and informed him a crowd was about to hang a Black man in the front yard. Quickly dressing and rushing across the street, the judge demanded that a path be opened for him so that he could reach the mob's victim. Crane was formidable in appearance—some said he resembled a horned owl—and his voice and manner commanded respect. He immediately tried to assist Lewis by lowering him back down to the ground. Badly bruised and bloodied, Lewis was struggling to breathe and seemed barely conscious. Under ordinary circumstances Crane would have recognized Lewis's face, as the bus driver was a familiar presence in lower Pike Street, where Crane had his law office. But now it was dark and the man's features were grossly disfigured. The judge did, however, recognize several men in the crowd, including the newspaper editor William Doty, the Reverend Hudnut, Dr. Walter Illman, and the police officers Bonar, Yaple, and Collier.

"The crowd was dense in all directions," Crane later testified. "I saw Collier do nothing except to come in and back out; I asked him if he was an officer; he said 'not now,' after which I lost sight of him; he did nothing I saw that was in aid of me or [Officer Yaple]." Seeing that

Lewis's whole body was quivering and that he was still alive, Crane asked Dr. Illman if he might yet be saved. Illman said yes, so long as he was taken at once to a hospital. When someone nearby informed Crane of the transgression with which Lewis was accused, the judge responded sharply that such matters must be left to the courts and that, in any case, the victim's face was so mauled and covered with blood, it was impossible to identify him with any certainty. Crane recalled that "just then someone caught hold of me and jerked me back. I turned and saw Dr. Illman. He said 'there is no use, Judge, we will only get hurt.'" Crane made one final try. The mob had flung the rope over the branch of the tree again and hoisted Lewis back up. Crane

THE LYNCHING OF LEWIS.

grabbed the rope and tried to haul it down but lost the struggle with those pulling hard from the other end. It must have been several moments later that Robert Lewis died, suspended in the air, while the crowd gaped upward from below. The gathering had by now grown to as many as two thousand people, drawn by the commotion—men for the most part, but also women, as well as adolescents like Clarence McKetchnie.

After the great din of the past two hours there came a noticeable hush, a striking absence of sound, as many stood for several minutes looking up at the result of their collective cruelty. The crowd began to stir, murmur, and move apart only when lightning flashed in the distance.

Crane returned to his house, where his family was waiting, fearful for his safety. A few minutes later came a hesitant knock on the door; Crane opened it to find Patrick Collier, wanting to know what the judge's wishes were. The judge replied curtly that it was rather late to be asking after his wishes, but said there was nothing to do now but to cut the body down and notify the coroner.

This was done and then, with the coming of the storm, it began "raining pitchforks," and Lewis's body was left where it had fallen for half an hour or more, untouched, in the mud, blood gathering at the mouth. In days to come, many swore that the uncanny arrival of so merciless a storm could be no coincidence, but was, per the *Tri-States Union*, a visitation from Mother Nature herself, "weeping and protesting in deepest tones." Some even feared the spirits of the valley's long-vanquished Indigenous people had been aroused.

FIVE

SOUTHERN METHODS OUTDONE

L ate on the night of Thursday, June 2, a telephone operator at the East Main Street tower in Newburgh, New York, relayed an unusually large number of calls from Port Jervis to New York City, many to the offices of the major newspapers. What she'd managed to overhear trickled down to a nearby hotel lobby, where several Newburgh men were sitting up late, smoking cigars. They discussed the rumor briefly, agreed it was most unlikely, and turned in for the night. Friday morning's headlines, however, brought irrefutable confirmation: FLIGHT OF THE BRUTE; OFFICERS OVERPOWERED; DRAGGED THROUGH THE STREETS; HEROIC ATTEMPTS TO CHECK THE FRENZIED PEOPLE IN THEIR MAD WORK; and, finally, SOUTHERN METHODS OUTDONE. At a moment when the lynching of Black people was widely viewed as an epidemic limited to the backwaters of the former Confederacy, its appearance in New York State was a frightening reminder that the contagion could very well spread North.

Port Jervis was condemned by its upstate neighbors. Middletown decried "a scene rarely witnessed in this section of the country"; Goshen wept at "the ghastly fruit of lynch law"; while Kingston foresaw "a disgrace to Orange County which will require a long time to fade away."

The New York City papers immediately dispatched to Port Jervis their most seasoned crime reporters, who were provided desk space at the Farnum Building. Roundly their articles conveyed a sense of shock and dismay. The *Tribune*'s man wrote in disbelief that "in a civilized community in the state of New York a mob of men should ignore the officers of the law, drag a wretched negro through the public thoroughfares, choke him, kick him, and club him, and then in the view of 2,000 people string him up to the limb of a tree, almost in the shadow of a church." Intoned a solemn *New York Recorder*, "The leaders of the mob . . . have on their hands the red, indelible stain of murder . . . What is wrong [in the South] cannot be right here." From far across the land the *Los Angeles Herald* concurred, noting that Port Jervis had *"unsectionalized* the rage for lynching."

To a degree, shock over what had occurred related to the fact that Orange County was associated with historic scenes of the American Revolution and the formative decades of the Republic—General Washington's headquarters at Newburgh (where on August 11, 1870, Frederick Douglass spoke to thousands in celebration of the ratification of the Fifteenth Amendment), the founding of the U.S. Military Academy at West Point, the voyages of the steamboat inventor Robert Fulton's *Clermont*, and the cultural heritage associated with the stories of Washington Irving and the verdant landscapes of the Hudson River School artists, such as Thomas Cole, Frederic Church, and Asher Durand. Now, the *Orange County Times* cited as shallow Port Jervis's pretensions of progress and civic virtue, noting that the "addition of a supply of shot guns and a kennel of blood hounds . . .

would enable it to claim comparison with the most lawless and desperate Southern community." The *New-York Tribune* piled on, fretful that murder by mob in a town so close to Manhattan would reflect poorly on the larger city itself, and would be "pounced upon by advocates of outrage in the South as a prime vindication of their own worst excesses."

The headlines were correct that the death of Robert Lewis had resembled a "Southern" lynching in almost every detail—a cry of sexual outrage, the quick actions of a posse, the forcing of the accused to a hurriedly chosen place of lethal punishment. But the Port Jervis lynching, an example of what scholars of violence refer to as "spontaneous vigilantism," lacked the ritualistic staging typical of many Southern lynchings. In its suddenness it felt unreal; the participants appeared to one another frenzied and wild-eyed, yet it was grounded in the same white insecurities that characterized the practice in warmer climes.

———•—•———

For days, white Port Jervians could talk of nothing else, the *Gazette* noting that Lena McMahon "was such a decided favorite with a wide circle of friends that it would have been impossible for anyone to calm the public mind." Even many residents who had not been present at the lynching remained badly shaken by the unsettling reports of the sadistic violence carried out by their neighbors and friends, and of the victim's dying agonies. This anxiety was best personified by the cries of an unbalanced white citizen who claimed to have walked all the way from Port Jervis to Middletown, where he was arrested for raving in the street: "Don't kill me! I didn't do anything! Save me! Oh, if they should kick me as they did that poor [man]!"

After a day or two, a more subdued mood overtook the town, as whites gathered on street corners and debated solemnly: *Why here? Why us?* It was the beginning of a collective head-scratching as to how Port Jervis had come to this end, yet the town's self-reflection somehow remained largely incurious about underlying racial factors. "The reasons which are held to justify mob violence in the South have no force when applied to this case," a Philadelphia paper wrote. "[Black people] number only a small minority of the population . . . in the main they are peaceful and law-abiding and are as worthy of protection. The courts are also well-organized, and there is no reason to suppose that any unnecessary leniency would have been extended to the prisoner."

A more candid editorial in the *Tri-States Union* conceded: "We never imagined such crimes would be enacted in this beautiful valley. The magnitude of the disgrace is most keenly felt. We mourn like a stricken household." But although cognizant of having committed a great wrong, white Port Jervis's focus stayed for the most part on its own wounded reputation and was noticeably lacking in regret and compassion for the lynching's actual victims: Robert Lewis, his family, his friends, and his neighbors. In the throes of the lynching, some antagonists in the mob had egged on a general assault on the entire Black community. Such an event was a kind of sequel that was too common in many Southern lynchings and had perhaps been avoided in Port Jervis only due to the sudden downpour. This last fact was likely not lost on Port Jervis's Black residents.

In place of sympathy or reassurances of goodwill, many whites were content to add insult to injury, much as the media issued offensive and damnable statements pointedly void of regret. The *New York Times*, in lamenting the mob's actions, observed that "it is not to be denied that negroes are much more prone to this crime [sexual assault] than whites, and the crime itself becomes more revolting and infuriating to white men, North as well as South, when a negro is the perpetrator and a white woman is the victim." The *Herald* dared cite a benefit in that "there will be ample opportunity for some months to come for the women of Port Jervis to go abroad without an armed guard to protect them from insult." Closer to home, a Monticello sheet served up the odious "consolation" that despite all that was wrong with Lewis's murder, "there is deep in the breasts of thousands of parents, husbands, brothers, and lovers—warm-hearted, noble Christian men they are too—a feeling of serene satisfaction that the earth is no longer encumbered with this animal in human form." A paper in Pennsylvania, the *Honesdale Citizen*, mocked the notion that its neighbor Port Jervis had to apologize as "nothing but maudlin snivel."

At first, Robert Lewis's mother, Mrs. Jackson, a laundry worker in Paterson, New Jersey, expressed doubt that the reporters contacting her could be referring to her son. He went by various names, she explained, including Bob Martin, Robert Jackson, and Robert Murray, as well as Bob Lewis. She herself went by the name Jackson, from her marriage to Henry Jackson, also known as Happy Hank. Robert, she explained, had worked at a livery stable in Port Jervis beginning in 1886 but had returned in 1890 to stay with her in Paterson, where he was arrested on suspicion of assaulting a white woman, although the charges were dropped.

Mrs. Jackson, in showing a reporter from the *Paterson Morning Call* a photo of Robert, allowed that "he was like other young men and often got into trouble." She said he had left Paterson for good in summer 1891 and, back in Port Jervis, had been hired to work in the stables at the Delaware House. "My mother, whose name is Sampson [the wife of Henry Sampson], lives in Port Jervis, and she often tells me of Bob and his doings. He used to come home frequently but has not been here since he called for his skates last winter."

Not having heard from the Sampsons that anything to do with Robert was amiss, Mrs. Jackson telegraphed at once to learn if word of the lynching was true. When the worst news was confirmed, according to the *Call*, it "caused considerable excitement among the colored residents on 16th Avenue, and the neighbors flocked in upon the stricken woman to offer their sympathy." The grief among Mrs. Jackson's acquaintances was shared and personal, for many had known Robert Lewis as a boy and young man, but the way in which he had been killed was particularly unnerving, a psychological assault on the Black community at large. At the relatively modest distance between Port Jervis and Paterson, as at far greater removes, the terror-istic message that total white dominance could at any time be re-asserted through unforgiving violence was carried into the homes and hearts of all Black people.

On Friday morning, June 3, the Orange County coroner Joseph Harding, accompanied by reporters, arrived at Carley & Terwilliger's Front Street furniture emporium—which doubled as a mortuary—to examine the remains of Robert Lewis. Harding had been out of town on a fishing trip on the evening of June 2 and had been called back expressly to deal with the situation. The body was in a pitiful condi-tion, revealing the extent of the beating and torture the victim had endured. His face, terribly swollen, led Harding to conclude that Lewis had died by strangulation.

Tellingly, town authorities were concerned that a large proces-sional funeral for Lewis might incite more white violence and initially

94

suggested interring him discreetly in a potter's field. Black Port Jervis would not have it. The African American community, which resided in noncontiguous parts of town—on the Acre near the Delaware, along Kingston Avenue close to the Neversink, and at the end of North Orange Street—had little if any history of collectively challenging white officials. But the deceased was neither vagrant nor tramp, and given the unusual and contradictory accounts of his crime, he may not have been guilty of anything at all. "You've killed Bob Lewis as if he were a dog, and now you're going to bury him like a dog," accused one member of the community, while insisting on a dignified service. When officials of Port Jervis balked, saying the village allotted only fifteen dollars for a burial, Black residents responded within hours, contributing the additional funds needed for a grave at Laurel Grove, and for use of the small chapel near the cemetery gate.

It was the custom at Carley & Terwilliger's to allow in friends and neighbors who wished to pay their respects. Several white guests, however, were seen reaching into the pine casket to remove relics, including strips of clothing and even strands of the deceased's hair. The collecting of items associated with a lynching—as proof that one had a tangible connection to so powerful an enactment of white domination—was a mania already familiar in the South. Such macabre desecration, however, was not something the coroner Harding or the undertakers had thought to guard against. This was a terrible violence to Lewis's community, Black people having long suffered from white folks' disregard for their dead. And given the mutilation and violation of a lynching, the laying to rest of a loved one was a doubly sacred ritual, as was the importance of respectful treatment of the deceased. But so frenzied became the assault on Robert Lewis's remains, Black mourners grew alarmed that the souvenir hunters would tip the casket over. Demanding the help of police, they drove the offenders from the building. "Finally, the crowd had to be shut out entirely," reported the *New York Sun*, "as Mr. Carley said that the negro would have been carried off piecemeal otherwise."

(Collection of the Minisink Valley Historical Society)

News of the heinous incident spread swiftly in regional papers, enabling outsiders to lay additional scorn on the white people of Port Jervis. Yet this was a sociopathy that proved to afflict white people not only of Port Jervis. It was reported that some relics of the lynching had already traveled to New York City, where, at Worth's Museum, five dollars bought the sick thrill of walking "in the shoes in which the Negro Bob Lewis had been lynched." Other souvenirs turned up in

Goshen and Otisville, the bearers taking handsome sums for a piece of rope or clothing, or other more hideous mementos. Days later men, women, and children were still hacking away at the maple tree upon which Lewis had been murdered, extracting large chunks of bark and leaving it looking storm-ravaged. Enterprising young "urchins," said one news account, were boarding trains passing through town to peddle some of the smaller pieces to travelers.

The village was known for its graceful leafy avenues, and many trees had wooden enclosures around their base so that they would not be scraped by passing wagons. But any such instinct for preservation was forgotten now, and E. G. Fuller, the owner of the property where the tree was located, had to appeal to the authorities because "the bark has been cut away in dozens of places, and it will soon be killed if [the tree] does not have police protection." (The cruel irony that police were now summoned to rescue the tree upon which a man they'd failed to save had died was nowhere recorded.)

By the time of Robert Lewis's funeral, on June 4, strict precautions were in place. At the Tri-States Chapel outside the entrance to Laurel Grove, both the coroner Harding and Chief Kirkman stood guard over the hearse. To minimize the chance of disruption, Lewis's body remained inside the carriage while a memorial service was held in the chapel. Only Lewis's mother and invited mourners were admitted. The white minister, the Reverend J. B. Taylor of Drew Methodist Church, the institution once led by the Reverend Crane, encouraged his listeners to allow the Almighty to judge both Robert Lewis and the perpetrators of the lynching. "It is best for us all to be silent," he said. "I have no words of condonement for anybody, either the party here whom we follow to the grave or for the leaders of this shameful tragedy. Even in a mob every man is looked on as an individual." The Black community had not threatened any protests, but Taylor concluded by admonishing his listeners, "Go your way with the single idea to do what is right. Pray avoid doing anything that looks like retaliation."

From the chapel the entourage went on foot and by carriage to a section of the grounds along the Delaware River in view of the large boulder known as the Tri-States Rock, where the states of New York, New Jersey, and Pennsylvania meet. Only a few days before, one of the more somber moments of Decoration Day had occurred here, and many of the graves still held the fresh bouquets that had been placed on them during the observance. Happy Hank was buried nearby, in a section reserved for war veterans.

Robert Lewis's coffin had remained closed all day, but just before it was lowered into the ground, the undertaker raised the lid a few inches so that Lewis's mother could see his face one last time. When Mrs. Jackson saw what had been done to her child, she became agitated and shrieked uncontrollably. Even after Lewis was in his grave and mourners had strewn handfuls of dirt over the coffin, along with some wildflowers and lush grasses they'd found growing nearby, his mother refused to leave the place. Resisting those who tenderly compelled her, she cried in her sorrow, "How can I go away?"

———•—•———

At Barber's pool hall, Philip Foley worked as a billiards marker, a job that entailed keeping score of patrons' games, arranging tables and equipment, and occasionally serving players drinks. It was a decided step down from being the representative of a New York City insurance firm, but ever since leaving jail he'd struggled to regain his footing, and he seemed to have accepted his changed circumstances.

Before parting from Lena on the afternoon of June 2, as she was escorted away by her mother after the assault, Foley had vowed that he would find out who had attacked her. But there's no evidence he tried. Instead, he spent part of the afternoon at Nolan's Saloon before reporting for his evening shift at Barber's.

Meanwhile, at the little house on West Street, John McMahon returned from work late in the day and learned what had befallen Lena. He collapsed and remained for several minutes prostrate on the floor. When told where Foley was, he rose, muttered a few words to his wife, and stormed out of the house. "I never before saw a face so distorted with anger," said the newspaperman Charles Young, who had gone to West Street in response to reports of the incident. "He saw me and said, 'If I find Foley, I'll kill him.'"

Ten minutes later the doors of the pool hall burst open and McMahon entered, "in a half-crazed state of mind." He would not yet have known that Robert Lewis would implicate Foley in the assault, but he had heard enough already to be furious—that Foley had spent hours secluded with Lena, first on the hill above Carpenter's Point, then by the river, at the very least exposing her to potential scandal. The factory girls had watched Foley hesitate to come join Lena after her attack, and McMahon may have assumed from this bit of gossip that Foley had seen the assault and done nothing to intervene; and as he knew that Foley frequently fraternized in Grab Point, he may have concluded there was a connection between Foley and Lena's Black attacker. All of this after a judge had ordered Foley to leave town, and Theresa had told him in no uncertain terms to keep his distance from Lena.

McMahon approached the younger man, telling him he was "placing him under arrest." Foley made a savage lunge with a pool cue and ran for his life. The father chased Foley outside, around the block, and then back into the pool hall before Foley managed to escape out a back door. "He wanted to catch me but I was too fly for him," Foley later boasted. "I got rid of the old man, and went on the outskirts of the town and stayed all night with a friend."

In the darkness of the predawn hours of June 3, some Erie workmen on the night shift in the rail yards west of town saw someone
lurking in a nearby lumberyard. They assumed it was a tramp, waiting to sneak aboard Number 12, the 4:17 a.m. train to New York City,
and notified the police. But when officers arrived, they found instead
the nattily attired Foley, whom they were already seeking in connection with the McMahon case. They handcuffed Foley and took him
to the Ball Street lockup.

He denied having had anything to do with the assault on Lena.
"Do you suppose that if I had been connected in any way with that
scrape, that I would have been around Port Jervis?" he demanded.
"Why, I had all the chance to skip out to New York. I tell you I am
innocent, and I want you to send a copy of your paper to the young
lady so that she can see I have told you the truth." His claim was
somewhat borne out by the previous day's railroad timetable. There
was a scheduled train that departed toward the east—Middletown,
Goshen, New York City—at 10:00 p.m., and three heading west into
Pennsylvania, at 9:20 p.m., 11:50 p.m., and 12:30 a.m. He might
have availed himself of any of these departures and been gone
scot-free.

Foley later said that it was only when police took him into custody
that he learned of the lynching of Robert Lewis. This seems improbable. He may have been oblivious to the mob's seizure of Lewis and
the chaos sweeping the village as the lynching occurred, but his hiding in a lumberyard at 4:00 a.m., hoping to slip undetected onto an
outbound train, suggests he did learn about it at some point during
the night—as well as the extremely unsettling detail that Lewis had
named him as a coconspirator.

He would very soon come to appreciate having been placed behind bars, for when he awoke in his cell midmorning, it was to the
sounds of a crowd outside on Ball Street, close enough that its words

were plainly audible. Guards saw him wince when a prominent voice from the street exclaimed, "String him up where [Lewis] was strung up!"

Port Jervis was "a nice town," Foley would later tell the press, but not for strangers who had "no show" there. Already he had remained long after many men with his difficulties would have left. His considerable obstinacy might be chalked up to a resilient character, or his devotion to Lena. But even he was not fool enough to think he could dissuade a lynch mob.

———•·•———

Determined not to surrender another prisoner to lawlessness, the authorities decided it best to transfer Foley to Goshen, twenty-three miles away, for safekeeping. They ordered the Goshen train to back right down to the foot of Sussex Street, thus alleviating the risk of taking Foley in an open conveyance along Front Street to the depot. The constabulary closely guarded the one-block route from the jail to the railroad tracks, joined by a number of law-abiding citizens who had volunteered to assist the police if needed. Nonetheless, after Chief Kirkman personally walked Foley from the jail to the train, it inched its way out of the yard through a crowd of grumbling men who, it was noted, "would have torn the prisoner limb from limb had they been able to lay hands on him."

It appears that Foley's alleged complicity in the crime against Lena had already been generally accepted as fact. As a result of this assumption, Robert Lewis was reduced to being little more than a cog in a white man's villainous scheme, a tool for a frustrated suitor seeking revenge on the McMahons. Foley "was undoubtedly the girl's lover," a Pennsylvania paper wrote, "and he may have taken this means, horribly base as it may seem, to shake off any hold which the girl may have had on him by reason of the promises made her." The *Paterson Call*, taking a keen interest in the case because of that city's connection to Robert Lewis, floated the theory that Foley had arranged for Lewis to playact a scene in which he attempted to ravish Lena, so as to create a melodrama that would make his own shortcomings appear forgivable to her parents. This speculation was based on a rumor making the rounds in Port Jervis that Foley had offered five dollars to other Black men to stage such a charade.

"Two negroes came here last night and told me that they knew of two other negroes besides Lewis that Foley put up to assault my daughter," John McMahon told a *New York Sun* reporter. "I don't blame Lewis as much as I do that villain Foley. I got to the scene of the lynching after Lewis was dead, and I said to the boys there, 'you've hung one of them, but the worst one is out of reach now. Foley is the one you ought to have hung.'" Theresa echoed the sentiment, saying she had not been at the lynching, "but if I had been, I would have tried to save Lewis for trial, and I would have said 'let the black n***** go; the white n***** is the one to hang.'"

No one knew quite what to believe, but so vehement was the disgust for Foley and so revolting all the various theories of his complicity, Robert Lewis was in many minds already half exonerated. Even some who had excitedly urged on his murder now came to suspect, with only mild contrition, that Lewis, alive, might have helped seal the fate of the true fiend. It was even possible to hear one white person quietly admit to another, "He was really a pretty decent Negro, as I knew him." The *Tri-States Union* outlined the situation:

In P.J. Foley the people of Port Jervis seem to have a more despicable character than the negro Lewis, whom certain unknown people recently lynched. The negro claimed that Foley induced him to assault Miss McMahon. It now turns out that Foley, as the lover of the girl, systematically blackmailed her, compelling her to give him money from time to time to prevent his making certain exposures. It is a bad piece of business all around, but, compared with Foley, the lynched negro appears honorable in his brutal manliness.

So it was that whatever negligible remorse the town had expressed at having lynched a neighbor and fellow human being was quickly supplanted by a new kind of regret: that it had committed a most unfortunate error. As a cooperative witness in court, Lewis might have enabled prosecution of the most villainous malefactor in Port Jervis history. And by preserving Lewis for the law, the citizenry would have not only done the right thing but also escaped the infamy their murderous impatience had wrought. Whether Foley was a Lothario, a loser in love, or something far worse—a man who derived satisfaction from seducing country girls—it was clear the town had come off badly in the business.

——— ·•· ———

White Port Jervians in the immediate aftermath of the lynching took comfort from any number of rationalizations: lynching was wrong but Robert Lewis deserved it; the reputation and sensitivity of a violated white woman licensed the summary judgment and execution of the perpetrator; the courts were too slow and therefore lynch law was inevitable. These conceits would persist for many years. But publicly, at least in the columns of local papers and the opinions of quoted officials, the town committed to bringing those who had instigated the lynching to justice, perceiving this as its only chance at redemption.

Some argued that the mob had been made up of strangers— "thieves and loafers, rough railroad employees who chanced to be in town," as the *New-York Tribune* would have it, many of whom "had spent the day in the liquor stores of the town." This exculpatory reasoning, that the lynching could be blamed on outsiders and inebriates, was hardly original, as it had been occasionally invoked in the South. In Port Jervis, specifically, such a theory played on the uptown-downtown divide between middle-class, churchgoing moderation and the intemperate pleasure-mongering of Front Street.

Public opinion was not unanimous, however, in accepting this too-easy rationale. In its bones, Port Jervis knew better. If the town wanted to prove the lynching did not reflect its true character, that better nature would be exhibited only if swift justice were meted out to those who had trampled on law and legitimate authority. With the help of the reputable courts of Orange County, the guilty would be held accountable before the world. Such an expectation rested on what the scholar Jason Sokol terms "the Northern mystique," the faith that the Northeast part of America, home to Lexington and Concord, Independence Hall, the abolition crusade and the Ten-Hour Movement, was surely the nation's enlightened heart and soul.

The North had fought in the great sanguinary conflict to maintain the Union, and it had triumphed, while the people of the Confederacy had paid the price for their obstinate defense of enslaving fellow human beings: near-total regional devastation, born of an ill-conceived war. And the South's spectacular cruelty in the postwar era—night rider terrorism, ballot box intimidation, convict labor, lynching—revealed the bottomless nature of its depravity.

The North, without much effort, could and did hold itself superior to such a place, even as it elided from its own memory the pillories and dunking stools, the witch trials and the genocide of Indigenous peoples, as well as the enslavement of African Americans, which in New York State had proved a far more durable custom than white people cared to recall. On the verge of the twentieth century, Black citizens in Port Jervis were educated most often in inferior circumstances, if at all. They rarely rose above menial jobs as laborers, household servants, and nannies, and struggled to survive at the margins of white-dominated society. But "in the region's collective history," Sokol concludes, "the narrative of freedom had no room in it for these less savory realities."

———·•·———

Part of that conveniently neglected history includes Orange County's "other lynching." It had occurred at Newburgh in the spring of 1863, when the Civil War had entered eastern Pennsylvania and the fears and prejudices generated by the conflict were at their height.

Ellen Clark, an Irish woman in her thirties and recently arrived in America, came to the Newburgh courthouse on June 19, 1863, to ask the wife of Sheriff Hanmore about the possibility of obtaining work as a maid. Mrs. Hanmore told her she knew of nothing available. Clark was leaving when she encountered Robert Mulliner, a Black man doing yard work on the grounds. He said he had heard that a family who lived nearby was looking to hire a housekeeper and would pay eight dollars a month. Clark, unaware he was a prisoner on a work detail, agreed to follow him to their house. When they took what he said was a shortcut through a wooded area, he knocked her down and began tearing at her clothes, threatening to kill her if she cried out. Clark later refused to say "what he accomplished," but eventually slipped from his grasp and got away, although not before he struck her and took her purse containing "all of her money"—about two dollars.

Mulliner fled the area. The next morning, however, he was spotted by police from Newburgh and a local constable on the opposite side of the river as he walked along a road toward Poughkeepsie. Pretending to be travelers headed his way, they offered him a ride in their wagon, then seized him the moment he climbed aboard. He was returned to Newburgh, where word of his alleged attack on Clark had already spread among the town's Irish American laborers and dockworkers, some of whom said they knew the injured woman's family back in Ireland. Irish hostility toward African Americans in Newburgh was, as elsewhere, not uncommon. A Hibernian mob had crashed a traditional New Year's Eve service at the African Methodist Episcopal Zion Church on Washington Street in 1860, smashing several windows and tearing the front door off its hinges, and a second similar assault occurred in 1862.

Sheriff Hanmore and other authorities at the Newburgh courthouse briefly debated moving Mulliner to Goshen for his own safety, as a rough-looking group had gathered outside, demanding he be handed over. The officials chose to wait, hoping the crowd would soon lose interest and disperse. Instead, within minutes its numbers swelled, and men drunk on "rum and anger" began "thundering" at the door with a sledgehammer. A priest, E. J. O'Reilly, arrived and bade them to go home, but his pleas were ignored, and when Sheriff Hanmore emerged to declare he would face down the mob at any cost, he was hooted at and warned that the "discharge of his revolver would be the signal for a general attack, and that neither himself nor those acting under his orders could live five minutes."

As at Port Jervis, civic-minded men came forward to join Father O'Reilly in trying to calm the situation, including the district attorney, the chief of police, the proprietor of an inn, and a judge named C. F. Brown, who was roundly distrusted as "a damned abolitionist." These Good Samaritans had managed to get the sledgehammer out of the mob's hands when a rumor arrived that Ellen Clark had expired from her wounds. The crowd, infuriated, reclaimed the hammer and resumed pounding.

Mulliner then shouted through the door, offering to give himself up if he could be hanged lawfully. Southern sheriffs had been known on occasion to advise prisoners, regardless of guilt or innocence, to choose a dignified execution at the hands of the state rather than risk being torn apart or otherwise hideously put to death by a mob. What was unusual in this instance was that Mulliner himself had proposed the idea. But if anyone heard his proposal, they did not reply.

In moments, it ceased to matter. The wall was broken through, and Mulliner was seized and dragged into the yard, where, it was reported, "he became the football of the maddened wretches . . . The basest animal passions dictated his death, and if any cruelty or indignity was left undone, it was because it was not thought of in the frenzy of the moment." His body was then strung up in a tree on the courthouse lawn, from which it hung for several hours.

As the Mulliner lynching occurred, Confederate forces were making their deepest incursion into the Northern states. General Robert E. Lee and his troops were in east-central Pennsylvania, a threat alarming enough to prompt the building of defensive entrenchments at Philadelphia. Within days the war's two opposing armies, led by Lee and his federal counterpart General George Meade, would meet at Gettysburg. In the context of this anxiety-provoking news, Mulliner's alleged crime against a young Irish woman may have animated deeply held Irish American resentments of African Americans, for whose freedom Irish boys by the hundreds were dying at places like Gettysburg. The mob had been enflamed by an assault on a countrywoman, but also by the sudden proximity of the war.

For this same reason the Mulliner lynching can be seen as prologue, perhaps even part inspiration, for a far greater protest over "the Negro's war," the New York City Draft Riots, which began two weeks later with demonstrations outside recruitment offices in Manhattan. The initial spark of the conflict was the announcement of a new draft call-up, and the accompanying reminder that men of means could, for three hundred dollars, hire a substitute to go in their place. As ever, the draft's heaviest burden would fall on the working poor. Protests at places of recruitment led to acts of arson throughout Lower Manhattan and vicious attacks on Black persons of all ages; men were beaten, stripped of their clothes, and lynched from trees and lampposts. The four-story Colored Orphan Asylum on Fifth Avenue, home to two hundred children under twelve and a staff of fifty, was set afire, the occupants escaping only at the last moment by a back door. A young Black girl found hiding under a bed was murdered. Elsewhere, Black waiters and servants were hauled from their places of work to be assaulted in the street, and whole blocks of Black residents in what today is fashionable SoHo were rousted and scattered. Many fled for their lives, to Brooklyn, Staten Island, and New Jersey; those unable to get away appealed to police, who took hundreds in at police stations and armories.

To the sounds of gunshots and clanging fire bells the city teetered and collapsed in near-total chaos. Hooligans and gangs from the Five Points neighborhood, taking advantage of an overwhelmed police force and the absence of soldiers, indulged their worst tendencies. Widespread looting, arson, and pitched battles between cops and mobs armed with clubs, knives, and guns rocked Lower Manhattan. The publisher Henry J. Raymond in his *New York Times* discredited the idea the upheaval's cause had anything to do with conscription, characterizing it instead as "a craving for plunder [and] a barbarous spite against a different race." He exhorted city officials, "The mob must be crushed at once. Give them grape, and plenty of it." In perhaps the bloodiest confrontation of the three days of upheaval, an outnumbered police unit at Broadway and Amity Street (now Third Street) stood its ground against a riotous army of several thousand trying to smash their way south to the financial district and police headquarters on Mulberry Street. Ordered by their officers to hold their position at all cost, the embattled cops swung freely, striking rioters dead with single blows from their batons. By the time the riots were quelled five days later with the arrival of federal troops fresh from the battlefields at Gettysburg, more than a thousand New Yorkers had perished.

The Newburgh lynching of 1863 is often recalled in connection with that of Robert Lewis at Port Jervis in 1892 because both occurred in Orange County. But the two lynchings, separated by almost thirty years, occurred in dramatically different contexts, almost different worlds—the first in a singular moment of national doubt and stress, the latter at a time of relative prosperity and optimism fed by accelerating technological progress. Yet when viewed from the twenty-first century, what becomes visible are the underlying racial and ethnic tensions they shared, as well as the numerous striking resemblances between the twin incidents.

It had been members of the 124th New York Regiment, the illustrious Orange Blossoms well represented by Port Jervis men, who took part in a tawdry incident in Newburgh at the Civil War's end, when they "caught a stray Negro and commenced to amuse themselves by tossing him in a blanket," as recorded by the local press. "The men declared that they had fought for the country, but not for the Negro." The fears and resentments the war provoked among white Americans were of course most fully alive in 1861–1865, but they lingered three decades later in Port Jervis. In June 1892, with the town's own substantial population of war veterans and others drawn from the surrounding countryside for its massive Decoration Day commemoration, word of an assault by a Black man on a fellow veteran's daughter would have enraged its grieving men, soldiers still in spirit, primed by an event of memorialization powerfully evocative of the trauma and sacrifices of their youth.

The Port Jervis *Tri-States Union* noted on June 3, the day after the lynching, that "to avenge a crime, black enough of itself, but not so heinous as ever unreliable rumor made it appear, a merciless mob dragged the wretch a distance of a quarter of a mile and then yanked him up to a limb of a tree."

What did that mean, "but not so heinous as ever unreliable rumor made it appear," and why did this and other significant doubts about the case not receive further examination? Some of the newspaper's reluctance was doubtless borne of a discretionary self-censorship. Late nineteenth-century U.S. newspapers served up no end of lurid true-crime stories, heavy on innuendo but cautious with certain facts, particularly those that might compromise the reputation of a white woman. There was a continual tension between newspapers' urge to publish (and profit from) multiday sagas of elopements, poisonings, cheating spouses, and sexual crimes and their need to remain discreet. The word "rape" was rarely if ever used; instead, euphemisms such as "ravished," "outraged," or "violated" were employed, and the journalists who churned out this gripping copy often relied on stereotyped ethnic and gendered characterizations to explain human behavior, ignoring potentially revealing truths as they went. A Black man who assaulted a white woman was commonly depicted in animalistic terms, as a "brute," a "beast," a "coon," an "ape," or a "monster." Occasionally, he pounced stark naked from his woodland ambush. The white posse pursuing the alleged criminal through swamp and forest was invariably made up of "determined men," while newspapers often found ways to indirectly urge on a lynching with not-so-subtle "observations": "It is said the ultimate price is demanded," for example, or "we hear there is no room in the jail."

The result was that news stories about lynching became compelling reading for whites precisely for their pulpy nature and faux discretion. Well-crafted euphemism can be an art form in the hands of journalists inclined to exaggerate innocence and heroism and assign bestial or less-than-human qualities to the ignoble. In seeming reaction to women's expanding freedom to live and work independently of patriarchal authority, newspapers were never at a loss for stories of young women boldly venturing forth and coming to grief at the hands of conniving predators, abductors, or duplicitous married men. These cautionary tales carried an obvious moral, juxtaposing a stereotype of women's innocence with men's supposed worldliness and competence to assist in a crisis. Another lesson frequently imparted was that neglect of one's parents was fraught with risk. An editorial admonishment of Lena McMahon that ran in the *Orange County Press* shortly after Lewis's lynching reminded female readers, "Women have great power. Let us then use it by upholding all around us—by being genuine women. We cannot be genuine without being true to ourselves; we cannot be true to ourselves without being true to our parents; we cannot be true to our parents without heeding their advice."

Such well-natured homilies were offset by muted yet highly suggestive renderings of sex and violence that emphasized the female victim's vulnerability and subjugation. Of Lena McMahon's plight in Port Jervis, Pennsylvania's *Allentown Morning Call* wrote with typical embellishment:

> [Robert] Lewis hid behind a tree until the young woman came up, and then he jumped out and seized her. He caught her by the throat, and with his other hand he bent her body back over his knee. She tried to cry out [but] the man threw her almost breathless to the ground. She lost consciousness for a while, but recovered and made a terrible outcry. Some boys . . . heard her outcry and crept up on Lewis but he heard the underbrush crackling, and, jumping to his feet, drew a murderous looking revolver from his pocket . . . He held

the pistol near the girl's head and declared that if they molested him or made an attempt to take him prisoner, he would first blow the girl's brains out.

Narrativized renderings of this kind made for such popular reading that "family stories," fictional serialized accounts of domestic strife, often involving a stricken young woman—something like a TV miniseries of our time—ran side by side with news columns in many dailies, and advertisers also frequently emulated the form. On June 1, the day before the Lewis lynching, Port Jervis read a distressing "farewell note" from a "Mrs. Watkins" beneath the headline SHE COMMITTED SUICIDE:

> My husband—Forgive me if I cause you trouble, but I suffer so. You do not know what these long, wretched nights are to me, and I am so tired, darling—the pain will never be better. It is not easy to take my own life, but I have been sick so long. Goodbye, my husband, I love you—your wife.

An attached comment advised,

> This is but one of thousands that give up, instead of using Dr. Miles' Restorotive [sic] Nervine . . . Go to D.J. Pierce's next door to the Post Office and get an elegant book and Trial Bottle free.

———•••———

For all Port Jervians it was an extraordinary experience to be thrust into the glare of national attention, to have reporters from big-city papers lounging on the portico of the Fowler House or accosting residents for their opinion along Pike Street. Equally novel was seeing the names of people one knew—John McMahon, Sol Carley, Officer Yaple, Judge Crane, Dr. Van Etten—in the pages of the *New York Herald* and the *New York Times*. For the family of Philip Foley, nationally published accounts of his arrest and alleged role in the lynching were the first inkling in a long while as to his whereabouts. If he hoped for succor from them, however, it was not forthcoming. His brother, J. P. Foley, a clerk in the office of the Worthington Steam Pump Company on Liberty Street in New York City, was so upset upon reading coverage of the Port Jervis case that he suggested Philip might have "forfeited his right to brotherly sympathy." A quote attributed to him by the *New York World* read, "If it is true he was in collusion with Lewis, it is a pity he was not strung up with the negro." He said further of Philip: "I cannot understand why he has turned out so badly. There appears to be a mean streak in him which cannot be traced on either his mother's or father's side." He explained that his brother had been born in Warren, Massachusetts, where their mother and sister still lived: "Mother is seventy-five years old and this trouble may prove fatal. He is the youngest of her three children, and naturally was always petted. He learned the trade of a machinist in Warren, and afterward worked his trade there and in Holyoke and in Boston. He came to New York, and for a time was engaged as pump salesman by the Gordon Steam Pump Company."

The *Port Jervis Gazette* agreed that Philip certainly once had prospects, and that "Foley is a good-looking young man and acts and talks in a manner which tends to bear out his repeated assertion that he comes of a good family and has had good opportunities for improvement and refinement." But his brother explained, "He took to drinking and idling, and I was several times called upon to pay his bills and money that he borrowed. I finally refused to have anything more to do with him."

The *Newburgh News* claimed that Foley had a history of alcoholism, petty crimes, and other mischief, including stealing clothes from acquaintances and roommates, and traced his recent movements from Holyoke to New York, then to Boston, then back to New York, before coming to Middletown and Port Jervis. "Foley has been of a sporting disposition," the *News* observed, "and exceedingly foppish in his dress. He has been inclined to boast of his conquests among the fair sex, but he was bright and sociable, and so had many friends." Foley vehemently denied a rumor circulated by the *News* that he had been betrothed to a young lady in Middletown in 1891 and then abandoned her.

The police held him initially on suspicion of having been an accomplice in Lewis's attack, but as even Lena denied this possibility and Foley's chief accuser was dead, it soon became apparent he might serve as no more than a material witness, as he had seen neither the assault nor the lynching. John McMahon, however, soon gave authorities reason to keep Foley locked up, filing a charge of blackmail against him based on letters he had sent to Lena in which he appeared to threaten her reputation if she did not loan him small amounts of money or keep her promises to meet him.

"I see they are trying to make a case of blackmail against me," Foley told a reporter. "Well, let them go ahead. I don't see how they can do it." He pointed out that the only cash he'd received from Lena was a loan of ten dollars, and that if he threatened her occasionally it was only to goad her into defying her parents' restrictions about seeing him. "All that I ever said to her in a letter was that if she did not meet me, I would write her father and tell him some things," Foley said. "Her folks have got no one to blame but themselves for this. They did not treat her well. She was a good girl, but her people wanted to get me out of the way."

Foley denied having improper relations with Lena or plotting to harm her, and never spoke of her disrespectfully in his many conversations with the press, even after she took her parents' side in the blackmail case. However, he warned reporters that if pushed too hard, he would "tell some stories . . . which will implicate several prominent people in the village." As he had spent considerable time in Grab Point, it's possible Foley was capable of exposing a number of men whom he had witnessed slipping in and out of the "houses of assignation" along Front Street.

The McMahons' instinct that Foley was bad news and Judge Mulley's condition that he clear out of Port Jervis now appeared prescient, for as the town reeled from unkind national scrutiny and the taint of an unforgivable act of racial violence, it was given to understand it also had a clever man in its custody, one who might know a few too many secrets.

———•—••———

As the alleged victim of a sexual assault, Lena expected that her privacy would be respected by the press and that details of the outrage she had endured were off-limits. But whatever restraint reporters displayed in this regard, they abandoned in depicting her physical recovery. Attending physicians were variously quoted as saying that her shoulder was broken, her neck badly bruised, and that her nervous system was so severely shocked, blood poisoning must result. She was reliant on laudanum. She was unbalanced in her mind. Dr. Van Etten had seen blood on her undergarments. One paper out of Middletown recorded that "great handfuls of hair [had been] torn from her head," while in Pennsylvania readers were simply told, "Miss McMahon died Friday morning at 8 o'clock."

Van Etten explained that Lena slept only with the help of opiates because although "the pains, aches and soreness are gradually leaving her, her sleep is nervous and unrefreshing . . . In her dreams she is

fighting the negro, and she awakes in a fright and somewhat deliri-
ous." The claim that Lena was *fighting the Negro in her dreams*—was
a journalistic trope that some local reporter (or perhaps Dr. Van
Etten) had likely nicked from Southern news coverage of another
lynching.

A curious omission from Van Etten's diagnosis is any discussion
of what had brought on the fugue state she reported experiencing in
New York City days before the lynching. As an older practicing physician in the town, and a near neighbor of the McMahons, it's also
likely he knew of the similarly mysterious incident from when Lena
was a child. It's possible Lena suffered from mild seizures of an epileptic character. Medical knowledge of epilepsy was still progressing
in 1892, and while the term used today for such events—"temporal
lobe epilepsy"—was not in use, the basic representations of the mal-
ady had been known since antiquity and would have been evident to
a doctor of Van Etten's experience. This was certainly one of the
central unexplored and unexplained elements in the case. If Lena's
inability to recall where she had been for two days and nights was
medical or psychiatric in nature, what was its cause? If instead she
was lying, what truths lay behind the lies? Anyone seriously investi-
gating the circumstances precipitating the murder of Robert Lewis
might also have asked why a clever young woman like Lena, if she
wished to conceal her actions, would concoct an excuse so incompe-
tently constructed and impossible to accept.

One detects in the local media's blend of facts and guesswork
a twin determination to scrub away the possibility Lena was in any
way complicit in what had befallen her, and to keep her reputation
and virtue at least perceptively intact. The alternative, that she had
defied her parents to run away with a flashy older man and possibly
transgressed acceptable sexual or even racial norms, could not be
countenanced. The white community itself seemed to disown such

suspicions. It preferred not to speak of or recognize the possibility that a bond or relationship between Lena and Robert Lewis existed.

In this way all three of the tragedy's protagonists served as scapegoats for unwanted social revolution—Lena, who independently attached herself to a man her parents disapproved of; Lewis, who dared to desire a white woman and did so forcefully, possibly in connivance with a white man; and Foley, that most contemptible rogue, who posed as a gentleman but was not one, and whose predatory heart pulsed behind a well-groomed facade.

Of course, it was the Black man's life that had been unjustly stolen, and his reputation co-opted. "Bob Lewis was none too good to hang, and society loses nothing by his death," the *Gazette* instructed readers. "He was a man of low, brutal instincts and would not hesitate to steal, rob or assault a person, male or female." He had been fired from the Delaware House "for making insulting remarks to female employees," and while at the hotel, "he stole food from the larder in order to satisfy the hunger of his white friend Foley. If rumor is true, he was arrested in Paterson at one time for making a criminal assault on a white girl. The fellow was mulatto with a penchant for white girls."

This last characterization of Lewis is one that has endured. Eddie Keys, a descendant of a large and historic Port Jervis African American family, recalls that the local Black matriarchy of the 1890s viewed Lewis unfavorably and as slightly pathetic for believing his light features made it possible for him to appeal to white women. His efforts in this regard apparently had limited success and at times struck his own friends and family as reckless. A Middletown cousin named Dusty Miller remembered cautioning him only a week before the lynching, "You'll never make old bones, Bob; you're living too fast."

SIX

THE VIGOROUS PEN OF
IDA B. WELLS

he year Robert Lewis was lynched in the streets of Port
Jervis, the major political story of the summer was the
two parties' nominating conventions and the impending
presidential battle between the Republican incumbent, Benjamin
Harrison, and the Democrat Grover Cleveland, a contest that reflected
in part the nation's struggle over civil rights. Republicans had tried
recently to expand voting protections and education for Black people
in the South; however, the country's prevailing mood, personified by
Cleveland and the Democrats, was for sectional reconciliation and a
retreat from further meddling by Washington in the South's affairs.

New York City had begun the decade with the launch of a popular
campaign to finance the construction of a tomb for Ulysses S. Grant,
the former general and president, who had died in 1885. It was the
eve of the city's great age of civic architecture, and New York fought
hard for the right to build the memorial, a project undertaken less in

honor of Grant's military defeat of the Confederacy than in the emerging spirit of national reunion. It was in New York that Julia Grant, the president's wife, made social calls to Varina Davis, widow of the president of the Confederacy, and General Dan Sickles reminisced with his Confederate counterpart James Longstreet about the Battle of Gettysburg, where they had met as lethal foes. Relegated to the hinterlands of compassionate inquiry among whites amid this reconciliatory jubilee was the imperative of ameliorating the remaining inequities between the races. "The Civil War ceased physically in 1865," noted Thomas Beer, a chronicler of the Mauve Decade, which closed out the century, "and its political end may be reasonably expected about the year 3000."

The North saw itself beset by new challenges. As of 1880, industrial workers outnumbered farmworkers for the first time in U.S. history, and with the growth of organized labor came frequent conflicts with capital and fears of "foreign" political movements (socialism, communism, anarchism) associated with agitation for working people's rights. Chicago's 1886 Haymarket Riot, and the subsequent trial and execution of its alleged anarchist perpetrators, had riveted the country, and in July 1892 the Homestead Strike near Pittsburgh would see murderous battles between steelworkers and their families and Carnegie Steel's hired Pinkertons. At the same time, American cities struggled with a host of social ills, including unemployment, inadequate housing, health crises arising from overcrowding, and the lack of care for children and families.

Meanwhile, the Civil Rights Act of 1875, the "Capstone of Reconstruction"—guaranteeing equal rights in public accommodations such as hotels, restaurants, theaters, and transportation—was in 1883 gutted by the U.S. Supreme Court. A federal elections bill, put forward in 1890 by Senator Henry Cabot Lodge of Massachusetts to safeguard Black voting rights in congressional elections, known by detractors as the Lodge Force Bill, was defeated. A similar fate met a federal education reform act sponsored by Senator Henry Blair of New Hampshire aimed at alleviating the rampant illiteracy in the South, particularly among Black children. In the former Confederacy a white conservative crusade known as Redemption proudly trampled into the dust the last vestiges of Reconstruction, as the federal government, worn down by the region's unrelenting resistance, abandoned its commitment to facilitate and defend full citizenship for African Americans.

Even Northern conservatives argued that those in Congress who overindulged the project of Black advancement did a disservice to the very people they aimed to help, coddling them with the false guarantee that the government would see to their needs. The concern that Black Americans not become the "special favorite of the laws," a phrase that emerged from the Supreme Court's ruling against the Civil Rights Act of 1875, grew familiar by repeated utterance. The related notion that it was futile, under any circumstances, to attempt to adjust social inequities through legislation was promulgated by William Graham Sumner, a professor of political science at Yale, whose observation that "stateways cannot change folkways" became a useful impediment to late-century equal rights efforts. Such dogma, hypocritically, did not keep Southern legislatures from passing laws—*stateways*—to restrict and disincentivize the Black vote.

So pervasive was the assault on the country's postwar idealism that in 1884, when Grover Cleveland won his first term, becoming the first Democrat to attain the White House since the war, fears arose he would seek to topple the great edifice of Reconstruction, the Thirteenth, Fourteenth, and Fifteenth Amendments, which had granted African Americans freedom, citizenship, and the franchise, respectively. Cleveland took a dim view of Reconstruction, which he considered a failed experiment, and held that Black Americans need make their way by their own initiative, not from reliance on government largesse. He lost the next presidential contest in 1888 to Harrison, who had more enlightened views on the subject, but who was unable to see reforms like the Lodge and Blair bills through Congress, nor a proposed constitutional amendment he favored to overturn the Supreme Court's 1883 ruling rejecting the Civil Rights Act of 1875. Now, in 1892, the two men were set for a rematch.

These political currents involving race had a lethal undertow: the conviction among many whites that Black people were perpetual outsiders, "citizens" in name only, who existed at the margins of American life and would never fully belong in it. This idea was nurtured by dubious "race science" theorists at elite universities and in the pages of the country's leading magazines. The geology professor Nathaniel Southgate Shaler at Harvard; the zoologist Edward Drinker Cope and the linguistics professor Daniel G. Brinton, both at the University of Pennsylvania; Frederick L. Hoffman, a statistician with the Prudential Insurance Company; and Lester Ward, a professor at Brown University and the first president of the American Sociological Association, were among those who questioned the very survivability of African Americans, given their alleged lack of initiative and resourcefulness and inability to control "the lower passions." Every Black man who raped a white woman, Ward posited, was driven by "an imperious voice of nature . . . to raise his race to a little higher level."

Noxious views like these crept into American homes in the pages of *The Atlantic*, *The Nation*, and *North American Review*, as well as syndicated newspaper pieces and editorials. "What of the common negroes?" asked a typical feature in the *Olean Herald* (New York):

Well, they are like their kind everywhere else—singularly like grownup children. They are, in fact, soft children of the tropics—a race suddenly transplanted from the lowest civilization and placed under the rigid requirements of the very highest, with only a century or two of training to fit them for it . . . They crowd the sidewalks, perch on the fences . . . swagger and shove, and if there is no policeman in sight are liable to be insulting to certain classes of white people. It is, however, but the exuberance of an untrained race, in whom a century or more of slavery and a quarter of a century of freedom have still left the tropical nature pretty strong.

This humbug of racial pseudoscience was not new. It had, however, been inadvertently reinvigorated by the appearance in 1859 of Charles Darwin's *On the Origin of Species*, a work often taken out of context to promote notions of the "survival of the fittest" and the alleged inferiority of African Americans, along with immigrant populations of Italians, Irish, Jews, and Chinese, as well as Indigenous peoples. One pernicious lie that would have held sway at the time of the Port Jervis lynching was that America's formerly enslaved people had simply not made good on the generous constitutional gifts they had been given, and thus had failed to thrive in the country's system of competition and opportunity. Such a conclusion conveniently neglected slavery's painful emotional legacy, as well as the practical difficulties for the freed people in gaining economic and political footholds, especially in the postwar South, where they were denied land, access to capital, and, increasingly, the vote. The lawyer and social justice activist Bryan Stevenson has argued recently that this white-imposed "narrative of racial difference," as it was amplified by nineteenth-century "experts," has perhaps been slavery's most harmful vestige, "the idea . . . that Black people are not as good as White people, that Black people are not fully human [and] are less evolved, less capable, less worthy, less deserving."

Despite the countless obstacles strewn in their path, formerly enslaved Americans had emerged as a significant political force, particularly where their concentrated numbers enabled them to vote for Black representation. As many as two thousand African Americans served in official capacities in the Reconstruction era, from county sheriffs to tax collectors to representatives in the U.S. Congress. But the new mobility and ambition of formerly enslaved men and women, as well as of the up-and-coming younger generation who had never known that condition, posed a distinct challenge to whites, who resented deeply the reality of Blacks attaining elective and appointed office and the expectation that whites need live "beneath the splay foot of the Negro." But nothing signaled the unwanted consequences of Black equality, or highlighted white hypocrisy, more keenly than the specter of physical relations between Black men and white women. This haunting projection of the white man's own adulterous sin led him to place Southern white womanhood high on a pedestal of purity and unblemished virtue, and to elevate as well the defense of its inviolate honor.

Lynching in the South thus served as a means of communal acclamation, soothing perceived threats in the white mind of Black political and economic advancement, of social equality and sexual "deviance," anxieties that were in turn compounded by young white women's increasing departure from home and smothering parental jurisdiction to seek independence and opportunity. The cry of diminishing white male authority in this changing world found both solace and amplification with the mob—righteous in its victimhood, blameless in its anonymity.

Under such self-induced pressures, white sensitivity to Black transgression was set routinely at a hair trigger; an alleged sexual offense demanded swift retribution. But any number of actual or perceived violations of regional norms, arising from "impudence," private disputes over wages or property, the refusal to give the right-of-way, and so on, could suffice to bring an act of lethal summary "justice." The *Chicago Tribune* tabulated deaths of Black men lynched for mule stealing, slander, and threatening to make political comments; others died for "being found in a white family's room" or for simply "being troublesome." The *New York Age* wrote of a Black clergyman pummeled by a mob in Georgia because he went about in a fine suit and "shiny shoes." As W.E.B. Du Bois would explain in his 1903 book of essays, *The Souls of Black Folk*, "[The South's] police system was arranged to deal with Blacks alone, and tacitly assumed that every white man was *ipso facto* a member of the police. Thus, grew up a double system of justice, which erred on the white side by undue leniency and the practical immunity of red-handed criminals, and erred on the Black side by undue severity, injustice, and the lack of discrimination." For the Black journalist Ida B. Wells, such an imbalance meant that "the unsupported word of any white person for any cause is sufficient to cause a lynching."

———•◦•———

On May 27, 1892, only days before Robert Lewis was lynched, President Harrison, in response to a resolution from a Black Virginia Baptist convention seeking a federal anti-lynching law, said, "[I] have asked that law-abiding men of all creeds and all colors should unite to discourage and to suppress lawlessness. Lynchings are a reproach to any community . . . and shame our Christian civilization." He conceded, however, that obtaining such a law would not be easy; murder was technically a state crime, and as the defeat of both the Lodge and Blair bills had shown, Congress was unlikely to overcome the unanimous Southern rejection of federal intervention in the region's affairs, or, for that matter, mounting Northern apathy on the subject. Much as the Grant administration had once pronounced itself weary of addressing the "autumnal outbreaks" of Southern voter intimidation and wanton violence around fall elections, so the Northern press had also grown comfortable with the idea that the South should be left to work out its own destiny.

Broader recognition of the lynching issue had been set in motion by the efforts of a handful of Black journalists and publishers, especially Ida B. Wells of the Memphis *Free Speech and Headlight*, and the Afro-American League, the country's leading postwar national civil rights organization, with a decidedly activist bent. It had helped lead the call for the May 31 day of fasting and prayer to protest lynching, with public observances planned in a number of Northern cities. "The courts of justice turn a deaf ear to our cries for protection, the dog is set upon us to drink our blood for human satisfaction," the civil rights attorney D. Augustus Straker proclaimed at a Michigan anti-lynching summit. He beseeched the heavens, "Oh, God! Wilt thou hear us?"

The petition for the May 31 Colored People's Day of Prayer was signed by more than a hundred well-known educators, writers, and jurists, including Booker T. Washington and Frances Ellen Harper, the renowned abolitionist, poet, writer, and civil rights leader. Also among the signees was T. Thomas Fortune, the influential editor of the *New York Age* and a founder of the Afro-American League, and Albion W. Tourgée, a former Union soldier and North Carolina judge whose popular novel *A Fool's Errand* (1879) gave an intimate, discerning account of the South's postwar intransigence. Tourgée, who would represent the plaintiff Homer Plessy in the 1896 Supreme Court discrimination case *Plessy v. Ferguson*, was one of the first prominent whites to raise public alarm about lynching.

In fact, it was the mass lynching of white people in New Orleans that had helped make the subject a focus of wider concern. On March 14, 1891, at a time of growing local fears of an active criminal underground known as "mafia" (a term new to the American public), a white mob had entered New Orleans's main jail and lynched eleven Italian Americans suspected of having conspired in the recent assassination of the chief of police, David Hennessey. Shot from ambush on a darkened street, Hennessey had whispered with his last breath a single word: "Dagoes." This lynching of men against whom nothing had been proved (six had already been acquitted), in a place where they had no chance to flee, became an international incident when Italy, offended by the terroristic slaughter of its nationals, broke off diplomatic relations with the United States.

The threat the New Orleans massacre raised, in a year that already had seen an obscene number of lynchings of African Americans across the South, was that mob law was transportable, that it could claim white lives as well as Black and trample established law anywhere, anytime it chose. In June 1892 this peril materialized at the corner of Ferguson and Main in Port Jervis.

Afro-American League members were understandably outraged by the manifestation of Judge Lynch in New York State, not forty-eight hours after the fast day set aside as a protest against lynching. Were such gross manifestations of violent intolerance to be emulated everywhere throughout America? The league's Newburgh chapter lost no time in decrying "the action of the angry mob upon Bob Lewis," who was "disgracefully lynched without law or justice." Their message concluded: "We offer our thanks to the President of the village [Obadiah Howell] for the efforts to protect the prisoner in such a perilous predicament. And we earnestly appeal to the citizens of the Empire State as American citizens to give us the protection that is due American citizens." That same week, New York governor Roswell Flower, in attendance at the Democratic National Convention in Chicago, responded to the league's efforts and the news from Port Jervis by offering a resolution condemning lynching for inclusion in his party's platform. It was quickly voted down by Southern delegates for its "possible implication casting some reflection on their state governments," prompting the Black-published *Freeman* of Indianapolis to quip, "It used to be said that while every Democrat was not a rebel, every rebel was a Democrat. By the same rule of reasoning, why may it not be said that while every Democrat is not a lyncher, every lyncher is a Democrat?"

The situation for Black Americans that summer, in Port Jervis and elsewhere, could hardly have been more bleak. The African American historian Rayford Logan would term the post-Reconstruction decades "the nadir" of the Black experience in America, a time of rampant lynching, voter suppression, convict labor, and the ongoing deprivation of rights and property. In Mississippi in 1890 a model piece of legislation—soon known as the Mississippi Plan—pioneered novel ways to extinguish Black voting through poll taxes, literacy tests, grandfather requirements, an "understanding clause," and myriad other forms of procedural harassment. These methods were then enacted by many neighboring states—effectively denying African Americans the franchise without appearing to violate the Fifteenth Amendment, the very trickery the reforms of the deceased but greatly mourned Lodge bill had been designed to confront.

———•◦•———

T. Thomas Fortune was committed to jarring awake a nation grown narcotically indifferent to the extent of Black suffering. A native of the Florida Panhandle, he had been an aide to Josiah Walls, the only African American elected to Congress from the state in the nineteenth century. In 1877, with Reconstruction drawing to a close, Fortune left politics for the challenge of newspaper publishing and within a decade was editing the *New York Age*, destined to become one of the nation's best-known Black publications of news and opinion. He

admired Walls and the other elected figures who had risen on Reconstruction's promise (Fortune's father, Emanuel, had been a state poli-
tician in Florida), but many had by now been driven from public life,
by both assaults on the Black franchise and the frequent and wrongful
stereotyping of Black officials as incompetent and corrupt. Like Frederick Douglass, Fortune believed it vital to defend Black people's
hard-won constitutional rights to equality and citizenship and conceived of a national advocacy organization as the best way to safeguard them. Protecting the vote was a priority, but the agenda of
Fortune's Afro-American League, whose first branch was founded in
Richmond in June 1887, took on multiple challenges, including
school segregation, lynch law, and the denial of equal access to public
accommodations.

"See here, young fellow," Fortune, in one exemplary protest, told
a bartender at New York's Trainor's Hotel who refused to serve him
because of his race, "you will fill my order, and if you do not, I will
remain here and ornament your establishment until you close in the

morning." Fortune was arrested but, with the aid of the attorney Mc-Cants Stewart, sued the hotel for damages. "Let us agitate! *Agitate!* AGITATE!" Fortune urged his readers. "Until the protest shall wake the nation from its indifference."

In the Negro Convention Movement, begun in Philadelphia in 1830 and active until the Civil War, free Black men and women—religious leaders, educators, artisans, joined by those in flight from enslavement—met in state, regional, and national gatherings to address issues of discrimination, white violence, abolition, and African American emigration. Useful in fostering solidarity, the conclaves, however, often led to little more than well-drafted resolutions. Fortune insisted his league would be an activist organization, one that would make demands, not simply agree on shared sentiments. He believed that whites were capable of changing their behavior and attitude toward people of darker skin, because "the heart of the nation is true to the sublime principle of justice," and would respond to advocacy that demonstrated the clear legitimacy of Black citizenship.

The league's hopes were raised when Benjamin Harrison won the 1888 election, although even with Republican control of the White House and both houses of Congress, the South maintained a powerful emotional edge. With the region's history of noncooperation, Klan violence, ballot box fraud, insistence that it alone "knew the Negro," and banner-waving legions of the Southern Redemption (for all its pomp and pageantry, more or less the white mob, now led by ex-Confederate dignitaries), the South's obstinance ultimately broke down the North's will to endlessly readjudicate the Civil War. Henry W. Grady, the *Atlanta Constitution* editor, in 1886 announced a "New South," one open to an influx of Northern business capital and with its "colored problem" sufficiently under control, a boast of Southern progress that Fortune swiftly punctured by noting how cruel and violently racist the New South remained, even a quarter century after Appomattox. When Grady in turn dismissed Fortune as an "Afro-American agitator," Fortune warned the editor, and assured his own readers, that the ubiquitous Afro-American was indeed an agitator, one who would sound "the death knell of the shuffling, cringing creature in black who for two centuries and a half had given the right of way to white men." In his place, Fortune hailed the coming not of a "New South," but rather of "a new man in black, a freeman every inch, standing erect and undaunted, an American from head to foot . . . who looks like a man! . . . and bears no resemblance to a slave, a coward, or an ignoramus." Shooing away white detractors like Grady as so many "croaking ravens," Fortune assured his followers: "No race ever had before in the history of mankind greater cause for organization, for self-reliance, for self-help than Afro-Americans."

Fortune's militance impressed other leading Black publishers and journalists, among them Wells at the Memphis *Free Speech and Headlight*, William Calvin Chase at the *Washington Bee*, and John Mitchell, Jr., of the *Richmond Planet*. Horrified by the South's brutality and indifference and Washington's failure to act, they saw with Fortune the critical need for bold words and effective action. The end of the Civil War and the opening of the vast theater of Reconstruction across the South, with its four million emancipated freedmen, had for many years soaked up what attention reformers and the nation paid the advance of equal rights. The Afro-American League thus represented for many Black activists a return to the prewar intensity of the abolition movement and the resistance to the Fugitive Slave Law of 1850, when the cause of liberation was national, and centered in Northern cities. Wells called the league "the grandest [idea] ever originated by colored men," as she admonished the Black America she so dearly loved to fight now or be "stigmatized forever as a race of cowards." By fall 1889, more than forty state and local chapters had formed.

The league saw one opening in creating legal precedents for its agenda by challenging racial discrimination in the North, common injustices such as prejudicial insurance rates for Black people and restaurants and hotels that illegally denied them service. While the success rate was modest, publicized cases of this kind, simply by being aired in the white and Black press, advanced the perception that such clearly obvious claims for basic racial equity were completely deserving. This work inspired several like-minded campaigns, including one in response to the lynching at Port Jervis.

"Whatever Bob Lewis's own crime, the community's was murder," declared the attorney Rufus L. Perry, Jr., of Brooklyn, leader of the Friends of Bob Lewis. In summer 1892, the group announced the first lawsuit of its kind in New York, seeking twenty thousand dollars in damages from the state on behalf of Lewis's mother, citing criminal negligence in his death. A graduate of the New York University School of Law, Perry, from his offices on Fulton Street, was already making a name for himself as Brooklyn's "Negro lawyer." His father, the Reverend Rufus Perry, was an influential community leader as head of a large Baptist congregation in the borough. The younger Perry's closest associates in the Lewis case were Dr. Robert R. Meredith, leader of the Tompkins Avenue Congregationalist Church in Brooklyn, and Louis Stoiber, an attorney and early advocate for the Legal Aid Society, which was founded in New York City in 1876 to assist indigent German immigrants.

Perry, Meredith, and Stoiber saw the Port Jervis lawsuit as the beginnings of what they hoped would become a permanent legal advocacy group capable of holding communities accountable for lynching. If mobs went unpunished in criminal court, as so often happened, towns and states could at least be brought to heel by court-sanctioned demands for financial restitution, a process that would at the same time publicly shame officials' abhorrent failure to protect a citizen's right to the presumption of innocence. Using a similar dynamic, some of the first state anti-lynching laws enacted in the early twentieth century would reach over the heads of the mob entirely, placing legal culpability at the doorstep of any sheriff who did not use the power of his office to deter an act of summary justice. In the context of Perry's lawsuit, Port Jervis's botched effort to safeguard the life of Robert Lewis seemed an open-and-shut case. As the *New York Herald* had scolded a few days after the lynching: "Four New York policemen could have prevented the mob on Thursday night from murdering Lewis, and one or two New York detectives would have before this caught several [of those responsible] and locked them up. Not a step has been taken to secure the arrest of the ringleaders. Not even a reward has been offered for the identification and arrest of any of the lynchers." Although a judge might sympathize with the Port Jervis police on account of the lynching's spontaneous nature and the overwhelming numbers unprepared law officers found arrayed against them, it seemed nonetheless a straightforward matter to conclude that local authorities had failed Robert Lewis.

It is unclear, however, whether the legal papers of the Perry group were ever served on Governor Flower. As the *Tri-States Union* pointed out, although a state statute of 1855 made counties and municipalities potentially liable for property damage caused by a mob, there was no corresponding fiscal remedy for loss of life, and a legal principle known as the doctrine of sovereign immunity tended to protect states from lawsuits involving violations of an individual's constitutional rights, such as the right to due process. The protection had been reaffirmed by the U.S. Supreme Court as recently as 1890, in *Hans v. Louisiana*. The upstate press took interested note of the innovative nature of the Perry suit but scoffed at its chances; the *Newburgh News* described it cynically as "a case where a negro is worth $20,000 more dead than alive." Perry assured Orange County newsmen that the case was already attracting attention, certainly a chief objective in and of itself, although at one point he seemed to compromise his movement's implied opposition to extrajudicial violence by declaring that "Lewis was merely a cat's paw in the hands of P.J. Foley, and if anyone deserved lynching it was he."

Per the consoling words of the Reverend Taylor at Lewis's funeral, Port Jervis's Black community, while profoundly shaken, had remained peaceful over the summer and showed no inclination to retaliate for the lynching. Some perhaps hoped that actual restitution might be won through Perry's lawsuit, or were simply encouraged by the strong critique of white authority the suit articulated. A likely more consequential threat to local white hegemony, however, came in words directed by one Black Port Jervian to local white Republican officials—the coroner, district attorney, sheriff, and judges—that a failure to bring convictions against the lynch mob would greatly diminish turnout for Republican candidates in the fall election. "If Lewis's murderers are allowed to go unpunished, mark my words, the Republicans won't carry Orange County this fall, or for many years," recorded the *Middletown Daily Argus*. "For years they have professed to be the friends and protectors of our race. Let them prove it, now that opportunity offers."

———•◦•———

There were few people in America better able than Ida B. Wells to think critically about what had occurred in Port Jervis. The young African American journalist from Holly Springs, Mississippi, had, through her Memphis writings of the 1880s and early 1890s, established herself as one of the sharpest minds in the nation's press. Yet she had learned the dark reality of lynching in the worst possible way—not as a reporter but through personal loss. As recently as the fall of 1891, "like many another person who had read of lynching in the South," Wells conceded, she "had accepted the idea . . . that although lynching was irregular and contrary to law and order, unreasoning anger over the terrible crime of rape led to the lynching, that perhaps the brute deserved death anyhow, and the mob was justified in taking his life." This impression evaporated swiftly in March 1892, when her friend Thomas Moss and two of his Memphis business partners, Will Stewart and Calvin McDowell, were arrested on trumped-up charges for repulsing an attack on the store they owned, the People's Grocery, then stealthily taken from jail in the middle of the night and lynched. Their actual "crime" had been to operate a business that competed with one belonging to a white man.

Manufactured allegations of various kinds, Wells found upon further inquiry, were at the heart of many other lynchings, although a good number involved the most inflammatory charge, a sexual offense against a white woman. The latter could be relied on for purposes of incitement, so it was often included, no matter the original cause of complaint. And because whites viewed any intimacy between a Black man and a white woman as criminal sexual assault and refused to acknowledge the possibility the relationships were consensual, the likelihood of lethal consequences was ever present. By early May 1892, Wells had grown contemptuous enough of this hypocrisy to declare in the *Free Speech and Headlight*:

Nobody in this section believes the old threadbare lie that Negro men assault white women. If Southern white men are not careful,

they will over-reach themselves and a conclusion will be reached
which will be very damaging to the moral reputation of their women.

Publishing such volatile words in the South in the early 1890s
was beyond asking for trouble; it was suicidal. Wells, however, who
stood no more than five feet tall, had never lacked for daring. Following the deaths of both her parents in a yellow fever epidemic in 1878,
when she was sixteen, she had refused to hand her several younger
siblings off to the care of relatives and instead assumed sole management as head of her family. She taught at a one-room country school-
house in Mississippi, and later in Memphis, where she dabbled in
literary and theatrical club life and contributed articles to local African American newspapers. Her early pieces dealt with household
and women's health issues, but she soon branched out, penning eloquent critiques of politics and the struggle for equal rights. Of a decidedly activist bent, she once bit a conductor who tried to physically
evict her from a first-class railroad car, and in a similar incident in
1884, she brought and won a lawsuit after she was driven from a "ladies' car" and sent to the Jim Crow "smoking car" of a train. A DARKY
DAMSEL OBTAINS A VERDICT FOR DAMAGES AGAINST THE CHESA-
PEAKE & OHIO RAILROAD: WHAT IT COSTS TO PUT A COLORED
SCHOOL TEACHER IN A SMOKING CAR—VERDICT FOR $500, the
Memphis *Daily Appeal* headlined its account. The award, however,
was successfully appealed, the state supreme court ruling that her
sole intent had been to harass the railroad.

In May 1892, when her incendiary words about white women
and lynching ran in the *Free Speech and Headlight*, she was in New
York City. In her absence the paper's offices were vandalized, while
the *Memphis Scimitar*, assuming the author of such a calumny to be a
man, threatened "to brand [the editor] in the forehead with a hot iron

and perform upon him a surgical operation with a pair of tailor's shears."

T. Thomas Fortune had long followed Wells's Memphis writings and, aware that she could not safely return home, offered her work on the *Age*. In exchange for the subscription list of the *Free Speech and Headlight*, he and co-owner Jerome B. Peterson gave her a quarter interest in the *Age* and a salary to write weekly pieces about the South. "Having destroyed my paper, had a price put on my life, and been made an exile from home for hinting at the truth, I felt that I owed it to myself and to my race to tell the whole truth now that I was where I could do so freely," she vowed.

"Miss Ida B. Wells has added her vigorous pen to the pugnacious quill-quivers of the *New York Age*," applauded the *Detroit Plaindealer*. "If those sneaking, cowardly, Negro-hating Memphis copperheads think they have gained anything by this arrangement, they are welcome to it." Indeed, Wells lost no time in returning to her criticisms. In a June 25 article for the *Age*, she noted that "the miscegenation laws of the South only operate against the legitimate union of the races; they leave the white man free to seduce all the colored girls he can, but it is death to the colored man who yields to the force and advances of a similar attraction in white women."

Her June 25 comments were part of a seven-column *Age* exposé titled "The Truth About Lynching," in which Wells provided numerous dates and names involved in known lynchings and attacked the overworked reports that Black men were raping white women. Ten thousand copies of the issue were distributed, one thousand in Memphis alone, the first excerpts of what would become *Southern Horrors: Lynch Law in All Its Phases*, Wells's book debut and the country's first incisive outline of the lynching plague. It showed convincingly "that lynching represented the very heart, the Rosetta Stone, of America's troubled relationship with race," notes one appraisal of the book's publication, and helped establish Wells as a national figure.

The next month, Frederick Douglass, writing in the influential *North American Review*, lent the issue historical perspective, terming lynching by whites a response to Black people's advance since Emancipation. "I have frequently been asked to explain this phase of our national problem," he wrote. "I explain it on the same principle by which resistance to the course of a ship is created and increased in proportion to her speed. The resistance met by the negro is to me evidence that he is making progress."

Despite Wells finding a home in New York, she learned that whites' personal contempt for women of color was a Northern fact of life as much as a Southern one. Once, while commuting on the Fulton Street ferry, she was rudely shoved by a white man who cursed at her. She also discovered that the one thousand miles separating Memphis and New York City offered no guarantee of safety. Memphis whites had at last realized that it had been "that Wells wench" who had so cruelly libeled them, and the Black-owned Kansas City *American Citizen* reprinted their threat to "put a muzzle on that animal . . . We are onto her dirty sneaking tricks. If we get after her, we will make her wish her mother had changed her mind ten months before she was born. We have been to New York. Are we understood?"

Such a violent threat against a Southern journalist in exile, let alone a female journalist, was unnerving, particularly as it evoked the mood of surveillance and terror that had characterized the fugitive slave era of the antebellum years, when white slave catchers infiltrated the North, often working with corrupt Northern police and judges to capture self-emancipated Black people and return them to slavery. While sympathetic to her plight, the *American Citizen* questioned the sagacity of Wells's having humiliated white men in print in the pages of the *Free Speech and Headlight*. "Some medicine will not stay in the stomach when taken. Small doses, sugar-coated, would do better," it advised. "God could have made the world and all in it in one minute. He chose to take six days, in order, if for nothing else, to teach the Negro patience, moderation and conservatism."

Wells could not have disagreed more. She used strong words and had little patience for things half said, or for anyone who appeared willing to accept lynching as just the way things are. Her criticisms did not fall solely on the heads of lynching's apologists but were at times directed at prominent progressives. Frances Willard, president of the Woman's Christian Temperance Union and one of the country's most revered reformers, was taken to task by Wells for excusing lynching as an unfortunate outcome of Black men's weakness for drink, which Willard believed rendered them helpless to control their sexual urges; the result in the South, Willard had claimed, was that "the safety of women, of childhood, of home, is menaced in a thousand localities at this moment so that [white] men dare not go beyond the sight of their own roof-tree."

For Wells the perfidy of alleged Northern allies was one thing; the violent threats of Southern racists, who in print called her a "wench" and a "saddle-colored Sapphira"—or, as in the case of the *Memphis Scimitar*, offered, were she to return, to strip her clothes off in some public place and whip her in the manner of a slave—quite another. Wells was one of the first civil rights activists to understand that the hateful words of white people, especially pompous Southern officials and newspaper publishers, cited verbatim, worked as effective propaganda, depreciating the offender's voice as it highlighted the reasonableness of her own.

Her writings in the *Age* soon brought her to the attention of Victoria Earle Matthews, a Brooklyn journalist, and Maritcha Lyons, a teacher, who arranged a talk for Wells at Brooklyn's Lyric Hall on October 5, 1892, with the aim of raising enough money for her to

expand her anti-lynching work. Wells had taken elocution lessons as a young woman in Memphis, briefly entertaining thoughts of becoming an actress, but speaking before a packed house of prominent New York women reformers, as well as some who had traveled from Boston, made for an intimidating debut. She became so overwhelmed sharing the story of the early loss of her parents, and the vitriol aimed at her for having placed herself at the head of a campaign to halt lynching, that she could not keep her emotions in check. She broke down and for several moments was unable to carry on with her address.

It is difficult today to contemplate the crisis of the human heart, mind, and spirit that lynching presented, in its sickening depravity and nauseating frequency: corpses found in the morning hanging from trees; spectacle "executions" attended by picnicking crowds;

victims immolated and dismembered, their ears, fingers, and private parts sold as souvenirs; picture postcards made of such atrocities—all accomplished with complete disdain for the rule of law and often with passive or direct police collusion. Surely others shared Wells's fear and concern, but for a considerable time it must have seemed that she alone had stared directly into the abyss and knew the magnitude of the crisis.

Wells had to signal to other women on the platform to bring her a handkerchief so that she could wipe the tears from her face and continue. "Respectability was among the highest goals of middle-class Black women after the degrading experiences of slavery," the biographer Linda McMurry writes of the incident. "Without the backing of wealth and family, Wells had probably felt at times like an outsider in the elite social circles of Memphis." The warm reception by the women gathered in Lyric Hall "was a precious gift at that point in her life."

Wells returned the gift in kind. Regaining her composure, she blasted with a fiery eloquence the vindictive, unchangeable South, which, despite its loss in the Civil War, refused to reform and was instead taking the region backward in time, introducing strains of torture and violence as spectacle unseen since the days of the Roman Colosseum. With imagery that would echo in Martin Luther King, Jr.'s "I Have a Dream" address decades later, she called on her listeners to reawaken the great moral energies of the abolition movement, so as to

> rouse this nation to a demand that from Greenland's icy mountains to the coral reefs of the Southern seas, mob rule shall be put down and equal and exact justice be accorded to every citizen who finds a home within the borders of the land of the free and the home of the brave. Then no longer will our national anthem be sounding brass

and tinkling cymbal, but every member of this great composite nation will be a living, harmonious illustration of the words, and all can honestly and gladly join in singing "My country! Tis of thee / Sweet land of liberty, of thee I sing / Land where our fathers died / Land of the Pilgrim's pride / From every mountain side / Freedom does ring.

The event, described by the *Washington Bee* as "one of the finest testimonials ever [given for] an African-American," raised $450, far surpassing expectations. No one was prouder than Frederick Douglass, who wrote in a preamble to *Southern Horrors*, "Brave woman! You have done your people and mine a service which can neither be weighed nor measured. If American conscience were only half alive . . . a scream of horror, shame and indignation would rise to heaven wherever your pamphlet shall be read."

Douglass's praise, it has been suggested, represented a kind of generational transfer of the Black struggle in America, from his lifelong battle for emancipation and equal rights to a young woman's determination to secure an equally prodigious goal, an end to white terror and the bloodlust of the mob.

———•◦•———

June 1892, the month and year of the lynching at Port Jervis, as well as the beginning of Wells's advocacy on the national stage, marked the genesis of the anti-lynching crusade in America. This movement would accrue followers incrementally as lynching became, in the decades around the turn of the twentieth century, one of the very few issues impacting Black lives outrageous enough to arouse white concern. It also stimulated efforts by leading jurists and legal educators to examine what factors drove otherwise law-abiding citizens to take the law into their own hands, to become judge, jury, and executioner, or to stand by as dispassionate observers. The jurists' probing led them to question traditional forms of criminal justice and their possible deficiencies.

No serious scholar of the law supported lynching, yet the experts challenged themselves to find ways to streamline criminal prosecutions in order to meet several aspects of the problem lynching represented: the people's demand for retribution and punishment in something approaching real time; the belief that certain crimes could not be adequately punished by the courts; and the intense public frustration with the cumbersome rules and procedures of the justice system, of lawyerly double-talk, endless hearings, appeals, and obscure technicalities. In contrast, as a Delaware County, New York, paper argued with wry cynicism following Robert Lewis's death, "Judge Lynch permits no long delays or serious interruptions. His decisions are rapid, forced, and final. He allows no appeals to be entered, but sees that his orders are enforced and his judgements executed with dispatch. He has presided for many years [and] is well and widely known. While some of his decisions have been questioned, none are reversed, and very many have been approved by the best citizens, as [the] case seems to be in Port Jervis."

Certain cases brought these issues into sharp public focus. At the time of the Lewis lynching, a legal conundrum was working itself slowly toward resolution in New England; it centered on a white murderer named Frank Almy, whose much-publicized trial and long-delayed punishment had inspired numerous editorials critical of the law's inertia.

Almy, a "handsome drifter," had in 1890 been hired as a farmhand by the Warden family of Hanover, New Hampshire. He soon took a fancy to one of the Warden daughters, Christie, who reciprocated his amorous feelings. They walked the fields hand in hand in the evening and spoke of marriage. Her family, however, was far less enchanted with Almy, sensing, correctly as it turned out, that he was not who he pretended to be and was possibly some sort of grifter or criminal. In March 1891 her father refused to renew his work contract. Indignant, Almy left the property but returned secretly in early summer, making a hidden lair for himself in one of the barns. From behind its wooden slats, he could peer out and keep an eye on Christie. On July 17 he staged a surprise reunion with her as she strolled along an isolated country lane. Waving a gun to frighten away one of her sisters, he led Christie into the woods where, after a heated conversation and an alleged sexual assault, he shot her twice—once in the head, once between the legs. Investigators surmised she had rejected his plea that they run off together.

Dozens of lawmen and citizens scoured the hills for days without luck. Almy, it turned out, was right under their noses; he had gone back to his hiding place in the barn and managed to evade capture for a full month. He was caught only when he ventured out on a midnight foray for food.

Hanover was too small to have a jail, so Almy was held at a local hotel. To satisfy the public's intense curiosity and forestall any attempt to lynch the prisoner, authorities allowed visitors to enter and file quietly past the murderer's "cell," peering in for a moment on the fiend, who was shackled to a bed. Sometimes, to their thrill and horror, he directly returned the gaze. After a photograph of the captive glancing up from his bed was published, letters and flowers from female admirers poured in.

Over the course of two trials, Almy played skillfully to the gallery, speaking movingly of his love for Christie and insisting his had been a crime of passion, for which he blamed her family. The adoration he enjoyed from lovesick women, along with the trials' innumerable delays, infuriated a news-reading public (even as it remained glued to the story). Almy didn't go to the gallows until May 16, 1893, almost two years after his crime.

The issues surrounding the lynching of Robert Lewis differed greatly from those raised by the example of Frank Almy—most significantly, Almy had received a trial, in fact two—but the press did not hesitate to connect the cases, linking the public frustration over what appeared to be the legal system's overly considerate treatment of Almy to the Port Jervis mob's rush to "execute" Lewis. "Bob Lewis's crime was almost as atrocious as that of the New Hampshire murderer Almy," Pennsylvania's *Honesdale Citizen* noted, "and perhaps the leniency and spurious distinction accorded to that infamous ruffian by idiotic sentimentalists may have had something to do with the hasty justice of the Port Jervis people." The *Gazette* went so far as to excuse Port Jervis's rejection of the right to due process, saying that "lynch law is a terrible thing, but the man who possesses a decent instinct of respect for wife, mother, daughter, or sister, will prefer it a thousand times before the mockery of justice and law which permits a wretch like Almy to cumber the earth one hour after his guilt has been made known." If such criticisms are an accurate gauge of public opinion, it's possible Robert Lewis's life was taken from him as swiftly and brutally as it was at least in part as a result of the courts' perceived pampering of Frank Almy.

Other defenders of summary justice in the Lewis lynching spoke of the municipal savings realized, the *Elmira News* crediting Port Jervis's actions as potentially helpful to cash-strapped jurisdictional coffers, since "a wretch was quickly disposed of and a good deal of expense saved." Southern newspapers were known to make a related argument: that lynching offered a "shortcut" to an otherwise tedious civic duty, since the men who staged a lynching were, after all, likely the same men who would sit on a jury. Their service in "Judge

Lynch's court" was thus a no-cost alternative that achieved the same end.

The public disgust with justice overly deliberated and delayed brought forth many proposed reforms, including a return to corporal punishment such as public flogging and shaming rituals, both of which, it was proposed, would satisfy an aggrieved citizenry, reduce recidivism, and save on the costs of incarceration. To deal with sexual assaults, a few authorities, led by Judge Simeon E. Baldwin of the Connecticut Supreme Court and a founder of the American Bar Association, were willing to consider castration, "the surgeon's remedy," a vengeance admittedly so heinous it was expected to not only discourage rape but also diminish lynching, since even the most pent-up mob might be placated if assured that so exacting and appropriate a punishment awaited the accused. To expedite the law generally, experts weighed the elimination of peremptory challenges in jury selection, the abolition of the unanimity requirement in jury trials, and the suspension of the right of appeal.

As critics of these reforms pointed out, however, the law as practiced was already imbued with elements of vigilantism, emotionalism, and summary justice, biases that "chose" which criminals to suspect, arrest, and hurry to judgment, and influenced their sentences. This condition was present throughout the justice system, from the august figures who sat on the highest courts to the beat cop menacingly twirling his baton. Once would-be reformers recognized that removing some of the law's safeguards would not so much discourage lynching as increase the ways in which the justice system already resembled it, the urge for drastic change lost much of its fervor.

SEVEN

INQUEST

The coroner's inquest into the lynching of Robert Lewis convened on the morning of Monday, June 6, in the Corporation Rooms, a meeting place on Front Street used frequently for village business and civic purposes. The questioning was led by C. E. Cuddeback and H. B. Fullerton of the Orange County district attorney's office, and overseen by District Attorney Michael Henry Hirschberg. The coroner Joseph Harding told the ten members of the jury, "It is your duty to find the cause of [Robert Lewis's] death and those who are responsible for his death. He has come to his death by violent means under circumstances which have excited the entire civilized world." Hirschberg, in turn, exhorted the group, who sat fanning themselves with their hats, "You are to investigate; I to prosecute. I shall do my duty; you should and I believe will do yours."

Unlike the medical examiner system that became common in America in the late twentieth century and that, as its title implies, has a narrow scope of inquiry, the coroner's inquest, beyond its re-

147

sponsibility of ascertaining the cause of death, had a broader mandate, including the weighing of any issues of a criminal nature. It was more an investigation, however, than a trial. While there were witnesses, no cross-examination was permitted, and the inquest's verdict was not binding, although any subsequent grand jury hearing could refer to its conclusions.

In the Lewis inquest, Coroner Harding had availed himself of the assistance of three of the county's top prosecutors. There was, accordingly, the expectant atmosphere of an actual criminal trial, with standing-room-only public attendance and an ample press contingent. The start of the inquest was delayed as additional chairs were fetched from Carley & Terwilliger's furniture emporium to accommodate the overflow crowd.

Making small talk during the delay, one of the jurymen mentioned the "other Orange County lynching" and the eerie coincidence that the leaders of the Newburgh mob that in 1863 killed Robert Mulliner, having avoided serious punishment, had each met a violent end. One had been thrown to his death from a wagon, two others were killed on the Hudson River coal docks, a few perished in an explosion at a powder mill, and another became a railroad fatality. The juryman Ed Geisenheimer shifted uncomfortably in his seat at this allusion to the mysterious ways of fate. It was he, after all, who had scavenged and sold some of the most prized relics of the Lewis lynching, including the dead man's shoes.

Officer Simon Yaple was the first major witness. He testified that the wagon in which Robert Lewis was bound hand and foot had made it to within twenty-five feet of the door to the jail before a mob of at least three hundred to four hundred people pressed forward from all sides to seize him. Yaple also described the struggle beneath the tree on Main Street: "Every man in sight was trying to string up the negro, and not one in the crowd except [Officer] Bonar tried to

help me. The negro was hauled up again and it was two or three minutes before I could get to him again by forcing my way through the
mass on my hands and knees."

He named several individuals as ringleaders of the mob, although
most in their own turn in the witness chair offered alternative accounts of their actions. The railroad engineer John Kinsella told the
inquest a patently false story, claiming that when it became evident
the police would not be able to rescue Lewis, Ben Ryall had appealed
to him, saying, " 'John, can't you stop this, they have the wrong man.' "
Kinsella testified that he then "went out in the crowd and told the
boys to stop it, it was the wrong man. They said 'you go to hell; we
have the right man, and we know it.' " The grocer John Eagan, also
accused of playing a key role, swore that he'd approached the victim
merely to tap him on the shoulder and ask if his name was Lewis, to
which the prisoner had replied, "No, it is Murray." Eagan added, "I
then went directly to the McMahon house on Kingston Avenue, and
advised them to lock their house as the mob was coming."

Dr. Sol Van Etten denied the allegation that he had egged on the
mob with an exaggerated report of Lena McMahon's condition. He
did admit to speaking with many people on the day of the lynching
but claimed that his only critical remarks about Lena were shared
with Chief Kirkman, and then only to urge a diligent police search
for the young woman's attacker. Van Etten insisted that he never ut-
tered the words "if they saw the girl as I saw her and they had the
right man they ought to hang him," nor had he offered to pay the bail
bond of any of the lynchers—both persistent rumors.

Duke Horton testified that after Lewis had confessed to the crime
on the ride back to Port Jervis and complained about "what a scrape"
Foley had put him in, he'd also said that he hoped " 'you fellows [will]
make it light for me.' " Horton recalled that Lewis then asked him how
long a prison term he would get and that he had replied "five or ten

years," at which point Lewis, with terrible prescience, urged, "'Hurry up and get me down there before a gang gets around.'"

By today's standards, the inquest progressed swiftly, finishing its work in only five days. But the experience, to many in the village, was discomfiting, as it meant continued scrutiny from the outside world. The *Gazette*, after only two days of testimony, urged the participants to end the agony and resolve the revolting business as soon as possible. "The lynching was bad enough," it posited. "Why add to the horror by prolonging it?" Despite the assurances of the town fathers and county prosecutors, most residents doubted a true verdict would emerge. "When the probable action of the Coroner's jury is discussed, people smile significantly," the *New York Herald*'s man in Port Jervis observed. Witnesses lied on the stand rather than accuse their friends, while men, like Kinsella, who heard testimony of their own role in the lynching, then took the witness chair to carefully refute what had been said. The jury was willing to accept such clearly perjured testimony, and the added excuse was given that as the lynching itself occurred in murky twilight, in a blur of bodies and raised voices, certain identification of any of the participants was difficult. Even William Doty, who had tried to halt the lynching, confided, "I was right in among them, and to save me, I could hardly swear to a man who was urging the mob on. We were all too much excited." Sol Carley said the only man he recognized was Dave McCombs, the former police chief, while John Doty and Ben Ryall strained credulity by testifying under oath they had not known anyone there.

Officer Patrick Collier stated on the witness stand that he disapproved of the lynching, thinking it "too bad to mutilate a man that way until they found it to be the right man." But Yaple's testimony was that Collier "part of the time appeared to be assisting the lynchers." He'd even seen him try to put the rope over Lewis's head. Such damning testimony was humiliating for local authorities, but the examination of Officer Patrick Salley, who had been warned explicitly of the need to alert other officers to the danger of the crowd seizing Lewis and had done nothing to prevent it, was especially painful. Salley, who was "bounced" by President Obadiah Howell the day after the lynching, had joined the police force only six weeks earlier, likely expecting a quiet moonlighting job shooing people home from the saloons, not the role destiny had thrust on him.

"Why didn't you take a more active part in this affair?" he was asked.

"I did what I could."

But whether through a paralysis induced by the extreme violence he saw, or his fear of counteracting friends and acquaintances in the mob, certainly he had done very little.

"Didn't you know Yaple was struggling?"

"I couldn't tell."

"Didn't you see the negro kicked, cuffed, and dragged along?"

"I couldn't see."

"So, you left Yaple to get along the best way he could?"

"I struggled with no one, I pushed no one, tried to arrest no one."

"Did you know it was your duty to do so as an officer to arrest those who obstructed you?"

"Yes, sir."

"Did you make any attempt to interfere at the hanging?"

"He was dead at the time I saw him."

"Answer my question?"

"No, sir."

"You took no step toward cutting him down?"

"No, sir."

"Do you say you are unable to tell the name of a single person who took part in the violence?"

"I saw only officers Yaple and Carrigan, who were trying to put him in jail."

"Can you say who had hold of you or pulled you?"

"No one pulled me."

"You were in no one's way, then?"

"I don't know. I saw officer Yaple step to the wagon to receive his prisoner."

"Why didn't you step up?"

"I stepped within four feet of the jail but the crowd stopped me."

"You had a right to be there."

"Yes, sir."

"Did you see that violence was being offered to Yaple and Lewis?"

"No, sir."

"You saw the crowd pushing them, didn't you?"

"Yes."

"You had your club in your hand?"

"Yes."

"It was given [to] you to assist in preserving order?"

"Yes."

"Didn't you consider this a proper [time] to use it?"

"No. I had my club raised and kept it raised . . . I tried to get the colored man to the jail . . . Howell told me to do my duty. I tried to get in but couldn't. I stood with my club raised. I heard the crowd say: 'Don't use your club.'"

The experiences of the other lawmen that day, even those who helped battle the mob were, if not as pathetic as Salley's, nonetheless futile. Yaple testified that he had to fight to maintain his footing as the crowd shoved and tried to dislodge him:

When they got to the maple tree I was dragged away. Some had hold
of me by the collar. My club was taken from me. I saw a man climb
the tree and I tried hard to get to the spot, but the negro was already
up in the air. One man said he would kill me if I didn't get out. Pat
Collier cried: "If Yaple shoots, I've got a revolver."

Several officers mentioned an inability to wield their clubs because of the density of the crowd, while Yaple testified that the reason
he *was* able to recall certain faces was because he had struck them
with his baton. He repeatedly brought his "persuader" down on the
heads of men he knew, men apparently so determined to take part in
the lynching they were willing to absorb the blows.

The overall ineffectiveness of the policemen's clubs (Yaple at one
point lost his to the mob) raises the question of whether events might
have transpired differently had Yaple, who had his gun drawn, fired
into the mob to protect Lewis. The results may have been cata-
strophic, given the number of armed individuals present (there were
reports of spectators showing up with rifles), although anti-lynching
forces in later years would endorse shooting into a mob as one of the
few effective means of getting it to retreat or disperse. There have
been numerous examples in the nation's history—from the Boston
Massacre to the Astor Place Riot to Kent State—of police or soldiers
opening fire on unarmed protesters or strikers. In the instance of a
lynching, of course, the objective was not to confront protesters but
to reclaim authority from those in the act of illegally appropriating it,
and to defend the life of a would-be victim.

Judge William Crane testified that after he had rushed from his
house and across Main Street, he was able to push his way beneath
the maple tree. "I said [to Officer Yaple], 'have you your revolver with
you?' He said 'yes.' I said 'then protect that man.'" Crane straddled

Lewis's head and heard him gasping for breath. When he asked Dr. Walter Illman if Lewis would live if they got him away, Illman replied, "Yes, the man is all right, get him to the hospital." But Illman's words were overheard and deemed treacherous by those nearby. "Hang him!" a man shouted. "Don't let the doctor touch him!"

The crowd surging beneath the tree, seeing Yaple draw his gun and tiring of the resistance from Judge Crane and a few others, proceeded to sweep them away from the scene. "Judge Crane disappeared and so did I," the officer testified. "I went out of that crowd like a chip on the water."

Yaple recounted that in the immediate aftermath of the lynching, Patrick Collier approached him to say he was an undertaker (he was, it seems, tangentially connected to his brother William's undertaking firm) and to imply he could see to the remains of the deceased. Yaple, frayed and exhausted after fighting a mob for what seemed like hours, stared at him incredulously and asked, "You don't want to take charge after hanging the man, do you?"

To which Collier weakly replied, "There's $25 in it."

———•———

The most controversial aspect of William Crane's testimony was his allegation that it had been the careless words of Raymond Carr, son of the prominent Orange County lawyer Lewis Carr, Sr., that had doomed Robert Lewis. On its way up Sussex Hill the mob had paused before the Carr residence at 51 Sussex Street, perhaps expecting a word of praise from the village elder, who was well-known for his eloquent tributes to flag and country and who had addressed the Decoration Day crowd a few days earlier at Orange Square. But Carr was not at home, and he was certainly no advocate of lynch law. Carr, Sr., was not present at the lynching of Robert Lewis.

The view looking along East Main Street in 1919, with the E. G. Fowler
house on the right and the steeple of the Dutch Reformed Church in
the distance. The large tree visible in the right foreground was
possibly the tree from which Robert Lewis was lynched.
(Collection of the Minisink Valley Historical Society)

His son Raymond was, however. As William Crane stood over
Robert Lewis in an attempt to protect him, Raymond Carr leaned
down, held a lit match to his face, and cried, "You have got the right
man, boys; that is Bob Lewis." Crane put a hand on the younger
man's shoulder and told him to be quiet. Crane knew Raymond,
twenty-three, a recent Harvard University graduate, and respected
his family and thought he might cooperate. But instead, Raymond
repeated his identification of Lewis, adding, "Damn it! He ought to
be hung!" The mob buzzed in agreement. "Hang him! Don't let the
doctor touch him! Hang *all* the n******!" Raymond's outburst,
Crane told the coroner's jury, had likely precipitated Lewis's death.
"It was a critical moment," he testified, "at which a word either way
might be decisive. The crowd was momentarily quelled and there was

certainly an opportunity to save the negro, which was destroyed by young Carr's words."

Coming from anyone less respected than Judge Crane, so unflattering an account of the younger Carr's behavior might have been simply ignored. But given its source, the claim was one that the Carr family, and Port Jervis as a whole, would need to reckon with: Had the son of Port Jervis's most admired citizen caused the most shameful event in the town's history?

William, like his brother Stephen, was familiar with the Carrs, who lived across the street from Orange Square, not far from William's house on Main Street. William and Lewis Carr, Sr., were both prominent in Port Jervis legal affairs, and the previous summer of 1891, Stephen had gone camping with Raymond's brother, Lewis Carr, Jr.

Lewis, Sr., the family patriarch, a proud, much-honored personage (President Cleveland was a personal friend), wasted no time in denouncing Judge Crane's account. It simply could not be that his many good works, his decades of courtroom success and public service, were undone by one disastrous utterance from his son. While he had no choice but to publicly defend his boy, privately he must have been monumentally disappointed. In a moment of moral crisis, Raymond, instead of showing character and coming to the aid of those upholding the law, had stood with the rabble—had even, it appeared, goaded them on.

Prior to testifying at the inquest, William had invited Lewis, Sr., to his office to alert him, "My duty as a citizen will compel me to say that your son Raymond was the man who lit the match over the negro's face and whose words incited the mob to do their worst." The meeting, as expected, was not a pleasant one, with the elder Carr hotly contesting Crane's recollection, the judge holding his ground, and their raised voices heard up and down the corridors of the Farnum Building. Seeing heads poke out from office doors, Crane reassured his guest, "I was talking to you, privately, not to all these others." But Carr was far from appeased. Word of their unhappy encounter reached District Attorney Hirschberg, who sought to assure Carr that Raymond would have ample opportunity at the inquest to give his version of what had occurred.

In his own testimony Raymond admitted to identifying Lewis but denied uttering the words that led to the lynching: "I was downtown when I heard that the mob were up in front of our house. I hurried home, pressed through the crowd, and saw the negro lying flat on his face." Carr overheard Crane and Dr. Illman say it was too dark to see if the victim was dead or alive. Just then a young Black man Carr identified as "Drivers" (likely Edward Drivers, age sixteen) pressed through the crowd and asked if the man on the ground was Bob Lewis. "I then pulled a match from my pocket, lit it, and held it close to the negro's face," Carr testified. "I involuntarily exclaimed, 'this is Bob Lewis all right enough,' without thinking of the possible effect of my words."

He followed up with a letter in the *Port Jervis Index* that again countered Crane's version and chided him for basking in his new role as community hero. Certainly the Carrs, father and son, would have bristled at the immense outpouring of praise for those like Judge Crane, Officer Yaple, President Howell, and Reverend Hudnut, who "endeavored to save the fair fame of the village from the eternal disgrace which has been fastened upon it by this foul and indefensible deed." Tributes arrived from the *Boston Globe*, calling Judge Crane "the one cool man among a thousand passionate avengers," as well as the *Middletown Argus*, which lauded him as "a champion of humanity." A former Port Jervis resident, the Reverend A. M. Gliddon cheered that "in the midst of that exhibition of wretched, cringing, half-hearted, un-backboned crowd of male bipeds, it is a treat to see some real men."

Others in the town resented Crane's sudden elevation because they saw his actions as a betrayal—of his community, of his neighbors, of his race. There were attempts to warn him into silence, threats similar to those made against the prosecutors and President Howell, who had found his mailbox stuffed with hate letters from all over the country. Crane later recalled that a man came around his office, purportedly "on business," then quickly pivoted to the subject of the lynching and mentioned that "the boys were talking a little ugly."

If the town yearned to turn Officer Yaple and Judge Crane into heroes, however, who could blame them? Better to celebrate the goodness of a few of its neighbors than brood over the dishonorable behavior of the rest.

But why had *they* done right and others wrong? Yaple's weakness for drink could make him violently irresponsible, and no one would have thought less of Judge Crane had he dismissed his maid's interruption, pulled down the window shade, and gone back to his book. If the cowardice and pathology of a mob of hundreds of people bent on murder is a thing to ponder, more mysterious may be the courage of two.

———•◦•———

The last witness to testify at the inquest was the flagman Lewis Avery, who, like others before him, claimed to have witnessed only "part of the riot." He said he had pushed his way to the center of the crowd because he "wanted to see what kind of an animal it was that did that business," but swore he did not try to put the rope around Robert Lewis's neck or see who did, nor did he impede any police. He was in fact attempting to leave the area when he "fell down and several people trampled on him."

With a look of exasperation, Coroner Harding then rose to say he wished to hear no more witnesses who swore that they had done nothing wrong, had not interfered with the police, or had not harmed Robert Lewis, nor seen anyone else do so. It was unbelievable, he said, that "no one of the thousand or more people who were on the streets that evening resisted the officers, [yet] still the man was hung. In all my experience, I have never known of so many people who either couldn't or wouldn't see what was plainly before their eyes."

Thanks in large part to Yaple's testimony, however, eight men were cited by the inquest for assault and inciting to riot: the Front Street grocer John Eagan, the train engineer John Kinsella, the depot worker John Henley, the former police chief Dave McCombs, the flagman Lewis Avery, Officer Patrick Collier, James Kirby, and Bill Fitzgibbons. There was little expectation on anyone's part of actual consequences, typified by a reporter's sighting of Kinsella around this time taking his ease at a saloon, a "thorough-going sport" in "a very light cutaway suit, a Maltese-colored high hat and a giddy necktie, dressed for Saratoga rather than the bloody streets of Port Jervis."

Notably absent from the list was Raymond Carr. Jurors may have honestly believed Raymond's version of events over Judge Crane's, dismissed it as a young man's foolishness, or opted to give him a pass in honor of his father's reputation. The days and weeks ahead would be awkward enough without smearing one of Port Jervis's leading families.

It hardly mattered. The jury left the room and in one hour returned to say it had acquitted all the accused. Coroner Harding then read the verdict: "Robert Lewis came to his death in the village of Port Jervis on June 2nd by being hanged by his neck by a person or persons unknown."

Who were these *persons unknown*? Were they from out of town, as many Port Jervians contended, or perhaps stranded, out-of-work railway men? Or did the too-common expression that a lynching victim had died *at the hands of persons unknown*—the ubiquitous last word of coroner's findings throughout the South, now invoked here in Port Jervis—connote something else? Some mysterious process in which the men mobbing their neighbor Robert Lewis to death became, for a moment, not the *persons* they ordinarily were, but beings unknown even to themselves, instruments of some irreversible collective force akin to gravity? Perhaps, as the scholar Jacqueline Goldsby has observed, when "witness after witness swore under oath that the members of the mob were unknown to them, Port Jervis realized its dream of being a modern metropolis. Like a city teeming with millions, no one in the crowd at Lewis's lynching knew anyone else."

As for the willful blindness of the witnesses, "that [they] have deliberately perjured themselves is reasonably clear," complained the *New York Morning Advertiser*. Those who led the mob were known by many who testified, yet they were "able to throw no more light on the affair than if they had been in the heart of Africa when it took place." All were intimidated by the mob spirit. "They are afraid for their own lives," noted the *Advertiser*, "or afraid, at least, that their houses or barns may be burned. It is an exhibition of cowardice that is always present when mobs undertake to administer justice." This last point was doubly true, for the mob had not only "convicted" and summarily executed Robert Lewis; it had now literally acquitted itself.

The jury had clearly vacated its duty, and had certainly failed Robert Lewis. "The case will go on record as one of the most singular suicides ever reported," deadpanned the *Honesdale Citizen*. The most likely excuse was that the jurymen feared retribution from their neighbors. Yet it's also possible they were disinclined to take their duty seriously because of the suspicion, shared by the community, that "there is something back of the whole affair," that neither Lena, her family, nor the press had been forthcoming about what had occurred to prompt the lynching. If the precipitating facts couldn't be established, nor an honest account of what had taken place satisfactorily produced, how could citizens delegated to a jury be expected to approach their role? As one local journal pointed out:

> The thinking public doubts Miss McMahon's story, as it also does Foley's. The circumstances are too conflicting. If the young woman had practically no knowledge of her surroundings from Wednesday to Thursday morning, then she must have been crazy. Not a living female would or could be hired to stay overnight in Laurel Grove Cemetery, as she stated she did. The stormy weather and the delicate physique of the girl would knock that story in the head.

The folly of the coroner's inquest soon had an equally disappointing reprise at a subsequent grand jury hearing in Goshen, where many of the same names and faces reappeared. Gathered on the Mountain Express from Port Jervis to the county seat on June 22 were Lena and Theresa McMahon, Sol Carley, Duke Horton, Dave McCombs, Dr. Van Etten, and Dr. Walter Illman, along with Officers Yaple, Bonar, Collier, and Salley. The presiding justice, E. M. Cullen, noted his "great surprise that [the lynching] should have taken place in a county like Orange, which has been living under the law for two centuries." His solemn words, however, fell short of inspiring the jurymen to take their role seriously, for they soon became uncooperative. With brazen disrespect for the court, they added to the earlier list of men cited by the inquest the names of Howell, the village president, and other authorities. The *Tri-States Union* termed the prank "contemptibly malicious," and an irate District Attorney Hirschberg quashed the indictment for lack of evidence, scolding the jury for sullying Howell's good name and making a mockery of the severe offenses they had been charged with considering.

Hirschberg failed to break through the wall of solidarity among Port Jervis citizens and came away with little to show for the efforts of his office. Of course, what had occurred, or failed to occur, was not merely a poor reflection on the criminal justice apparatus of Orange County. It was a judgment on a community that had given only lip service to the notion of seeking justice, although it's true that those loftier ideals had been chiefly articulated by jurists, editorialists, and clergy. Ultimately, as many a prosecutor has learned to their misfortune, legal mechanisms rely on the conscientious performance of ordinary citizens—restaurant managers, grocers, saloon owners, railroad engineers—and in their silence and collective mendacity, Port Jervians had chosen to stand squarely behind lynching. "They cannot force grand jurors to regard as a crime the wild justice of mob law," the *Argus* concluded, "when the jurors feel in their hearts that the mob did the county a service by ridding it of a villain too vile for earth. The law is as powerless to punish the men who strung up Bob Lewis as is the ghost of their victim."

EIGHT

THE AUTHOR OF
MY MISFORTUNE

—————◦◦◦◦————

A
s the efforts to hold accountable the leaders of the lynch
mob foundered, a parallel legal drama was unfolding, involving the charge John and Theresa McMahon had leveled
against Philip Foley for blackmail. Foley dismissed the accusation as
baseless, as he had Theresa's earlier attempt to have him run in as a
vagrant. His "threats" to Lena, he insisted, were nothing more than
the playful scolding that might feature in any romance. If his tone
seemed forceful, it stemmed from his deep feelings for her, and as for
any exchange of money, she had voluntarily given him some when he
needed it—the kind of casual borrowing of small sums common to
any friendship. One of his letters to Lena, from Friday, May 20, introduced by the McMahons as evidence, read:

Dear Friend: I waited until the clock struck 12. Why did you not
show yourself—some good excuse, I suppose. Well, I will tell you

what I will do, as it seems impossible for you to let me in. If you will come out this afternoon and stay one, two, or three hours, I will leave here tomorrow (Saturday). You can meet me on the Matamoras bridge at 2 o'clock sharp. Answer. Phil

P.S. You may think you can keep this farce up right along, but you will find out your mistake. Why did you not write me and let me know your reason for not meeting me? By meeting on Matamoras bridge at 2 o'clock sharp you will save yourself a great deal of trouble. Phil

A second addendum read in part:

Friday afternoon—I have sent to your house four times since Tuesday. The party saw you at the window. Why did you not come down? I find that the only way for me to do is to show things up just as they have transpired. It will make a nice talk for the colored population in your section. You will find your mistake trying the racket with me, as I won't have it. I will look for you on Fowler Street Saturday afternoon at 2 o'clock without fail; if not, I will be obliged to give you a sample of what I can do . . . I will talk for business.

Despite Foley's innocent characterization of the letter, its manner is hardly kind; rather it sounds anxious and, yes, threatening—perhaps a sign that by late May her parents' campaign against him was succeeding and that Lena had begun to push him away. It is also possible that this was simply the most aggressive-sounding of the large batch of Foley's letters to which the family had access. All love affairs consist of retreats and advances, ultimatums and surrenders. Taken out of context by outsiders—the press and the courts—a private correspondence between lovers could certainly give rise to some false impressions. Foley at one point asserted that fourteen letters he had received from Lena, which had been entrusted to Constable Patrick Burns, his court-appointed bodyguard, would prove that they had agreed to marry. Indeed, on June 10, Foley from jail sent a letter to John McMahon asking formally for Lena's hand.

As for proving the charge of blackmail, Lena and Foley concurred in separate comments that she had probably given him over the course of their relationship no more than ten or fifteen dollars. "She is . . . quoted as saying that I threatened her with all manner of things unless she furnished me with money," Foley objected. "This she knows to be a falsehood . . . as all the money she ever let me have she gave to me willingly, and I can't understand now why she makes such false statements. She also states that there was nothing to expose in her conduct. I think the best place to discuss this point is when she is under oath on the stand as that is where honest people tell the truth."

It was this last, more menacing element in Foley's writing, as well as in some of his freely given remarks to the press, that most alarmed the McMahons. The exact nature of these threats to expose Lena remain mysterious, although it can be assumed that they related to behavior that both partners knew would be perceived as immoral and/ or transgressive, and that would damage her reputation permanently.

It is telling that for how frequently Foley's insinuations—those about Lena and those suggesting he had embarrassing information to disclose about other unnamed people in the town—were reprinted, the local press remained disinclined to probe for details, instead content to note occasionally, as if from a great and incurious remove, how baffling some of the reported "facts" leading up to the lynching appeared. But what were these potent secrets that threatened so much harm? Editors may have been inclined to discredit anything Foley said, but in general they didn't hesitate to quote him at length, and he tended to be forthcoming with his opinions, so it is difficult not to understand their failure to follow up certain leads as negligence by design.

Foley conceded to reporters he had erred in angering George Lea and alienating Lena's parents, and that he regretted some of his other actions, but insisted he would not be railroaded on a bogus blackmail charge. The local courts, he feared, would "shove him up whether he was guilty or not." His warning that he would share scandalous intelligence about members of the community was his attempt to immunize himself. If the blackmail case went against him, the town would in effect be calling his bluff. Who knew what cards he held?

He did seek the return of the letters Lena had sent to him prior to June 2, which had been seized by the court, but it's unclear if he ever got them or what became of them. It may have been in several people's interest that they disappear. Their absence is especially unfortunate, as it is hard to read Lena's proclamations following the Lewis tragedy without hearing the voice of someone else, most likely Wilton Bennet, the McMahons' legal representative, who would have had an interest in framing her public statements. For example, her earlier insistence that she had spent Tuesday night who-knew-where in New York City and Wednesday night in Laurel Grove Cemetery in Port Jervis, and had not met Foley until Thursday morning, seemed designed to cover up something; the lost night in the cemetery, after all, was actually the night she spent in Foley's embrace on a hill above Carpenter's Point and, later, on the banks of the Neversink. And while her efforts to retrieve her trunk suggest a determination to leave town, her recollection that she had risen that morning at her parents' house and then gone down to the riverside to "wait for the train to Boston" strains credulity. She didn't awaken in her parents' house, and her and Foley's remote refuge by the river would have been an inconvenient place to wait for a train, as it was a considerable walk from there to the Erie Depot on Jersey Avenue. "I will leave it to all intelligent persons," Foley wrote, "if it is reasonable that a person would go that distance out of his or her way."

Despite the widely shared sense of his complicity in the tragic events of June 2, Foley was never officially accused of anything related to the lynching of Robert Lewis. He was briefly jailed for his own protection and as a potential witness for the coroner's inquest, but was not called to testify. Surely, though, he knew there remained strong public feeling against him, and he was understandably apprehensive when he was brought back from the Goshen jail to Port Jervis for a June 14 arraignment and preliminary hearing on the blackmail charges. Some small boys, in imitation of their fathers, had congregated at the entrance to the Ball Street lockup, calling out Foley by name and tormenting him with choking sounds and the threat he would be hanged. He told a journalist he did not think he would sleep well, as "he did not know but that the mob would come for him in the night," despite an assurance from the formidable Constable Burns that "the first man who lays a hand on you will be a dead duck."

An enjoinder to the village that ran in the *Tri-States Union* may have put him somewhat at ease. "Foley will not be lynched," it vowed, citing proudly the town's newfound fealty to the right of due process. "There is not the slightest evidence of any disposition to interfere with the regular and orderly administration of justice. The law will be allowed to take its course."

The reassurance evidently had an effect, for the next morning, even as hundreds of people gathered for the hearing, Foley "looked as cheerful and serene as a May morning. His countenance, as he coolly read the morning paper, did not indicate that he had even a passing acquaintance with trouble." He was, as ever, sharply dressed, although even he would admit to being upstaged by Lena, who entered wearing a stunning light-colored outfit and took her seat to applause from the spectators and generous noises of support.

There was a blushing exchange of glances between the lovers, observed with discretion by the room, but the tender moment was shattered almost immediately by the arrival of Lena's parents. Foley shrank visibly under the intense gaze of Theresa McMahon. Then came a shrill cry of alarm as John McMahon made a determined rush for him. Constable Burns stepped in McMahon's path and, holding him firmly, announced that Foley was in his charge. "I don't care whose charge he is in," Lena's father roared as he struggled in Burns's grip. "He is the negro that ought to have been hung."

From his seat McMahon continued to curse and berate Foley, who had returned to reading his newspaper and made a point of not glancing up. Justice Mulley warned Lena's father, "I don't mean any disrespect to you, sir, only we must have order."

In her testimony, Lena explained that she had known Foley since October and had very much liked him, but in April, after his release from jail, she had begun receiving blackmailing letters from him in which he asked her to meet him and to bring him money, warning that if she did not, he would expose her to her father. "He would tell her father and all the world that she was not a good girl," according to an account from the *Rome Citizen* (New York), which claimed the letters were delivered by Robert Lewis or by John Westfall, a Black man who lived across the street from the McMahons.

"This money I gave him from time to time, in small sums," she testified. "He kept me in constant terror of him." So frightening were the letters, she said, she immediately burned them or tore them up. Foley, who was representing himself, cross-examined Lena, who appeared visibly nervous under his questioning.

"Wasn't the first letter you received from me in November?"
"I think it was."
"Did you ever send me any money?"
"Yes."
"How many times?"

"Twice. Once to Port Jervis and once to Goshen."

"Was it received through blackmailing?"

"Yes."

"Was the money given at all times through threats?"

"It was."

"Was it so when you met me on the street?"

"It was extorted by fear."

Theresa McMahon followed Lena to the stand. She related that she had learned from George Lea and others that Foley, however smartly dressed and well-spoken, was no gentleman, but a rake, thief, and degenerate, who stole liquor and peeked in at half-dressed chambermaids, and who kept company with gamblers and hedonists. "Learning that he had visited the house clandestinely afterward, I told Lena to have nothing more to do with him. I made a complaint of vagrancy against Foley before Justice Mulley. Foley has continually annoyed us, inflicting his presence on us. He has been seen at eleven p.m. coming from our cellar. He was around there at all hours. He kept Lena in terror, which was increased by the letters."

Foley did not cross-examine Mrs. McMahon, but instead read a prepared statement:

> I am 32 years of age and was born in Warren, Massachusetts. I am a machinist by trade, and have been an insurance agent and a traveling salesman. I have never prowled around the McMahon residence except when I had an appointment to be there. I never sent threatening letters demanding money. All the money I ever received from Lena was, with two exceptions, given to me in person.

After the hearing Foley told a reporter that the letters held by Constable Burns would prove that he and Lena were engaged to be married, and that if he was indicted in the blackmail case and went to trial, he would introduce them as evidence. But Justice Mulley refused to return the letters, delivering instead a stern reprimand. He reminded Foley that he had made his release from jail in March provisional on the condition that he leave town for good: "Do you remember what you promised me the last time you were in this courtroom? I had sentenced you to four months at Goshen but on your solemn promise never to return to Port Jervis I reduced it to two months. On the day succeeding your discharge you [were] back in Port Jervis again." When Foley mumbled a sheepish apology, Mulley demanded, "What kind of a man are you, anyway, to break such a promise?"

Foley had a good answer but did not give it. That he had done so because he was in love with Lena McMahon.

On the afternoon of Saturday, June 18, Lena went for a fitting with Miss Hensel, a dressmaker in her neighborhood. She stayed only a few minutes, however, making the odd remark that she might never wear the dress she'd ordered. Two hours later, when Lena had not come home, Theresa McMahon went to check on her, only to learn she'd left Miss Hensel's long before.

Minutes later, as Theresa anxiously hurried home, she encountered a family friend, John Kleinsteuber, who said he had seen Lena walking on the canal towpath a short time before, and that uncharacteristically she had failed to return his hello but had kept her head down and continued walking. John McMahon, informed of his daughter's disappearance and strange behavior, immediately rushed out the door, fearing she had gone to drown herself in the canal. Lena had been subpoenaed to testify in a grand jury hearing on Tuesday in

Goshen about the lynching of Robert Lewis, and her parents knew she greatly feared what others, particularly Foley, might say.

Helpful neighbor Sol Carley joined John McMahon, and they first walked and then recruited a friend's buggy to go along much the same route Carley had covered in pursuit of Robert Lewis two weeks before, inquiring about Lena as they went. They passed through Huguenot and Cuddebackville, growing more concerned as the miles passed and the twilight deepened. Finally, as they approached the Sullivan County line, they learned that Lena had been seen going up a little-used mountain road toward Otisville. Hurrying their pace, they rounded and climbed the road's steep curves and managed to overtake her just below the town. When her father called her name, she collapsed and allowed herself to be taken into his arms.

"From 2 o'clock until 10:30 p.m. she had walked 13 miles," the *Gazette* recounted the next day, "the last three miles over the roughest, steepest, loneliest and darkest mountain road in this section." Asked why she had left Port Jervis without telling anyone, she said she was "merely taking a walk," but allowed that she had considered catching a train from Otisville to New York. "She is of a delicate constitution," the article observed, "and it is feared that the fatigue and excitement of the long walk over the rough road may have unfavorable results."

Dr. Van Etten, summoned to West Street, examined Lena and pronounced her physically sound, but stepping out of her bedroom, he warned her parents in a hushed conversation that recent events—the assault she had suffered, the lynching, all the world's prying into her private affairs, the demands that she appear in court—inclined him to believe she might "never again be right in her mind."

A month earlier she'd been a young woman who sold candy and ice cream to neighborhood children in a small railroad town; now her name and intimate details about her appeared in papers across the country. Aspersions were freely made as to her character. The ghastly lynching, to which she was now inextricably linked, had changed forever her hometown, a place of once-happy associations, and she alone was at the heart of the unpleasantness. It was not a role she nor anyone else would wish for, no matter how many times the press remarked that she was smart as well as pretty.

"Miss McMahon's former companions and friends have endeavored to convince her that she stands as high as ever in the public estimation," it was reported, "but the young woman has brooded constantly over her misfortune." Her friends said Lena worried she was losing her mind, feared that Foley would expose her or that her family would send her to an asylum, and spoke of changing her name back to Gallagher, her birth name, and moving far away where no one would know who she was.

The coverage from afar was less sympathetic. The *New York Times* headlined its write-up LENA MCMAHON'S FREAK. Another out-of-town paper inquired: IS LENA MCMAHON INSANE? While conceding that she had undergone a terrible ordeal, some speculated that her bizarre behavior indicated she was concealing something. "There was, and remains, something mysterious and maddening about this young woman," it was said. "Reported moments of lucidity are countered by acts of behavior so curious that newspapers hundreds of miles away challenge her sanity."

Since the lynching, Lena had been pitied as a victim and hailed as a survivor, and her recovery had been watched and prayed for. The public had been supportive, even when the facts as presented seemed vague. But one man was dead, another was in jail, and the town's good name had been sullied likely beyond repair. Now her erratic behavior had itself become a factor, pumping more air into the story. Those who covered it, or read about it, were beginning to lose patience.

Remarkably, considering her trek up a mountainside in the dark on Saturday night and what appeared to have been a serious emotional collapse, Lena was in Goshen on Tuesday, June 21, dressed in a neat black dress with a black hat to match and a few pieces of attractive jewelry, having been assured she would not be required to testify before the grand jury considering indictments in the Lewis lynching. Minutes before the procedure began, she was handed a letter from Philip Foley about the blackmail charges her family was bringing against him:

> Dear Miss McMahon: As my thoughts have run in the same channel since I saw you last Tuesday in court and sat and charged me with blackmail, I wondered that day, as I have ever since, if that could be the same girl whom I spent a Wednesday night with ten days before under the trees at Carpenter's Point, who on the night we were in the woods together considered ourselves as man and wife to prove your love for me, and that she would stand by me no matter what her people said.
>
> I can't bring myself to believe that you did this with your own free will and brand me a criminal and deprive me of my liberty for the next ten or fifteen years. You perhaps had little idea what the penalty is for the charge you have brought against me. You know that I never made any threats that if you did not give me money, I would ruin you. You know that all I ever was mad about was when you would not meet me, but let me say little girl if it is any satisfaction to you to put me in state's prison and, knowing as you do in your heart, that I am innocent of any crime against you no more than I would against my own sister. Now for the wrong you have been doing me I pray God forgive you as fully as I do. I will leave my case in the hands of

Him who regards the good and punishes the guilty and, in years to come, when you are happy, think kindly of the one you branded as a convict to be pointed out by his fellow man for all time . . .

No matter what becomes of me, my feelings for you remain the same and will while life lasts . . . The letter I wrote your father [in which Foley offered to marry Lena] was in good faith, but I see by the paper you scorned it. Well, I forgive you but never can forget. Now, little girl, as this is probably the last time my hand will trace your name, will you write me and tell me if it is true that you are doing this, or, better than that, come here and see me. Good bye, Phil

Foley's letter was eloquent and expressive, with a grace note of religiosity. Was this Foley the slick pretender casting a spell, or was he, as he represented it, simply a good man in over his head? The offer of marriage he sent from his jail cell was not insincere, nor do his expectations of Lena's reciprocal feelings seem inappropriate or imagined. The proposal was rejected in Lena's name by her parents, but as the *Gazette* reported of her receipt of his letter of farewell, "it was a very affectionate appeal from him. Miss McMahon was very much agitated when reading the letter and it was hard for her to keep from crying. That the girl has an affection for Foley there seems to be but little doubt."

Later that week Lena was back in her shop, tending to customers as usual. She told a visitor she had little recollection of her wandering up the mountain toward Otisville, but that she did feel a bit sore from all the walking. She had resumed attending services at St. Mary's Church with her parents, at least once appearing dressed entirely in white, and, on June 24, in response to Foley's written plea (which had been printed in a local newspaper), published a contrite yet firm statement of her own, one likely crafted with the aid of her attorney Bennet and with input from her parents. In it she sought her parents' forgiveness for disobeying them and asked the town to respect her dignity. The letter is well written, even as the overly repentant tone and many of its claims seem substantially out of character:

As my name has been so freely circulated throughout the press of the country during the past few weeks in connection with the infamous scoundrel Foley, who has been airing his ignorance and viciousness in frequent letters from the County Jail, I wish, once and for all, in justice to myself, to refute and brand as malicious falsehoods the statements this person has seen fit to utter.

I first became acquainted with Foley when he assumed to be a gentleman, through the introduction of a mutual friend. He paid me some attention and I was foolish, as other young girls have been, to believe in his professions of friendship, and when I, in the indiscretion of youth, having had some trifling difficulty with fond and loving parents who endeavored to give me wise counsel and advice, resolved to leave home, this inhuman monster egged me on and endeavored to carry into execution his nefarious schemes to ruin and blacken my reputation forever.

When I discovered "the wolf in sheep's clothing"—the true character of [this] parody of manhood—I at all risks and perils resolved to prosecute him as he so richly deserves. I assure the public that the maudlin, sentimental outpourings from this person, who, relying upon the fact that I was once his friend, has seen fit to make me the victim of extortion and blackmail, have no effect whatever on me, and it will not be my fault if he does not receive the punishment he so richly deserves. There is nothing to prevent this man writing letters, and I do not consider it wise or discreet to pay any attention to them. I simply desire to say that his insinuations and allegations are falsehoods; that my relations with him have only been those of a friend. God only knows how much I regret that.

I cannot have my reputation as an honest, chaste and virtuous girl assailed by this villain without a protest, and I ask all right-thinking people who possess these qualities to place themselves in my position and then ask if they would act differently than I have done. The evil fortune that has overtaken me has been no fault of my own, and I trust that the light of truth will reveal this man as he truly is—the author of all my misfortune.

I do not intend to express myself again to the public concerning this matter, nor pay any attention to what this man may say or do. All I desire is peace and the consideration and fair treatment that should be extended to one who has suffered untold misery and whose whole life has been blighted by one whose heartiness and cruelty are only equaled by his low cunning and cowardice.

It was a purposeful document. In rejecting Foley's claims of innocence and his offer of marriage, dismissing him as a "parody of manhood"—a characterization as insulting as it was innovative—she had surrendered fully to her parents' and the town's opinion of him as a menace and a rogue. Although she could not disguise her own uncertainty about whether she had been blackmailed, she nonetheless signed on to the charges about which her parents were so adamant. While she made no mention of Robert Lewis, whose life had been cruelly snuffed out, or the implosion of the town itself, by implication these things were laid at Foley's feet as well.

About this time, a rumor surfaced that Robert Lewis, upon his capture, had said that his own instinct would have been to protect Lena from harm, had Foley not "ordered" him to attack her. This made no sense, as it's unclear whom he would have protected her from, if not himself. But the rumor, in conjunction with Lena's published letter, created a useful deflection: two local young people, Lena and Lewis, had in their innocence become playthings for Foley, a malevolent force, knowing and wicked. With Lena's helpful retrospection, Foley's character, or lack thereof, made the havoc that had resulted seem almost inevitable. In this calculus, the village's initial certainty that Robert Lewis had raped a white woman, and paid the ultimate price for his act, was diluted to the considerably milder suspicion that he, like Lena, had been misused by a sophisticated predator. The dapper salesman had toyed with them both, and with the entire town.

Lena's published letter, it seemed—and this was likely her advisers' intent—thus served as a kind of public directive. It pointed to a path forward, a way out, inviting all to share in her redemption, a self-absolution sanctified by Lena's saintly appearances at church. It was a gentle nudge to a still dubious town that the time had come to cease asking unanswerable questions. Put another way, it was time to move on.

———•◦•———

Lynching has a perverse relation to recorded history, for obfuscation is central to its purpose. The so-called people's justice is meant to leave no trace of its operations. It features no lawyers' arguments, no objections, no trial transcript or rulings from the bench. This determined forgetting has over the years functioned in Port Jervis like a kind of self-winding mechanism; for as each generation remained tight-lipped about what happened to Robert Lewis, there have been ever fewer facts, half-truths, or rumors to pass along, a loss of oral history abetted by the steady exodus of the town's youths seeking education and opportunity elsewhere. By the early twenty-first century, most residents—Black and white, new arrivals and descendants of older families alike—could honestly profess ignorance of the lynching that had unfolded down the street. The resulting silence makes the efforts of those contemporaries who did try to understand what occurred in the promising village on the Delaware all the more poignant.

T. Thomas Fortune of the *New York Age* publicly condemned the fate of Robert Lewis, but it was his colleague Ida B. Wells who, having just relocated to New York City, became intrigued by the case and was drawn to examine it. Learning of the accusation that Philip Foley had sent letters to Lena McMahon and her family that could be construed as blackmail, Wells posited that the mystery behind the lynching was likely a consensual relationship between Lena McMahon and Robert Lewis.

> The white man [Foley] . . . had been a suitor of the girl's. She had repulsed and refused him, yet had given him money, and he had sent threatening letters demanding more. The day before [a court examination] she was so wrought up she left home and wandered miles away. When found she said she did so because she was afraid of [Foley's] testimony. Why should she be afraid of the prisoner? Why should she yield to his demands for money if not to prevent him from exposing something he knew? It seems explainable only on the hypothesis that a liaison existed between the colored boy and the white girl, and the white man knew of it. The press is singularly silent. Has it a motive? We owe it to ourselves to find out.

Was the liaison Wells described the "something back of the whole affair," the secret many village residents sensed lay behind the lynching? As Wells knew, if Lena and Lewis had had a consensual sexual relationship, it was not something that would likely be reported in the newspaper. Anti-miscegenation laws had never been enacted in New York or New Jersey, but Northern states such as Ohio, Maine, and Rhode Island had kept theirs until the 1880s. Southern courts would shun acknowledgment of consensual relations between white women and Black men well into the twentieth century, and Port Jervis, in this regard like many a small conservative burg anywhere in America, was probably closer in sensibility to Albany, Georgia, than Albany, New York. Once the report of a sexual assault on Lena became known, and Lewis was named the perpetrator, the suggestion that a "proper" local young white woman who still lived with her parents was complicit in such a relationship would have been unprintable, except from the pen of Ida B. Wells.

In Port Jervis, in 1884, one such case had brought swift condemnation, probably because the white woman was cohabiting with a Black man and had borne mixed-race children. SHE DESERVED HER FATE: THE WHITE CONCUBINE OF A COLORED MAN DIES IN POVERTY, in the *Gazette*, related that Mary Dobson, partner of Bob Brodhead, had perished from starvation a week after her two Black children had succumbed to the same cause. The daughter of "respectable and well-to-do people," the paper lamented, Mary "was lost to all sense of shame and preferred the society of colored people to that of her own race." The mother was to be interred next to her children in the graveyard called "God's Acre" maintained by the Black settlement at the top of North Orange Street.

By summer 1892, Wells's inquiries had given her an appreciation of how intimate biracial relationships struggled against social norms and came to be deemed unpardonable transgressions. She'd learned of a Black coachman forced to flee Natchez when his white mistress gave birth to their child, and of a white woman, accused of receiving a Black man in her home, who had the presence of mind to say she had hired him to install some curtains. It's unknown whether Wells's theory of the Port Jervis case was based on her own investigation. Given the proximity of the village to her new base of operations in New York City, it's tempting to believe she paid it a visit by train. She would not have been recognized, and could have slipped in and out of town in order to make contact with the African American community, a method of incognito fact-finding she was in the habit of employing. It's an intriguing, if speculative, possibility.

It is telling that the mainstream media at the time of the lynching of Robert Lewis was unable to appear certain about something as central to the case as Philip Foley's name. In the several weeks that the lynching remained in the news, the papers continued to refer to him as either William, Peter, or occasionally "P.J." Only when signed letters between Lena and "Phil" surfaced as evidence in Foley's blackmail hearing did news sources begin to identify him properly. By coincidence, both the surnames "Foley" and "McMahon" would have held significance for the large Irish American population of Port Jervis, as "Foley" in old Irish means "plunderer," and "McMahon" is a name associated historically with persons of status—chieftains, bishops, and kings. Of course, the paradox about Foley is that while he has always been characterized as disreputable, his letters and his answers to reporters' questions often appear more credible and consistent with known facts than those of almost any other person involved in the Lewis case, with the exception of Simon Yaple and William Crane. Inebriate or con man though he may have been, Foley nonetheless comes across in history's documents as grounded, self-critical, and willing to reflect with candor on his predicament.

He managed to remain resolute even when assailed by a determined nemesis, a freelance private eye named Samuel A. Elwell. The detective told the papers he'd been tracking Foley for months before the lynching, and claimed to have a warrant for his arrest, although on whose authority it's not clear. "Mr. and Mrs. McMahon knew that Foley was utterly worthless," Elwell told the press, "and that he was wont to boast of his conquests with women, victories that were generally destructive to the vanquished. Why Miss McMahon harbored him is best known to herself. She knew what he was."

Elwell proffered at least a partial explanation of the connection between Foley and Lewis. "I see that Foley alleges he did not know Lewis. That is very strange in view of the fact that Bob Lewis was a go-between for Foley and Miss McMahon. He carried more than one note for Foley to the young woman." Elwell insisted he had, with his own eyes, seen Foley hand Lewis a letter to deliver to Lena McMahon and had even glimpsed the envelope with her address on it. If Elwell was right that Lewis was helping Lena and Foley arrange their secret rendezvous, it might explain how Lewis became involved with the couple on June 2, when Lena and Foley were eager to get Lena's trunk and money from her parents' house.

Elwell said he believed Robert Lewis was telling the truth when he told Sol Carley that Foley had urged him to assault Lena, although he did not offer any reason why Foley would do such a thing. Like many people, he was inclined to be suspicious of Foley, but also seemed to nurse a special grudge against him, and loudly rued the fact that the lynching had obliterated any evidence "of a clinching sort" that might have been used to ensure his downfall.

The detective was a conspicuous figure in Orange County. In an era when small-town police did not often conduct in-depth investigations, private operators like Elwell, sometimes in the employ of government agencies, the railroads, or large landowners, provided a needed service. He had been in the news as a leading figure in the investigation of the murder of Mrs. Noah Gregory, a Middletown farmer's wife; for tracking down a bigamist who married and eloped with "young Nellie McGill" to Jersey City; and for taking part in "a bloody affray" in Susquehanna, Pennsylvania, a gunfight with two tramps in which a policeman was wounded.

His career thrived to a considerable degree on his being glamorized in the press as a crimefighter, but he was unfortunately also known for using his skills in less acceptable ways, such as impersonating special deputies and falsely imprisoning suspects. A Newburgh paper took joy in lampooning him as "the Orange County Pinkerton," "the Sleuth-Hound," and "the Man Who Never Sleeps," while in Middletown he was thought "good at a good many other things than paying his bills."

But Elwell's theory about Foley and Lewis was not illogical. The two men would have met at the Delaware House, where Foley lived and Lewis worked. They shared common interests—liquor, gambling, and young women—and, for Foley, Lewis would have been an asset, educating him about the town, the police, and the "opportunities" one did not find advertised in newspapers. The Black man's knowledge of the area's backstreets and secluded places would have been invaluable to Foley, once it became necessary for him and Lena to meet in secret.

Was Detective Elwell trying to help clear up a mystery or simply looking to attach his name to a case receiving national attention? Foley took the latter view, and in a public letter sent from jail called Elwell a liar, pointing out that

> there was nothing in my actions to warrant this man in shadowing me as he said he did and if it is true, I'm sure I could have been found in Port Jervis any day for the past four months. He further says that Bob Lewis was a go-between between Miss McMahon and myself. This statement I brand as a bare-faced lie. The young lady can tes-

tify to the truth of this. I defy this man Elwell or any other to come and prove that I had even speaking acquaintance with this man Lewis. If my memory serves me right this same Elwell was shut up last winter for trying to beat a hotel bill at Elmira. I mention this so your readers may know that his character is not above reproach.

Elwell was quick to denounce this stain on his escutcheon, vowing, "Before the Grand Jury I will connect [Foley] so closely with Lewis that the odor of the African will be perceptible." But as Theresa McMahon and Detective Elwell had both, in their own ways, observed, there was only so much "connecting" of Foley and Lewis that could now be had. The papers might continue to malign Foley, but in lynching Lewis the town had destroyed whatever testimony "of a clinching sort" it might ever have had against him.

———•·•———

So it may be that the persistent disinclination of the white press to explore the reasons behind the lynching, or to ask Black residents of Port Jervis what they knew or thought about it, had prompted Wells to visit the town. She understood that mainstream media selectively lied, glossed over or ignored details, and neglected to pursue facts they feared white readers would not tolerate. But because it's unclear whether she ever did make the trip, it's probably safest to assume she made her judgment by comparing what few facts she knew about June 2 in Port Jervis with the details of numerous Southern lynchings she had reported on. And there are some contingencies that might support Wells's theory. Two sources—George Lea and Detective Elwell—said Foley and Lewis knew each other, with Lea reporting that Lewis had stolen food for Foley, and Elwell suggesting that he had helped Foley arrange his meetings with Lena. And Lewis, if reports of his confidence in his ability to court white women are true, may have begun to covet Foley's role over his own in the triangle.

There are other ways in which we might begin to ascribe more agency to Lena McMahon than the mainstream media was willing to do. What if, for example, Theresa's violent argument with Lena on May 31 had been escalated by some single piece of explosive news: that Lena was pregnant? This could suggest an alternative to the story Lena told of the scene at the McMahon house that Tuesday morning before the lynching, when Foley had appeared wanting to talk. Theresa forbade Lena from coming downstairs to speak with him and chased Foley away, the latter angrily muttering a threat as he left. Say Lena then lost her temper with her mother and perhaps announced her intention to leave town to have the pregnancy aborted, causing Theresa, a devout Catholic who, evidence suggests, may as a young woman have given birth to a child out of wedlock, to strike her daughter. While Lena would later explain her trip to New York City as a spontaneous response to her mother's severity, the reverse may have been true: that the trip was not to New York but to Middletown or somewhere nearby and had been planned with the objective of obtaining an abortion. Theresa may have learned of this plan and sought to intervene. While there is no evidence or record of a pregnancy, it could be one explanation for why Lena ginned up so bizarre and unbelievable a yarn about her visit to New York, her loss of memory over the course of two days, and her lie about having spent a night in a cemetery. It might also explain the degree of near-murderous anger expressed by both the older McMahons for Foley.

But assuming Wells was close to the truth in citing a relationship between Lena and Lewis, what, then, *had* brought things to a head on June 2? If there was a romantic link between Lewis and Lena, Foley would have become aware of it upon his release from jail in March. It was around that time that the parents' campaign against Foley began in earnest, ultimately inducing Lena to start keeping him at arm's length; Lewis would have been encouraged by such a development. Whether, as Foley claimed, he and Lewis had no more than a nodding acquaintance or, as George Lea asserted, they had been collaborators in petty crimes at the Delaware House, in this particular pursuit they would have been competitors. On the morning of June 2, Lewis then would have been incensed to learn that, without his knowing, Lena had returned from "Middletown" and had spent the night with Foley in the woods. Lewis, on his way to confront Lena, may have encountered Foley by the Monticello tracks and expressed his anger, at which Foley could have defensively told him to go make his own case to the girl—the origin of Lewis's contention that Foley had urged him to try to seduce Lena. Lewis's claim of Foley's influence, in this scenario, would have been a deflection from his own infatuation.

Theresa told a news correspondent she was convinced "that the plot to ruin her daughter must have been laid, as Lewis seemed to know her movements," and that Foley had something to do with it. But this possibility seems inconsistent with Foley's attentive behavior toward her in the days and hours before the alleged assault. If the attack on her was something he had encouraged, as the McMahons believed, what could have been the reason for it? Did Foley resent Lena's intention to go away and abandon him? Would he have subjected Lena to a violent sexual attack by another man simply to punish Theresa for having chased him from her door, making good on his parting threat to "get square with you yet"? Foley was a too-smooth operator, and a shady dude, but his arranging for a physical attack on Lena out of vengeance seems unlikely, given what we know.

Remember that Lena herself spoke against the idea that Foley had orchestrated the assault, telling a *Union* reporter that "if Foley was really guilty of having anything to do with Lewis, she wanted to have him punished, but she did not really believe that he had as far as she

could see." She also reiterated her view that the reason Foley remained hidden while the factory girls aided her was that he feared her
parents would learn he was behind the effort to secure her trunk so
she could leave town, when they had expressly warned him to stay
out of her affairs. As the *Gazette* asserted, "Miss McMahon . . .
certainly does not believe that Foley was in any way connected with
the crime of the negro and possibly she may consent to marry him. It
is a curious world."

Some reported facts may be assumed to have a greater degree of
certainty because they were corroborated by others. Clarence Mc-
Ketchnie saw Lena struggling with a Black man at the riverside, and
several other witnesses heard her screams and saw her injuries. The
possibility that Lena McMahon was raped cannot be dismissed.
However, if it was indeed Robert Lewis that McKetchnie saw, it's also
not out of the question that the dispute the boy witnessed concerned
money, and not sex or a broken love affair. As Lena was more finan-
cially stable than Foley, she may have been in charge of paying Lewis
for his services as go-between, and cash at the moment was not something she'd have been willing to part with.

Immediately after their encounter, Lewis allegedly gathered his
fishing gear and went away; Foley helped wash Lena's face, comforted
her, walked back to town along the railroad tracks, and then headed
to a favorite saloon. Lena, however, had no such option. She was hurt
and bleeding; witnesses had consoled her. Whatever the truth was
about the assault she'd suffered, she had no choice but to stick with
the story she'd initially told, of a sexual attack by a strange Black man.
If Lewis was indeed her paramour, he would have known better than
to blurt out that truth to Sol Carley. He would have understood, once
in the posse's custody, for the first time and perhaps in a sudden flash
of terror and recognition, what his and Lena's fight on the embankment looked like to others, and sounded like when described. He

seized on the slim chance that, based on some acquaintance he had with John McMahon, the situation could at least be partly explained. That he believed such a thing was possible can suggest only that he knew the incident, as others perceived it, did not fully match the reality—that what had been a spurned advance, a lovers' quarrel, or an argument over a few dollars was now assumed to be something far worse.

Once Lewis was lynched, three blocks from her home, at an intersection she would walk through nearly every day, a horrified Lena would have had no choice but to double down on what misrepresentations, if any, she had made of a sexual assault. If she were to confess to having lied, it would mean her false story had "convicted" Robert Lewis and sent him to his death. It's possible that herein lies the key to Lena's emotional and physical breakdown: that it had nothing to do with fears of what Foley might reveal in court about her promiscuity, but rather something far more damning—that in her weakness she had allowed an innocent man to be killed. She could only pray for absolution, hence the virginal attendance at St. Mary's and her carefully written public letter casting Foley as the prince of darkness.

Foley knew all of this, and understood his advantage.

————

Or perhaps it happened even a different way. Perhaps Lena was never attacked in the first place but had instead raised a phony outcry and even faked her injuries as part of a charade, perhaps orchestrated with Foley's knowledge, and either McKetchnie had believed the performance or else been complicit in its staging. Foley and Lewis, even if they had been privy to or involved in the scheme, may have, like Lena, been so focused on the intended effect on her parents, they failed to think through its potential, far more monstrous consequences.

To what end would have been this subterfuge? Uppermost in Lena's mind that day was obtaining her trunk and her money. Because she knew her parents would not comply with her wishes, the object of any staged deception would have been either to make herself into a pitiable victim, in order to win back their affection and embrace, or, more likely, to force her mother and father to feel ashamed for their mistreatment of her. How better to guilt-trip her abusive mother than to make her believe that she had driven her daughter from home, only to have her sexually assaulted by a Black man in the woods? Such a fraud on the part of a white woman attempting to throw suspicion onto an innocent Black man, in full confidence that other white men, including police, would automatically believe her, was not unheard of. As was rumored at the time of the lynching, the charade in the Port Jervis case might have indeed been conceived with the aim of softening the McMahons' opinion of Foley, who, after the "assault," might appear in a more favorable light, perhaps even as Lena's protector (although Foley, if that had been the plan's design, missed his cue to make a heroic entrance). And it may have been Lena, not Foley, who had been the master architect of that plan.

Whether Lena created a false scenario on her own, or had others' cooperation, the problem then would have been that the protagonists played their parts too well. Once the act was instigated, its features were impossible to reverse. If she'd imagined she could call the public's attention to the allegation that she'd been violated by a strange Black man and not have people mobilize on her behalf, she was tragically mistaken. And once the saga was unspooled and had engulfed the town, she and anyone else in on the scheme would have been far too abashed to concede it had been make-believe. This may be why Foley appeared to the factory girls unconcerned about Lena's injuries, why he and Lena stepped aside to have a whispered conversation, and why he then sought to quell the girls' curiosity and further involvement by telling them to go away and not mention what they'd seen. If, as Dr. Van Etten maintained, Lena was *fighting the Negro in her dreams*, it was possibly not because she'd been traumatized by her attacker, but because she was haunted by her role in the death of an innocent man, with whom the truth need also perish.

NINE

THE BLUNDERS OF VIRTUE

O f the 1,134 recorded lynchings of African Americans between the years 1882 and 1899, the lynching of Robert
Lewis was the only one known to have occurred in New
York State. Those who defended Port Jervis's reputation in the aftermath of the incident were not entirely wrong in believing their village
singularly unlucky; the travesty of the lynching could, after all, have
come to pass in almost any small town where an alleged sexual assault
by a Black man on a young white woman took place, serving as a trip
wire for white men's racist and gendered insecurities. Once the inquest and the two Orange County grand juries had completed their
unproductive work, many relieved village residents took comfort in
the idea that what had occurred was aberrational, certainly not Port
Jervis as they knew it. Was it not now possible to hope that, as in all
things, "bygones would be bygones"?

No one had been held accountable, the last of the out-of-town
reporters had gone home, and the surviving principals soon moved

away—the McMahons to Boston, the Carrs to Albany. Dr. Van Etten died and was carried with all appropriate pomp and tribute to his eternal rest in Laurel Grove; William Crane eventually moved to California. Ida B. Wells, frustrated by America's inert response to lynching's horror, sailed for England in the hope of arousing British opinion, a strategy used effectively by the abolitionists a half century earlier and recommended to Wells by a hero of that movement, Frederick Douglass.

In Port Jervis, local newspaper mentions of the incident eventually diminished, then disappeared, and the town, as if by an unwritten concord regarding the subject, fell gratefully into a collective hush.

Yet a notable signatory to the pact of silence and forgetting had been overlooked: William Crane's ever-observant younger brother, Stephen. It was understandable—and probably inevitable—that Stephen Crane, a literary artist who derived his imaginative tales from real-world experiences, would not neglect the events of June 2, 1892, and that from his pen an exposé of the village's darkest hour would make its way into the world.

By the evening William had pushed his way into the center of the lynch mob to try to save Robert Lewis, the Crane family had been prominent in Port Jervis for more than a decade. The Reverend Jonathan Crane's leadership at the Drew Methodist Church had been as worthy as it was influential, but he died suddenly in 1880, only two years after the family had arrived, and his widow, Mary Peck Crane, moved back to New Jersey, leaving behind several of her older children who chose to remain in Port Jervis. Stephen, then eight, went initially to stay with an older brother, Edmund, who lived with his wife in Sussex County, New Jersey, although he was soon back in Port Jervis, along with his mother and brother Luther, who returned in summer 1880 to live with older brother William, who was seventeen years Stephen's senior. In addition to being a respected jurist and civic leader with a large, commodious house on Main Street, William was an aspiring lyceum speaker and had presented a talk to the Port Jervis Young Men's Literary Society titled "That the Intellect of Woman Is as Great as That of the Man." Stephen and his brother shared a number of interests, including an obsession with the history of the Civil War, a subject in which William was so well versed he gave popular lectures on the Battle of Gettysburg to veterans who'd fought there. William was also an early patron of his brother's writing career, which began when Stephen was still in his teens.

It is thought William suggested the idea for the title of Stephen's 1893 novel, *Maggie: A Girl of the Streets* ("Maggie" having been a childhood Port Jervis neighbor of the Cranes'), a realistic account of a young woman of the Bowery, abandoned by family and friends, who is driven by poverty into prostitution and ultimately to an early death. He also handled for Stephen the paperwork needed to free one thousand dollars from the younger man's inheritance so that the book could be published in a private edition. Despite the author's ingenious promotional scheme of paying four men to ride the New York City elevated for a day, each conspicuously reading a copy, the book sold poorly.

His initial literary exposure had come when the *New-York Tribune* from February through June 1892 published his *Sullivan County Sketches*, humorous and fanciful recollections set in the countryside northwest of Port Jervis, where the Cranes often went to camp and hunt. While it has never been proved conclusively, it's likely Crane gathered material for his best-known work, the Civil War novel *The Red Badge of Courage*, through his acquaintance with local veterans of the 124th New York Regiment, the Orange Blossoms, who had seen action in numerous battles, including Fredericksburg and Gettysburg, as well as the Battle of Chancellorsville, fought in late April and early May 1863 in Spotsylvania County, Virginia, and which provides the immediate backdrop for the novel. There were scores of veterans resident in Port Jervis, and although Stephen Crane was born six years after Appomattox, he would have had ample opportunity to hear these men's stories in the village parks, saloons, and barbershops.

"As children they had stood at the corner of Main and Elm and every minute or so seen a man pass wearing the veteran's cap of the Grand Army of the Republic," the literary critic Larzer Ziff notes of Crane's generation. "They had felt the sense of lost adventure, of having been born too late for the stirring events which had reached into every village, however remote, and called forth its young people to do battle." But Crane was not seduced by sentimental war glory or similar "flapdoodle." His book relates the travails of a young Union soldier who awakens to the falseness of war's lauded virtues. The result is a compelling psychological portrait, an antiwar war story the likes of which had rarely if ever been composed, depicting one man's crisis as he weighs the moral challenge of whether to join or flee carnage so seemingly pointless and absurd. What he had heard in the tales told by his Port Jervis veterans were not memories of victorious charges or cheering crowds, but recollection of old men, thirty years out of uniform, many never healed in body and spirit, whose gaze as they spoke lingered long and unfocused on something far away, visible only to themselves. The author's gift for reproducing inner monologue and surreal detail lends the work its fierce authenticity.

The Red Badge of Courage was an immediate success upon its appearance in 1895, went on to influence American writers from Ernest Hemingway to Norman Mailer to Michael Herr, and has never been out of print. "At the center of Crane's myth," the novelist and critic Ralph Ellison would observe, is "the mystery of the creative talent with which a youth of twenty-one was able to write what is considered one of the world's foremost war novels when he had neither observed nor participated in combat."

What story would so original a talent tell of the lynching of Robert Lewis?

———•◦•———

Given the intimate quality of life in the village, it's not unlikely that Stephen Crane and Lena McMahon knew each other, at least by sight. They were approximately the same age; Stephen's older sister Agnes taught at the Mountain House School when Lena was a student there. An 1882 record of public-school classroom assignments show Lena in Miss Olmstead's class at the Mountain House and Stephen Crane down the road in Miss Reeves's room at the Main Street School, which was across the street from Judge Crane's later residence at 19 East Main, and only a few blocks from where Lena would eventually manage her sweets shop. After a day writing on his brother's veranda, Stephen might well have ended a late afternoon stroll at the confectionery, dawdling uncommittedly over a dish of Lena's ice cream, spoon in one hand, cigarette in the other.

Like Lena's, Stephen's intellectual promise was recognized early. He knew his letters by age three and, according to family lore, was within a year reading the works of James Fenimore Cooper. Schoolmates would later call him "Stephen Cranium." Slight of build and often sickly as a child, he compensated with a fierce creed of outdoor life and physical exertion—hiking, boxing, hunting, and baseball. While attending Syracuse University, he started as catcher for the varsity team, where he excelled sufficiently to consider turning pro. "Small, sallow, and inclined to stoop" is how the Midwestern author Hamlin Garland remembered Crane, "but sinewy and athletic for all that . . . a capital catcher of curved balls."

Stephen often found Port Jervis too crowded and citified for his tastes and grew to prefer the pine forests at the six-thousand-acre Hartwood Club, located in nearby Forestburgh, New York, a hunting preserve William had helped found. Those who knew him would later recall Stephen writing in a wicker chair shielded behind a large lilac bush on his brother's porch, or walking swiftly along Main Street early in the morning, head down, lost in thought, on his way to board the Monticello Line train to Hartwood. The novelist Willa Cather's impression when she met the young author was of someone who "went about with the tense, preoccupied, self-centered air of a man who is brooding over some impending disaster . . . His eyes [were] the finest I have ever seen, large and dark and full of luster and changing lights, but with a profound melancholy always lurking deep in them."

Despite his love of the outdoors and strenuous recreation, Stephen, after leaving college without graduating and beginning his career as a freelance journalist, gained a somewhat less wholesome reputation. He smoked constantly, ate abstemiously (his pet peeve was watching others take inordinate pleasure in their food), and developed the untidy habit of scribbling notes in ink on his cuffs. Haunting the Bowery for material, he picked up much of its rough vernacular, and began swearing prodigiously and with a freedom that worried some of his longtime friends.

Crane was as engaged with questions of morality and man's obligations to self and society as had been his reform-minded parents; however, where they were concerned with people's lack of self-control and the threats modern life posed to one's character, Stephen was drawn to contemplate the ways a person is fully revealed in morally ambiguous circumstances and perhaps rises above the instinct for self-preservation. How does one make, or fail to make, virtuous choices in moments of extreme crisis?

This questioning informs many of Crane's works, and toward the end of his short life it was piqued by the need to capture a story of futile heroism—the march of a lynch mob through the streets of Port Jervis, over the remembered footsteps of his own once-cherished playgrounds, and his brother William's exemplary stand against an egregious wrong.

Stephen had been in Port Jervis, staying at William's house, until shortly before the lynching, but had left on or about Decoration Day to return to the Jersey shore, where he was a stringer for the *New-York Tribune* and contributed occasional pieces to the *Asbury Park News*.

A devoted follower of the day's headlines, Stephen would have immediately learned details of what had occurred in his hometown, particularly as it involved his brother. He would have been shocked and saddened, for he was fond of Port Jervis, knew intimately the locations connected to the incident, and was acquainted with many of the townspeople the articles mentioned, such as Raymond Carr and his father, as well as Dr. Van Etten, who was one of his brother's neighbors.

That a "Southern" spectacle lynching of an African American citizen had made landfall in his hometown was deeply troubling, for he saw at once its fearful implication, that, as Wells had written, "the black shadow of lawlessness in the form of lynch law is spreading its wings over the whole country." It was characteristic of him that he took it personally and felt a moral duty to respond. Likely he rued the fact he had not been there, and in his mind's eye saw himself at his brother's side, using his athlete's body and knowledge of how to land a punch to beat back the mob and help rescue its tormented victim.

Later that summer he sought an assignment from the American News Service to report from the South, perhaps to better understand the phenomenon of lynch law. The bureau rejected his request and dispatched him eventually to cover a drought on the Great Plains, but the Port Jervis lynching remained a preoccupation. The themes of summary justice, mobbism, abandonment, and the loneliness of unjust fate resonate in many of his short stories, including "The Blue Hotel," "The Bride Comes to Yellow Sky," "The Open Boat," and "When Man Falls, a Crowd Gathers."

That last story is Crane's most literal published rehearsal of the Robert Lewis lynching, telling of an Italian immigrant who suffers an epileptic seizure and collapses on a Manhattan sidewalk. "It was as if an invisible hand had reached up from the earth and had seized him by the hair," he writes of the tale's subject. "He seemed dragged slowly, relentlessly backward, while his body stiffened convulsively, his hands clenched, and his arms swung rigidly upward . . . Those in the foremost rank bended down, shouldering each other." Crane adds, "Once they struck a match and held it close to the man's face. This livid visage suddenly appearing under their feet in the light of the match's yellow glare, made the throng shudder. Half articulate exclamations could be heard. There were men who nearly created a battle in the madness of their desire to see the thing."

In early biographies of Crane there are accounts that he also created (and destroyed) a story he called "Vashti in the Dark," about a young Methodist preacher from the South who kills himself after learning his wife has been raped by a Black man in the forest at night. One of Crane's biographers, the poet John Berryman, suggests that the author burned the story after it was rejected by publishers. No copy survives. Stephen Crane was a brilliant literary craftsman, but he also wrote impulsively and sometimes turned out short pieces in haste to meet his financial needs. In disposing of "Vashti," he may have recognized that he had not yet mastered the nuance and perspective that the subject demanded and that he hoped to bring to it.

At the height of his fame following the publication of *The Red Badge of Courage*, in 1896, Crane became enmeshed in an incident that would expose the very challenges of moral self-measurement he so vigorously examined in his fiction. On the night of September 17, he appeared at the Jefferson Market Courthouse in New York City on behalf of Dora Clark, a young woman of twenty-one he knew through his research into the world of the Tenderloin district, the west side mecca of New York nightlife. Crane had witnessed Clark's arrest for soliciting on the corner of Broadway and Thirty-First Street and believed, as she did, that the charge was trumped up. Charles Becker, the arresting officer, Clark said, was acting on a grudge held by a fellow officer named Rosenberg whose crass romantic overtures Clark had rebuffed.

Crane, who attended the ensuing hearings, thought of himself as a journalist who transcribed the soul of the New York underworld without actually belonging to it; the police, however, saw instead a literary celebrity out to blacken the reputation of one of their own. "Thin and pale, with straight hair plastered down on a curiously shaped head," a press account from the courthouse described him, "a young man who does not look brainy, but who has proved he has brains." Although warned by a sympathetic desk sergeant to back off for his own good, Crane refused to retreat, averring, "I consider it my duty, having witnessed an outrage such as Becker's arrest of this girl, to do my utmost to have him punished. The fact that I was in her company, and had just left what the detective called a resort for thieves, prostitutes, and crooks, does not bear on the matter in the least. I had a perfect right to be there, or in any other public resort anywhere else in the city where I choose to go."

Such arrogance, however, played poorly with the police, and he failed to anticipate how his fame might be used against him. He was blindsided by Becker's attorney, who produced a live witness (a building janitor) who asserted that Crane cohabited with prostitutes and lived off their earnings. Police insisted the writer also smoked opium. The latter claim was bogus, and the others either exaggerated or outright lies, but the publicity had its intended crushing effect. It was an embarrassing comeuppance for a young man from Port Jervis who had, it seemed, gotten in over his head.

If there was any consolation, it was that he had acted honorably, with an automatic generosity of spirit, manfully upholding the belief that "a wrong done to a prostitute must be as purely a wrong as a wrong done to a queen." As the author of *Maggie: A Girl of the Streets*, he had little choice but to act as he did. But the Dora Clark debacle showed him also that "the inopportune arrival of a moral obligation can bring just as much personal humiliation as can a sudden impulse to steal or any of the other mental suggestions which we account calamitous." In this instance it hindered his future access to police sources and cost him his budding friendship with the police commissioner, Theodore Roosevelt, as well as the sense of being at home in New York City.

Crane described his creative process to Willa Cather by saying that even when he possessed factual information, he often chose not to cite it directly but rather to allow his imagination to reorder it. "The detail of a thing has to filter through my blood," he explained, "and then it comes out like a native product, but it takes forever." It took five years from the lynching of Robert Lewis for Crane to write *The Monster*, his highly imaginative novella loosely based on the crime. While casting virtually all the actual details of the incident aside, he presents a gothic horror story set in a claustrophobic small town, making his own use of both the common descriptor "monster" in sensational accounts of allegedly dangerous Black men, and the late Victorian era's morbid fascination with disfigurement.

The story is set in "Whilomville," his lightly fictionalized Port Jervis. Henry Johnson, a Black groom and carriage driver, rushes into a burning house to rescue Jimmie Trescott, the young son of his white employer. While he is carrying the child to safety, chemicals stored in Dr. Trescott's laboratory explode, leaving Henry gravely injured. When Henry is at death's door, the citizens of Whilomville, Black and white, recall him fondly and praise his heroism; but nearly all, including his fiancée, Bella Farragut, whom he has courted at her family's house in "Watermelon Alley," want nothing more to do with him after, with Dr. Trescott's medical attention, he makes a miraculous recovery. His is "an unwelcome return from the dead," for he no longer has a face and has become hideous to behold.

Before the fire Henry was a bon vivant, a stylish dresser, a man noticed and remarked upon as he strolled through town; now he has become an apparition. An uproar ensues when he instinctively tries to resume some of his former activities, for his countenance is so dreadful the town cannot bear to gaze upon him, and he is accused of frightening children and young women.

Dr. Trescott's friend Judge Hagenthorpe pays the doctor a visit to share Whilomville's concerns. "Perhaps we may not talk with propriety of this kind of action," he confides,

> but I am induced to say that you are performing a questionable charity in preserving this negro's life. As far as I can understand, he will hereafter be a monster, a perfect monster, and probably with an affected brain. No man can observe you as I have observed you and not know that it was a matter of conscience with you, but I am afraid, my friend, that it is one of the blunders of virtue.

"He saved my boy's life," Trescott reminds his guest. "What am I to do? He gave himself for—for Jimmie. What am I to do for him?"

"He will be your creation, you understand," replies the judge. "He is purely your creation. Nature has very evidently given him up. He is dead. You are restoring him to life. You are making him, and he will be a monster, and with no mind."

"He will be what you like, judge. He will be anything, but, by God! He saved my boy."

"Well," Hagenthorpe says quietly, "it is hard for a man to know what to do."

One of the blunders of virtue . . . It is hard for a man to know what to do. Like Dr. Trescott's determination to cure Henry and care for him, so William Crane forced his way into a mob to stop a lynching and, at least momentarily, brought Robert Lewis back to life. But much as Judge Crane is rudely tossed out of the circle of men intent on lynching Lewis and is accused of disloyalty by old friends, so Dr. Trescott and his wife are made to pay for their moral decency. His patients one by one desert him, and Mrs. Trescott is shunned by society, her husband left to count the unused teacups she had set out for her usual Wednesday ladies' parlor gathering, as she curls up in an armchair to weep.

Stephen Crane's story of fear and intolerance "in an environment traditionally associated with neighborliness and good will" takes place in what the scholar of the American short story James Nagel calls "a middle-class utopia," a country town of contented merchants, churchgoers, and working people, children's Saturday-afternoon birthday parties, evening band concerts, and a village barbershop habituated by gossipy white men. It is Crane's "town of Once-upon-a-time [literally the meaning derived from the archaic term "whilom"], the ideal American small town of memory and imagination." But Dr. Trescott's miraculous medical interventions force Whilomville to know for real what had previously been a nightmarish figure of journalistic styling and numberless headlines. The Black "guilty monster," as Robert Lewis was called, in Henry Johnson has become an actual one. Crane pokes beneath the metaphor to expose it as a form of avoidance, to reveal how the vernacular language of race suppresses meaning. Much as slurs and offensive naming serve as power dynamics between peoples, all the terms used by whites to describe Black people, whether cruel, grotesque, or comic, had the effect of dehumanization. By the tale's end, however, the real "monster" is revealed: it is Whilomville's intolerance and bigotry, the same blind hatred that William Crane had witnessed as he stood over a trembling, bleeding Robert Lewis.

Although the word "lynching" never appears in the book, it lurks threateningly in the text's ellipses. When the chief of police comes to tell Dr. Trescott that Henry has been out "scaring everyone," and Trescott inquires if Henry has been hurt, the officer replies, "No. They never touched him. Of course, no one really wanted to hit him, but you know how a crowd gets. It's like—it's like—." Other allusions to Port Jervis are more literal. "Must say he had a fine career while he was out," the chief of police says:

> First thing he did was to break up a children's party at Page's. Then he went to Watermelon Alley. Whoo! He stampeded the whole outfit. Men, women, and children running pell-mell, and yelling. They say one old woman broke her leg, or something, shinning over a fence. Then he went right out on the main street, and an Irish girl [Lena McMahon] threw a fit, and there was sort of a riot. He began to run, and a big crowd chased after him, firing rocks. But he gave them the slip somehow . . . We looked for him all night, but couldn't find him.

Later, when Henry is caught, the chief confides, "I thought I'd better let you know. And I might as well say right now, doctor, that there is a good deal of talk about this thing. If I were you, I'd come to the jail pretty late at night, because there is likely to be a crowd around the door."

Much as Judge Crane was visited by interested acquaintances curious to know his intended testimony in the Lewis case, a delegation of friends arrives to intervene with Dr. Trescott. They warn him his reputation and medical practice are at risk, and suggest Henry be sent to a farm out of town or to a public institution. "It's the women," they insist. Henry is no longer a familiar, acceptable presence in the community, but a strange Black man, whose thoughts and intentions cannot be divined. What he is capable of—what he *might* do—no one can be sure. Yet Trescott ultimately refuses to send him away.

Shunned by all, the Black coachman begins to lose his mind and, having learned to avoid trouble by no longer venturing into town, sits all day on a bench in Trescott's garden, talking and humming to himself, his face hidden by a veil. In the book's ultimate scene young Jimmie Trescott and a group of other boys dare one another to approach Henry as he sits motionless. Jimmie, the little boy whose life Henry saved, has taken to exhibiting him to other youngsters. Suddenly the boys move back as the apparition, sensing their presence, rises and mounts a box.

The monster on the box had turned its black crepe countenance toward the sky, and was waving its arms in time to a religious chant. "Look at him now," cried a little boy. They turned, and were transfixed by the solemnity and mystery of the indefinable gestures. The wail of the melody was mournful and slow. They drew back. It seemed to spellbind them with the power of a funeral.

Henry Johnson has become "a wailing mourner" at his own funeral, writes the literary scholar Elizabeth Young, which "marks the symbolic murder of the Black man by the world that has made him a monster."

Port Jervians who read the novella when it appeared in *Harper's Magazine*, or later in book form, and knew of the Crane family's connection to the Lewis lynching, would have readily grasped its judgment on the town. William must have informed his brother of that reaction in early 1899, for Stephen responded from his home in England, "I forgot to reply to you about the gossip . . . I suppose that Port Jervis entered my head while I was writing it but I particularly don't wish them to think so because people get very sensitive and I would not scold away freely if I thought the eye of your glorious public was upon me." Stephen held out the promise that he would eventually rejoin his brother and the rest of the family in their hometown. "My idea is to come finally to live at Port Jervis or Hartwood," he assured William. "I am a wanderer now and I must see enough but—afterwards—I think of P.J. & Hartwood."

———•—•———

Stephen would never be reunited with the citizens of Port Jervis, so did not learn their opinion of his story firsthand or face their condemnation. He had contracted tuberculosis while living in New York, where the disease was prevalent in the tenement districts he frequented, and then fell ill with malaria in Florida in 1896, a condition which in turn was likely exacerbated by his going to Cuba in 1898 to report on the Spanish-American War. He eventually returned to England, having moved there with his common-law wife, Cora Taylor, in 1897. They had rented a five-hundred-year-old mansion in Sussex known as Brede Place, a rambling manor with no plumbing, heat, or electricity, but a stone fireplace thirteen feet wide. William, aware that Stephen's health was failing, tried to convince his brother to return to America; however, Stephen chose to remain abroad. He was popular in England, where he was whimsically known in literary circles as the "Red Badger," and had good and influential friends in Henry James, H. G. Wells, Ford Madox Ford, and Joseph Conrad. His chief objection to returning home likely had more to do with Cora's past. They had met in Jacksonville, where she had been the manager of a nightclub and an elite bordello, the Hotel de Dream, a fact he knew would embarrass his family and become fodder for the tabloid press.

"I have managed my success like a fool and a child but then it is difficult to succeed gracefully at 23," Stephen wrote to William shortly after completing *The Monster*. "However, I am learning every day. I am slowly becoming a man." By late 1899, his health had deteriorated, however, not helped by his smoking, the couple's drafty lodgings, and the continual stress of his and Cora's precarious finances. Diagnosed with pulmonary congestion, Crane was moved in late spring 1900 to a clinic at Badenweiler, in Germany's Black Forest, where the regional climate was thought to possess curative powers. He died there early on the morning of June 5.

Port Jervis residents have occasionally advanced likely sources for Crane's reconstruction of their town in *The Monster*, pointing to several Victorian homes with adjacent carriage houses, homes of once-beloved physicians, and even some specific three-alarm house fires of memory, such as an April 1885 conflagration at the home of Dr. Charles Lawrence, whose son Frederic was a close friend of Stephen Crane's. Trained as a pharmacist, the physician may well have kept a small chemical lab at the house (which still stands at the corner of Fowler and Ball); and as something of a father figure to Stephen as well as a leader in public education in Port Jervis and a temperance man, he would have made a plausible model for Dr. Trescott.

William Crane's daughter Helen, in a short memoir of her famous uncle Stephen, recalled that her father believed *The Monster* was based on a Black coal hauler in Port Jervis named Levi Hume, who had a form of cancer that deformed the flesh on his face. The literary scholar Jacqueline Goldsby, however, suggests that William, while believing the character of Dr. Trescott to be based on himself, remained uncomfortable enough with the book's connection to the Port Jervis lynching that he, unconsciously or not, put forward his view about Levi Hume, if such a person even existed, deliberately as a way of keeping allusions to Robert Lewis at arm's length. Stephen Crane had envisioned *The Monster* as being included, and working in contrast, with the other, more pleasant *Whilomville Stories*, tales of his hometown and boyhood published in book form in 1900; it would certainly have given that collection a different cast. But after the author's death, William, as his brother's literary executor, separated it from the first edition. Judge Crane's obfuscation about the likely model for the novella's main character, and his setting it apart from the other localized tales, probably contributed to the century-long delay in scholarly notice being paid the connection to the Robert

Lewis lynching, although he was not alone in contemplating other sources for his brother's last work.

Many Port Jervians thought the character of "Henry Johnson" had emerged from the tragedy of Samuel Hasbrouck and Theodore Jarvis, two Black Civil War veterans struck on July 4, 1879, by a premature discharge from a cannon being used in an Independence Day celebration. Jarvis died from his wounds. Hasbrouck lost an eye and was permanently disfigured, a handicap that did not diminish his prominence in the village, where he served officially as a paid "dog slayer," shooting unmuzzled strays (including once, by mistake, a beloved pet belonging to George Lea). Hasbrouck's scarred, unsettling features, encountered routinely by fellow villagers, ensured that the July Fourth accident was not forgotten, as did the rumor that Theodore Jarvis's ghost regularly walked the towpath at twilight.

Race relations in America at the turn of the twentieth century were themselves a restless and deeply troubled spirit. "[*The Monster*] continues to fascinate," writes David Greven, precisely "because of its acute responsiveness to the violence, terror, and sheer incoherence of its national era's unresolved racial crisis and also essential uncertainty." Mark Twain, writing during the waning idealism of Reconstruction, sent two young men, one white, one Black, down the nation's mightiest river in a mutual flight for freedom. A generation later, Black Americans had become marginalized to the vanishing point, and Stephen Crane, in a bravura fictionalization, conjured a Black man who literally cannot be looked at. Ralph Ellison was much taken with Crane's body of work, terming *Maggie: A Girl of the Streets* "the parent of the modern American novel," but he responded with particular interest to *The Monster*. Who was the character Henry Johnson, after all, if not, like Robert Lewis and the many other victims of racial injustice, an *invisible man*?

Stephen Crane—along with his brother William and *The Monster*'s Dr. Trescott—had chosen to confront a question largely evaded in late nineteenth-century America: How should a conscientious white person respond to the most egregious forms of racial prejudice? "Despite the prosperity and apparent openness and freedom of the society, it was as though a rigid national censorship had been imposed—not by an apparatus set up in Washington but within the center of the American mind," Ellison wrote. "Now there was much of which Americans were morally aware but little which they wished to confront in literature, and the compelling of such confrontation was the challenge flung down to Crane by history."

It is fitting in a way that *The Monster* was Crane's last book. His older brother had done that which intrigued Stephen most: he had, in a moment of supreme mortal danger, chosen to do what was right. Unlike his devout father, Stephen did not possess faith in the inherent virtuousness of human beings; he believed that if there was any good in the world, it must reside in the selfless acts of which we are sometimes capable.

———

William Dean Howells, editor of the *Atlantic Monthly*, termed *The Monster* upon its appearance, "the best short story ever written by an American." When in 1897 Crane had read parts of the manuscript aloud to close friends in England, however, several were unimpressed, pronouncing the tale weird for its rude juxtapositions of the familiar and the strange and complaining of its lack of resolution.

One such colleague was the American novelist and *New York Times* London correspondent Harold Frederic, whose reports to the United States of the British popularity of *The Red Badge of Courage* had helped nurture its fame back home. The subheading of Frederic's glowing January 1896 *New York Times* review referred to the book's youthful author as "An Unrivaled Battle Describer," and compared favorably the innovative psychological perspectives Crane had introduced to the startling breakthroughs in human motion study achieved in the late 1870s by the photographer Eadweard Muybridge. But he disappointed Crane by labeling the new tale misbegotten and offensive and urging him to destroy it.

Frederic's opinion was hard to dismiss, as he knew as well as Crane the social and psychological terrain in which *The Monster* was set; his own popular novel *The Damnation of Theron Ware* (1896) was a realistic depiction of the impact of modernity on issues of faith in upstate New York, where he had been raised. Crane, who rarely allowed himself to be provoked, vehemently defended his latest creation. He had anticipated the short novel would help ease his financial woes, and he may have felt Frederic, who had earlier urged Crane to pursue reportage rather than imaginative tales, was accusing him of trying to profit from a sensationalized horror story. Crane insisted that readers would not be shocked by the inclusion of a faceless character and would appreciate the "sense" of the story, a portrait of a quintessential American town in crisis. When Frederic broadened his critique to include the Joseph Conrad novel *Lord Jim*, about the moral lapse of a ship's first mate haunted by his cowardly abandonment of passengers after an accident at sea, Crane, who prized his friendship with Conrad, erupted, slamming the table and "smashing a luncheon plate."

The incident caused a lasting rift between Crane and Frederic, although the *Times* reporter was not the only person to deplore the disfigurement of Henry Johnson. Richard Watson Gilder, the editor of the *Century Magazine* who had rejected *Maggie* years before as lacking in sentiment and restraint (in Crane's opinion "because the story was too honest"), sent the manuscript of *The Monster* back at once to Crane's literary agent, saying, "We couldn't publish that thing with half the expectant mothers in America on our subscription list."

Conrad, however, had no hesitation in praising Crane's achievement, remarking, "The damned story has been haunting me . . . I think it must be fine." It was soon picked up for publication by *Harper's*, which ran the full novella in its August 1898 issue. The following year the book publishers Harper & Brothers put out a Crane collection that paired *The Monster* with "The Blue Hotel," about the killing of an offensively behaving foreigner in a Colorado saloon.

Julian Hawthorne (son of the novelist Nathaniel Hawthorne) took Crane to task for setting up so awful a conundrum in *The Monster* and then offering no answer for the dilemma it posed. He dubbed the work "an outrage on art and humanity" and suggested that "something is fundamentally out of gear in a mind that can reconcile itself to such a performance . . . It is one thing to be humorous when writing a history of the French Revolution, like Carlyle; and quite another to be humorous about the tiny trivialities of a New York country town. Anybody can look down on that, and see the fun of it."

An unsigned 1901 review in *Academy*, however, allowed that "if Mr. Crane had written nothing else, this book would have wrested from the world an acknowledgement of his curious, searching gifts, and would have made him a reputation . . . The quick, nervous, prehensile mind that in an instant could select the vital characteristics of any scene or group, is notably here, and here also in superabundance is the man's grim fatalism, his saturnine pleasure in exhibiting (with bitter, laughing mercilessness) the frustrations of human efforts, the absurd trifles which decide human destiny."

If *The Monster* baffled Crane's contemporaries, it remained misunderstood by critics and literary historians for many decades. Some deemed it an uncanny tale of a monster and his maker, like Mary

Shelley's *Frankenstein*, or an occult yarn akin to Ambrose Bierce's "An Occurrence at Owl Creek Bridge" (a story Crane hugely admired). Others interpreted it as an indictment of small-town myopia and close-mindedness in the vein of Sinclair Lewis's *Main Street*.

Ralph Ellison was the first to note the story's background of racial violence and lynching, writing in 1960: "*The Monster* places us in an atmosphere like that of post–Civil War America, and there is no question of the Negro's part in it, nor to the fact that the issues go much deeper than the question of race. Indeed, the work is so fresh that [today's] daily papers tell us all we need to know of its background and the timeliness of its implications." The Crane biographers Paul Sorrentino and Stanley Wertheim picked up on Ellison's suggestion and included news articles about the Robert Lewis lynching in their definitive chronicle of the author's life published in 1994; two years later the literary historian Elaine Marshall's essay "Crane's 'The Monster' Seen in the Light of Robert Lewis's Lynching" introduced an interpretation that has subsequently been built upon by several other scholars, most notably Jacqueline Goldsby. Through the real-world brutality of the Port Jervis lynching, and Crane's fictionalized allegory of racist paranoia, the facade of the quaint village's neighborliness is exposed. *The Monster* reveals "truths not socially accepted for almost another hundred years," notes the critic Chester Wolford. "The story is, indeed, an excoriation of social conditions for [Black Americans], but more important . . . , it is an excoriation of all communities, all societies, in all places and times."

Crane's aim with *The Monster* was to offer a compelling fiction that would serve as social critique, echoing in its disturbing imagery the powerful emphases of *Maggie: A Girl of the Streets*. He may not have imagined that nearly a century would pass before the connection between it and the lynching of Robert Lewis would be made, or that the town's long collective silence about the matter would lend special value to his unearthing of its moral ambivalence surrounding the incident. As Goldsby suggests, "Reading *The Monster* should lead us to rethink the forms that writing and contemplating history assume, and the kind of cultural work that literature can be expected to do in history's wake." Crane's method of capturing history, allowing "the detail of a thing . . . to filter through my blood, and then it comes out like a native product," resulted in a work that is both timeless and memorable. Read alongside the known details of the lynching of Robert Lewis, it resembles a missing page from a family scrapbook, a candid sepia-tone snapshot of Port Jervis, New York, and the United States, on June 2, 1892.

EPILOGUE

———◦◦◦◦———

A t Hawk's Nest, the leafy heights above the Delaware River west of Port Jervis, early fall produced a flare of vibrant color, signaling summer's keenness to depart.

In September, the Orange County Court at Goshen adjourned without Philip Foley's blackmail case having come to trial; it was put over to the court's next term, scheduled to resume at Newburgh on November 21. On November 11, however, Foley was released on five hundred dollars bail and walked out of the Goshen jail after five and a half months behind bars. It was unclear who had come up with the money, although rumor pointed to his family; for despite having denounced his brother in a New York paper, J. P. Foley did eventually take a leave of absence from his job to come to Goshen to render what assistance he could.

Foley celebrated by getting drunk in the nearby town of Monroe. He then boarded a westbound train and, after refusing to pay his fare, was forced by rail employees into the smoking car with a lit cigar in his mouth. When he complained he was being mistreated and only wanted to get to Port Jervis, the conductor, who recognized him, laughed and advised he'd likely be more roughly handled when he reached that destination. After word of his antics on the train became known, a Middletown headline announced: FOLEY HAS NOT IM-PROVED (AND YET HE IS TOO GOOD-LOOKING A FELLOW TO FALL SO LOW).

Finding himself in complete agreement with the subhead, and deciding he'd had enough of Orange County, Foley jumped bail and disappeared. There were whispers that officials were secretly fine with his flight, even that his departure had been engineered. The evidence in the blackmailing case was thin, and the county, already exposed as incapable of holding anyone accountable for the lynching, may have thought it prudent to avoid another public relations disaster by washing its hands of the matter, along with Foley himself. Possibly he was offered the same kind of bargain Judge Mulley had given him the previous spring. But this time, no doubt a great deal wiser, he'd seized the opportunity and fled.

Sol Carley had in the intervening months struggled to distance himself from his role in the lynching. But whenever the freight train on which he worked as a flagman pulled into Goshen, Black residents emerged to taunt and curse him for having delivered Robert Lewis into the hands of the mob. Soon the verbal protests escalated and were accompanied by rocks, bottles, and brickbats raining down on the roof of the caboose where Carley sought refuge. After one torrential barrage, he abandoned his post entirely, ran to the main depot, and caught a passenger train back to Port Jervis. Eventually he secured safer employment as a conductor.

Simon Yaple replaced Abram Kirkman as Port Jervis's chief of police in fall 1892. The town's dreadful summer had clearly soured Kirkman on the position; he stepped down after only three and a half months on the job, his unease evident as early as a week following the June 2 lynching, when he'd left town on a family vacation in the midst of the coroner's inquest.

That Yaple was the right man for the position became plain at once. On October 17, when the milkman Ephraim Shay stepped away from his horse cart for a moment, three tramps seized the coin box he'd left on the seat and ran off down Jersey Avenue. Informed of the heist, Chief Yaple raced in a wagon to Duffy's Saloon, where it was believed the robbers were spending the loot. They weren't there, but a minute later he caught sight of them fleeing up a nearby railroad embankment. When they ignored his command to halt, he drew his gun and fired, killing one of the men as the others vanished into the woods.

Coroner Harding found the deceased had no identification but determined he was about thirty-five years of age and likely had a nautical past, as his right arm had a tattoo of an anchor, his left a woman reclining on an urn of flowers. Fourteen dollars was retrieved from his pocket.

The regional press prominently featured news of the shooting, leading the *Tri-States Union* to complain that on account of the Robert Lewis lynching Port Jervis had gained "a reputation for sensations, and even events of a commonplace character take on a sensational aspect." Shooting a fleeing suspect of a felony was not unacceptable police procedure at the time, and Yaple, after a brief inquiry, was cleared of any wrongdoing in firing his weapon. The papers, in commending him for his courage and quick thinking, acclaimed him "a terror to evil doers."

The following spring, however, he was abruptly removed from office, the victim of local patronage jockeying and perhaps lingering irritation among some residents for his having provided names and testimony at the lynching inquest. The *Union* bemoaned his firing and complained about the reappointment to the police ranks of Patrick Collier. Patrick Salley was also reinstated, while Patrick Burns, the onetime protector of Philip Foley, was appointed street commissioner, a job for which he had no qualifications. The article lamented the Democrats' "determination to reward [the] Irish."

Yaple took the end of his career in law enforcement in stride, returning to his former calling as a blacksmith. He opened a new smithy on lower Pike Street that was soon so busy it required the purchase of a new anvil.

The local press would rarely revisit the subject of the lynching in the coming years, but the one-year anniversary of the killing of Robert Lewis, on June 2, 1893, found the *Gazette* reflecting that:

> the lynching . . . however unfortunate it may be considered by the law, has had an appreciable effect for the better upon the morals of the town. This affair, together with the shooting of a tramp by ex-chief of police Yaple . . . has led criminals to give Port Jervis a wide berth. For more than one month (January) no criminals were brought before the police justice, a state of affairs altogether unprecedented in the history of Port Jervis, or for that matter, any other village or city of its size in this part of New York State.

The paper went on to equivocate that while it was unlikely anyone would ever be held accountable for the lynching, "scores of men and boys were equally guilty and to punish one or two for the crime of the entire mob would not be exact and equal justice." This, of course, was a fallacy, as lynch mobs always had a core of inciters, cheerleaders, and determined sadists whose "leadership," and culpability, were blatant.

At about the same time, Philip Foley resurfaced. "[He] now affects eyeglasses and wears a dudish-looking summer suit, and is very stunning in appearance," noted a reporter who spotted him. "So much so, few of his old acquaintances recognized him, and those who did were rewarded only with a look of scorn." While making the rounds of the Front Street saloons, Foley let it be known he had come to town to settle a score with Officer Collier. It's not clear what their dispute was, but as Collier was a boorish ruffian and Foley a roguish gent, it may have involved some insult to Foley's manhood. Collier managed to get the jump on the notorious visitor and locked him in the Ball Street jail, for Foley a place of distinctly unhappy associations. He then notified the sheriff's office that he'd arrested Foley, to see if Goshen wanted him back for a resumption of the blackmail case, but, sensibly, it appears, no one returned the call, and Foley, free to go, left Port Jervis and was never seen again. As for the consistently unreliable Collier, he was soon made chief of police.

Port Jervians no doubt studied the *Gazette*'s musings about the anniversary of the lynching, but in general they took a tight-lipped attitude toward any recollection of their collective sin, as if to exorcise it by silence. Meanwhile, it appears that the Black community also found it best to say little, or nothing at all. The collective hush would soon acquire the quality of the eternal.

Those who had suspected supernatural elements at work in the pounding rainstorm that had coincided with the death of Robert Lewis, however, found new cause for concern on the afternoon of September 7, 1893, when a rare tornado descended from the western hills, ripping shutters and shingles off houses and propelling them like missiles through the air, toppling the steeple of Dr. Crane's Drew Methodist Church and sending men, women, and children running for their lives.

"Sheltered on all sides by mountains, Port Jervis has hitherto enjoyed a singular immunity from violent wind storms," the *Union* observed the following day. "Their force has always been broken by the barriers which nature has erected on all sides of this favored locality. A genuine cyclone is therefore something unknown to us." Weirdly, the storm seemed to concentrate its force on the blocks between Orange Square and the intersection of Main and Ferguson, where the lynching had occurred. As a result of the carnage, it was reported, "an arc lamp was carried over into 'hangman's tree,' and had hung there all night."

Probably the only known twentieth-century rendering
of the lynching of Robert Lewis is this April 1955 magazine
illustration by Brendan Lynch.

In late July 1894, Lena McMahon checked into the Cosmopolitan Hotel in New York City, a popular stopping place for people from Orange County, as it was close to the railroad ferry that brought Erie passengers across the Hudson from Jersey City. She registered as

Lena Gallagher Dowling, Gallagher being her birth name and Dowling the last name of Will Dowling, a professional jockey she claimed to have married in Boston the previous year. For several days she was seen rarely, leaving her fourth-floor room only for meals. Then, on August 1, she walked to the nearby Chambers Street Hospital, a city-operated clinic, and told the receptionist that she had given birth to a stillborn child and that it could be found in a washbasin drawer in room 174 at the hotel.

The clinic summoned police, to whom Lena identified herself as Lulu G. Dowling and said she was employed as a bookkeeper, although under further questioning she admitted she was Lena McMahon of the Port Jervis lynching case. A *New York Herald* reporter who rushed to the scene saw "a tall, stately looking young woman, with clear-cut features, large brown eyes, and a modest and refined demeanor." He concluded: "A mystery seems to surround her." A Detective Kehoe, who went to the hotel and discovered the deceased infant, a female, in the drawer as Lena had indicated, remarked that Lena was a clever girl who "had acted very shrewdly" in concealing her condition and had refused to name the infant's father.

Theresa McMahon, notified by authorities, hurried to New York. Introduced by Lena as her "friend," Theresa told doctors and police she did not know why or how Lena came to be at the Cosmopolitan Hotel, but that the baby had been expected, and that she had once visited Lena in New York during the pregnancy. Theresa explained that Lena's husband, Will Dowling, was "a traveling man" from New York City and presumably the father of the child. Lena said that Dowling had abandoned her and that she had prepared for having the baby unassisted by reading books on alternative birthing methods.

Word of Lena's unfortunate plight put her back in the news in Port Jervis, stirring to life the very "tongue of scandal" she had so desperately wanted to flee. The story of a husband named Dowling was discredited. An alternative rumor, sworn to have originated with Lena herself, was that she'd recently been cohabiting with Phil Foley in Brooklyn. It was also known that she had visited John McMahon in Boston nine months earlier and that it was there she "got in trouble." The fact that her father did not rush to Lena's side at news of the stillbirth, as had Theresa, struck some who knew the family as odd, as he'd always been so demonstrably protective of her. Theresa, in an unguarded interview with the *New York Evening World*, seemed to suggest that her husband had left her and Lena, but upon the story's being cited in a Port Jervis paper she denounced it as false, writing to the editor: "Please do not add more to the already great sorrows of our family." Asked if Lena's new difficulties were connected to the Robert Lewis lynching, Theresa allowed that "ever since that time, she has acted very strangely."

Theresa, on advice of the authorities, had Lena committed to Bellevue Hospital. Because she had to answer a charge of murder read against her, she was housed in the prison ward. The coroner eventually ruled, however, that an autopsy of the infant showed the child had never breathed, and thus had been born dead, although a physician attending the examination noted that the absence of proper medical care during the delivery had likely been a contributing factor. Lena convalesced at Bellevue until the end of August, when her mother brought her back to Port Jervis. Friends who had not seen her in months gathered around in support. It was evident she was much shaken by her recent experience, and they expressed concern she was so exceedingly thin. One, Florence Kadel, later recollected that after the loss of the baby, Lena "didn't stop screaming. And when she had no voice left, her mouth still looked like she was screaming." As Lena herself had long feared and anticipated, she was committed by her family to a residential asylum, the Middletown State Homeopathic Hospital, where she remained until her death in 1937.

Or such was the rumor. The truth was likely more mundane. The 1895 Port Jervis directory still shows Lena as the proprietor of the confectionery at 34 Kingston, although by 1897 not a single Mc-Mahon is listed as a resident of the village. The U.S. Census of 1900 finds her living in East Cambridge, Massachusetts, under the name "Ellen Gallagher," with her adoptive parents John and Theresa McMahon and three boarders. Her occupation is listed as "music teacher."

John McMahon died on the last day of 1902, mourned by his local war veterans' lodge and survived by his adopted daughter and his wife. Theresa may have died soon after, for the census trail turns cold. It seems most likely Lena's dream of regaining her anonymity came true, and as Ellen Gallagher, so common an Irish name it could be worn as a disguise, she slipped unrecognized into the maelstrom of the new century.

As many had predicted, the lawsuit for damages against New York State filed by the Brooklyn attorney Rufus Perry, Jr., on behalf of the Friends of Bob Lewis, gained significant publicity but little in the way of legal traction. The *Middletown Argus*, eager to have the last word, advised smugly that if legal do-gooders truly wished to "put an end to the lynching of negroes, there is just one way in which [they] can do so, and that is to put an end to the brutal crimes which make lynching possible."

Perry, unfazed, continued to prioritize the need to relieve Black people's exposure to racially motivated violence. He subsequently helped found Beulah Land, a "model town for the negro race," on three thousand acres near Jamesport, Long Island. The *Brooklyn Eagle* cheered the endeavor, noting, "The negroes of North and South

Carolina, who are wondering just what is going to happen next in the lynching line, are naturally expected to jump at this chance to find a Beulah Land on earth, where they may not only be safe from indiscriminate hanging, but where they may grow fat and prosper on the best the land can afford." When it became apparent that opposition from local whites at Jamesport would likely doom the project by impeding the necessary land acquisition, however, the plan's investors withdrew.

An undeterred Perry fought on in ways large and small, leading an effort that secured a ban on a Coney Island attraction known as "Negro Ball Dodging," in which whites hurled baseballs at Black men's heads as they appeared in the openings of a cloth or wooden facade.

The Black female activists of Brooklyn who had given Ida B. Wells an early New York platform saw her influence grow through the 1890s. Wells lectured widely in America on the strength of *Southern Horrors*, as well as subsequent publications including *A Red Record: Lynchings in the United States* (1892–1893–1894) and *The Reason Why the Colored American Is Not in the World's Columbian Exposition* (1893), a broadside about the exclusion of Black American accomplishment from the Chicago World's Fair. Despite the compassionate reception for her message in progressive and African American reform circles, the mainstream U.S. press and most elected officials remained largely unmoved by the imperative of combating lynch law. In the footsteps of American abolitionists who had successfully visited England a half century before to rouse influential British support, Wells embarked on two lecture tours there, arranged by Catherine Impey, an English Quaker and editor, and the Scottish reformer Isabella Fyvie Mayo. No longer reticent before audiences, Wells managed to fire an intense British reaction, resulting in published expressions of horror at the savagery of lynching, as well as an extensive letter-writing campaign by leading Britons designed to shame Southern editors, statesmen, and business leaders.

Her efforts were no doubt instrumental in prompting Representative George H. White of North Carolina—the last standing Southern Black congressman of the nineteenth century—to introduce on January 20, 1900, in the House of Representatives the first bill for a federal anti-lynching law. It was denounced immediately by the usual suspects and never made it out of committee; indeed, when White was voted from office the next year, both houses of the white-controlled North Carolina legislature, long contemptuous of his fierce advocacy for equal rights and embarrassed (before their fellow Southern racists) by his lingering official presence in Washington, passed resolutions of thanksgiving.

Characteristically, he did not go quietly. Standing alone in the well of the House chamber, he gave a memorable valedictory address, declaiming:

> This, Mr. Chairman, is perhaps the Negroes' temporary farewell to the American Congress, but let me say Phoenix-like he will rise up some day and come again. These parting words are in behalf of an outraged, heart-broken, bruised and bleeding, but God-fearing people, faithful, industrial, loyal people, rising people, full of potential force . . . The only apology I have for the earnestness with which I have spoken is that I am pleading for the life, the liberty, the future happiness, and manhood suffrage for one-eighth of the entire population of the United States.

He went on to challenge white America's eliminationist views toward Black people by founding, in the spirit of Perry's Beulah Land and in partnership with the poet Paul Laurence Dunbar and the educator Booker T. Washington, a community in southern New Jersey called "Whitesboro," where Black people could purchase affordable homes and live free from white intimidation and authority.

T. Thomas Fortune and Ida B. Wells also saw the urgency of encouraging African Americans to shrug off their conditioned feelings of helplessness. "We do not counsel violence, we counsel manly retaliation," Fortune wrote. In a few reported instances, Black people had used the threat of armed retaliation to successfully thwart white violence, leading Wells to advise her readers: "The lesson this teaches and which every Afro-American should ponder well, is that a Winchester rifle should have a place of honor in every Black home. The more the Afro-American yields and cringes and begs, the more he is insulted, outraged and lynched." She herself had begun carrying a gun in her purse after the Memphis lynching of her friend Tom Moss. "I felt that one had better die fighting against injustice than to die like a dog or a rat in a trap. I had already determined to sell my life as dearly as possible if attacked. I felt if I could take one lyncher with me, this would even up the score a bit."

Behind their call for self-protection was their awareness that white terroristic control, once characteristic of the small-town South, was now emerging in Atlanta and New Orleans, as well as Northern communities such as Port Jervis. There was a significant riot in New York City's Tenderloin district in summer 1900, with police joining enraged whites in randomly beating Black men and women up and down the blocks of Manhattan's west side, pulling them off streetcars and out of restaurants. The fracas was sparked by the stabbing death of an undercover cop by a Black man, and fueled by Irish American resentment of inroads made by newly arrived Southern Blacks seeking employment. A similar explosion of uncontrolled white violence struck Atlanta in 1906, ripping the city apart and causing extensive damage.

Terror as a white response to Black advances, deep-seated white contempt for Black people generally, and the frenzied sadism of the mob, Wells saw, were easily replicated anywhere.

The concern prompted by the Port Jervis lynching, as well as others that occurred where they were "not supposed to," or else those that involved white victims, eventually began to catalyze broader apprehension in the nation's editorial pages and from its church pulpits. "Let this mob spirit continue unbridled," one Georgia paper predicted, "and the victims will not always be Negroes. When a howling, blood-thirsty, unreasoning mob starts into stringing up white men without a hearing, lynching will not be viewed with such complaisance."

In August 1908 in Springfield, Illinois, a mob of several thousand whites assaulted the Black community after the sheriff successfully spirited out of town two Black men being held on charges of rape and murder. The violence lasted for two days and nights and left nine Black people dead, with hundreds of homes and businesses destroyed, and ended only with the arrival of the National Guard. Three years later Zachariah Walker, a Black mill worker in Coatesville, Pennsylvania, shot to death a deputy attempting to arrest him for public drunkenness. Walker, who'd been injured in the confrontation, was taken to a hospital, but was then seized by a furious horde of townspeople who stormed the institution and took him, along with the bed to which he'd been chained, and burned him alive on a nearby hillside before several thousand men, women, and children.

A primary destination for Black people migrating north in the early years of the century was Chicago, where white vigilantes continually harassed residents of the rapidly growing Black neighborhoods. On July 27, 1919, at a Lake Michigan beach, white and Black youths were throwing stones at one another when a Black teenager, Eugene Williams, was struck in the head and drowned. Police refused to arrest the young white man responsible, even after he was pointed out by witnesses. The dispute set off three days of fistfights, vandalism, shootings, and arson, with police either collaborating with white rioters or turning a blind eye to their actions. When order was finally restored, the city tallied twenty-three Black and fifteen white fatalities, more than five hundred people wounded, and almost one thousand families made homeless.

Duluth, Minnesota, an industrialized harbor town at the southwest corner of Lake Superior, was the site of a horrific triple lynching in June 1920. A white mob, misled by exaggerated newspaper accounts of the alleged rape of a seventeen-year-old white girl, smashed its way into a downtown jail where several Black roustabouts from a traveling circus were being held on suspicion. Members of the mob seized Elias Clayton, Elmer Jackson, and Isaac McGhie and hanged them from a nearby lamppost.

———•◦•———

It was the 1908 violence in Springfield, Illinois, two hundred miles south of Chicago, that proved a turning point in the struggle against lynching. Reports that the hometown and final resting place of Abraham Lincoln had been desecrated by horrific racial violence were, to the outside world, most unsettling. Young white men who plundered the Black community were heard to shout, "Lincoln freed you, we'll show you where you belong." Meanwhile, some affluent whites were reported to have idly watched the destruction from the comfort of their automobiles. William English Walling, a Kentucky-born labor reformer, toured the city in the rioting's aftermath, and his article, "Race War in the North," appearing in the *Independent*, served as a national call for activists to reinvigorate the biracial energies of the abolition movement. The following year, white progressives and Black activists (veterans of both the Afro-American League and the Niagara Movement, a group of Black lawyers and rights advocates led by W.E.B. Du Bois and the Boston publisher William Monroe Trotter) founded the NAACP, one of whose early initiatives was to expose the evil of lynching. The new organization's methods included the kind of rigorous investigations of lynchings that Wells had long recommended, for "the colored man has no facilities if he has the courage to tell his side of the story."

The NAACP sent its white investigators south, posing as casual visitors or parties interested in land or timber purchases, to extract as much information as possible from local whites. Many white Southerners, it was found, were more than glad to speak about a recent event of such consequence in their community. Black representatives, such as James Weldon Johnson and Walter White, who chiefly sought information from the Black community, often learned the details of alleged crimes that had been distorted or ignored by white publications. The subsequent NAACP reports went to newspapers, elected officials, and leading clerics, and proved an effective way to awaken broad disdain for the cruelty and madness of mob justice, depicting it as anarchism and as un-American, a message that would resonate with the public in the wake of the Bolshevik Revolution and the First World War.

From 1920 until the 1940s the NAACP, frustrated by the Southern states' unwillingness to investigate let alone prosecute those responsible for lynching, waged an all-out campaign for a federal anti-lynching law. It was led by the organization's executive secretaries Johnson and White and given vocal support by Eleanor Roosevelt, Pearl Buck, and tens of thousands of allies and contributors. Little remembered today, the demand for the legislation was one of the most fervent and widely supported reform campaigns of the inter-war years. An important breakthrough for the effort came in 1923, when the U.S. Supreme Court ruled in *Moore v. Dempsey* that a trial could not be held in a mob atmosphere, with crowds gathering out-side the court, hollering through open windows, or otherwise intimi-dating the proceedings. The decision affirmed the principle that any denial of due process was a concern of the federal government, but despite substantial support in Congress, the push for a federal anti-lynching law could not overcome the by-now-familiar Southern resis-tance to federal meddling, or President Franklin D. Roosevelt's fears of alienating Southern support for the New Deal.

Although often at odds ideologically with the NAACP, the Inter-national Labor Defense (ILD), a legal arm of the Communist Party USA, went south in the 1930s to defend Black victims of so-called "legal" lynchings. In such proceedings the court conducted the mere formality of a trial, sometimes completed in as little as fifteen minutes, designed to bring a preordained verdict of guilt and possibly a death sentence. The most famous of the ILD efforts were the multiple trials of the Scottsboro Boys, nine Black teenagers ages thirteen to nineteen who were arrested in Alabama in 1931 and accused of raping two white women aboard a freight train. Led by the New York attorney Samuel Liebowitz, the ILD won key appeals at the U.S. Supreme Court that enlarged defendants' rights. These included *Powell v. Ala-bama* (1932), which established access to adequate defense counsel as an indispensable part of the right of due process, and *Norris v. Ala-bama* (1935), which found that excluding Black citizens from jury service violated the Equal Protection Clause of the Fourteenth Amend-ment. The Supreme Court justices were livid when they learned that, just before the files in *Norris* came before them, someone in Alabama had tried to belatedly add Black names to the relevant lists.

Despite the lack of physical evidence and inconsistent witness

testimony, highlighted by the recantation of one of the two female ac-
cusers (who went on a national fundraising tour on behalf of the defendants), Alabama refused to acknowledge its gross overreach in
bringing the charges of rape, to admit that the Scottsboro Boys were
innocent, or to allow its reputation to be blemished by being seen to
"lose" to "Communist" lawyers. The state needlessly prolonged the
legal proceedings as well as the incarceration of the men for several
years, the last not leaving prison until 1950.

An innovative homegrown source of effective agitation in the
1930s was the Association of Southern Women for the Prevention of
Lynching, led by Jessie Daniel Ames, a former telephone operator
who put her knowledge of the technology to good use. Ames enlisted
other Southern white women to invoke their status as the nominal
"beneficiaries" of lynching to keep local police in line. At the first
notice a Black person had been taken into custody, the association's
phone trees lit up, letting individual sheriffs and jailers know for certain they were being watched, and that if they knew what was good for
them, their prisoner best be safe and sound come morning. The
NAACP, in a related effort, created a program to honor sheriffs who
demonstrated fealty to the law, from which several colorful tales
emerged of lawmen (or their wives) holding would-be lynchers at bay
with a loaded shotgun, or otherwise securing prisoners from vigilantes at great personal risk.

In response to the stalemate in Congress over a federal anti-
lynching law, Justice Department lawyers during the Second World
War found something of a workaround in revived anti-Klan conspiracy statutes dating from Reconstruction, valuable if neglected heir-
looms from the nation's legal attic, in need of a light dusting off but
technically still in effect. These included Sections 51 and 52 (later
241 and 242) of Title 18, the "Conspiracy Section" of the U.S. Criminal Code. Section 51 derived from the Enforcement Acts, three bills

passed in 1870 and 1871 to safeguard Black Americans' voting and other civil rights under the law and to confront the Ku Klux Klan. The laws punished crimes in which "two or more persons conspire to injure, oppress, threaten, or intimidate any citizen in the exercise or enjoyment" of their constitutionally guaranteed rights, or in which "two or more people go in disguise on the highway for such a purpose." Section 52, which had originated in the Civil Rights Act of 1866, forbade those who "under color of law" acted to deny citizens the right to due process. After numerous attempts by Justice Department attorneys to use these statutes in Southern federal courts, and much legal push and pull about what constitutional rights they actually protected, the U.S. Supreme Court in *United States v. Price* (1966) affirmed that due process of law is a federally guaranteed right under the Fourteenth Amendment, and that citizens taking part in a conspiracy along with a policeman were also acting "under color of law." From this ruling came the first conviction of a lynch mob in the modern era and perhaps the first in the South since Reconstruction, when, in 1967, Assistant Attorney General for Civil Rights John Doar won guilty verdicts in the case of six members of the Mississippi White Knights of the Ku Klux Klan, as well as the colluding Neshoba County deputy sheriff Cecil Ray Price, in the 1964 Klan-police conspiracy murders of civil rights workers James Chaney, Andrew Goodman, and Mickey Schwerner.

These legal affirmations of the right to due process; reforms to guard against prisoners being relinquished to mobs; moral suasion generated by the efforts of the anti-lynching crusade, particularly the NAACP; white Americans' and the media's increased perception of mobs as un-American; and the editorials of Southern moderates lambasting the practice as anachronistic and immoral were among the factors that ultimately turned the country against this most egregious form of racial violence. The first year to pass without a single recorded lynching anywhere in the United States was 1952, although the decade was not without other incidents of racial violence, including the legal lynching of Willie McGee in 1951, the abduction and murder of Emmett Till in 1955, and the lynching of Mack Charles Parker in 1959.

McGee, of Laurel, Mississippi, convicted of rape, was put to death in the state's portable electric chair, which could be moved from one county courthouse to another, following six years of retrials and appeals. Despite the efforts of the authors William Faulkner and Jessica Mitford, the performers Josephine Baker and Paul Robeson, as well as the pleadings of a bold young civil rights attorney from New York named Bella Abzug, the Mississippi State Supreme Court refused to recognize the hidden truth of the allegations against McGee—that his accuser, a married white woman, had been his lover in a consensual affair.

Parker, alleged to have molested a white woman stranded on the highway at night in a broken-down automobile, was dragged fighting and kicking from a jail in Poplarville, Mississippi, bundled into a car, shot to death, and hurled into a river. The U.S. Justice Department attempted to use the newly renovated federal conspiracy laws against the suspected mob. However, a Southern federal judge hostile to the Justice Department's aims, and a decidedly unresponsive grand jury, quashed the prosecution.

Emmett Till's 1955 murder outside Money, Mississippi, became worldwide news given his young age (he was fourteen years old) and the allegation that he'd "wolf whistled" at a white woman, Carolyn Bryant, who had been working the counter in a grocery store. Film clips of the trial of Till's alleged killers—Carolyn's husband, Ray, and his half brother J. W. "Big" Milam—were recorded and flown nightly from the airfield in tiny Tutwiler, Mississippi, to New York to be aired on network television. Many Americans watched in consternation as an all-white jury acquitted both men, who the following year admitted to the crime in a well-paid interview for *Look* magazine. Mamie Till, Emmett's mother, condemned Bryant, Milam, and white America in toto when she insisted the coffin at Emmett's funeral be left open so all could see what monstrous violence had been done to her son. A photograph of the boy's grotesquely mutilated face, printed initially in *Jet* magazine, endures as an iconic image of the country's capacity for anti-Black cruelty and intolerance.

So thoroughly has this odium continued to infect policing and the justice system, it takes little imagination to recognize the link between the national crime of lynching as it was known to Ida B. Wells and the many racial injustices with which we still contend: racial profiling, police brutality, racial bias in the courts and in the nation's penal system, and disproportionate punishments, including the death penalty. Statistics on race and capital punishment today correspond closely, on a state-by-state basis, with the pattern of lynching more than a century ago. "We've regularized and sanitized it until we're down to white tiles, a gurney, and an intravenous drip," observes the scholar Eliza Steelwater. "What was an event has been downgraded to an occurrence, then to a parody of a therapeutic procedure."

Spectacle lynchings no longer occur in America, yet the *spectacle* of bystander-made cell phone videos and police body-cam footage serve in not dissimilar ways as witness to, and as amplification of, the summary executions of Black people. With the internet, the audience for such images has expanded into the millions, as the disturbing narrative loop plays seemingly without respite—ubiquitous, continuous, viewable by the click of a mouse. Like their nineteenth-century antecedents, such images sicken all decent human beings and retain the especial capacity to retraumatize and terrorize Black people. The term "lynching" has often been misappropriated in recent years, sometimes for trivial purposes that cruelly mock its deadly meaning, but after the world watched the Minneapolis police officer Derek Chauvin kneel on George Floyd's neck for an excruciating nine minutes and twenty-nine seconds, many viewers knew intuitively what they had seen.

———•◦•———

As with other communities in the Lower Hudson Valley whose prosperity and identity are linked to an earlier time, Port Jervis has struggled over the last few decades to regain a sense of pride and purpose. The town was ravaged by the disappearance of railroad jobs in the 1950s, and its thriving commercial center was soon made redundant by the arrival of an interstate highway that bypassed the town, as well as the opening of shopping malls in nearby Middletown. Although it won formal designation as a city in 1907, it still resembles in abundant ways the village where the lynching of Robert Lewis occurred. East Main is still lined with handsome dwellings, including that of Judge Crane (which, suitably, now serves as offices for a law firm). Almost every residential side street has its share of rambling Victorian homes with the occasional bay window or wooden tower. Front Street has retained many of its nineteenth-century commercial buildings, the majestic peak of St. Mary's still looks down disapprovingly at what was once Grab Point, and many sites involved in the Lewis incident are similarly unchanged, including the riverside flat with its shade trees and embankment where Foley left Lena reading a book on an otherwise unremarkable late spring noontime in 1892.

One of the town's major landmarks, the Tri-States Monument at the tip of the peninsula that contains Laurel Grove Cemetery, is now situated directly under a bridge for Interstate 84, from which emanates a steady, dull roar of cross-country highway traffic. Some of the most prominent examples of the town's architecture—the Farnum Building, the opera house, city hall—are gone. A deadly building collapse on Pike Street in 1971 led to understandable concern about the structural integrity of other old addresses in the downtown area, and, in retrospect, to what some current residents now regret was an overly aggressive program of urban renewal. While the wrecking ball may have been required in the interest of public safety, the loss of many distinctive edifices left gaping holes in the town's appearance, which are only now being addressed in revitalization efforts.

Memorabilia from the glory days of the Erie Railroad and the Monticello Line dot the town, and there remains a steadfast affection for railroad history and lore. The Erie Depot where Lena caught the 2:28 to New York City still stands, an impressive example of late Victorian civic design, although it no longer performs its original function. The Erie repair shops, in their day a sprawling complex so large it would have been visible from outer space, are long paved over; a solitary locomotive turntable is preserved as a curiosity; an adjacent parking lot serves customers of a Walgreens, a Burger King, and a modest strip mall.

The film director D. W. Griffith, who between 1909 and 1911 shot some of the country's earliest motion pictures in Cuddebackville, about nine miles northeast of Port Jervis, so loved the riverine scenery of the area that he described the bend in the Neversink there as "altogether the loveliest spot in America." But watery nature has repeatedly shown its less pleasant side here, bringing river floods and "ice gorges" that take out bridges and overwhelm low-lying acreage. Rising waters have encroached several times on Port Jervis streets, causing significant property damage.

On May 1, 1900, it was reported that the stone marking the grave of Robert Lewis had been damaged by relic hunters and a portion taken away. But a further, final indignity awaited. When one of the region's seasonal floods in the early twentieth century turned the lower part of Laurel Grove Cemetery into a lake many feet in depth, an embankment above the Delaware River collapsed. It is believed Lewis's final resting place was among those that slid into the strong current and were swept downstream toward the sea.

The story may be apocryphal. Based on the earlier evidence of vandalism, it's possible it was the stone, not the grave, that disappeared, and given the town's eagerness to forget its intolerant past, the lore that the victim of a notorious lynching was literally carried away may be a bit too convenient. Still, anyone who has witnessed a flood or ice gorge in the region knows better than to discount the potential for annihilation.

The Ku Klux Klan was brazenly active in western Orange County in the 1920s and 1930s, burning crosses from Point Peter overlooking Port Jervis and across the Delaware on Heaters Hill in Matamoras. The organization held banquets, marched in their regalia along Jersey Avenue, and maintained a women's auxiliary known as the Daughters of Betsy Ross. Although there was no formal segregation in Port Jervis, well into the mid-twentieth century Black residents understood there were places—a beach, a roller rink, a popular lunch counter—at which they were unwelcome.

Even as, for most white Port Jervians, concern over the lynching vanished over many years as surely as had Robert Lewis's remains, the Black community long endured the lingering effects of their white neighbors' unforgivable act of racial violence. An African American man who grew up in Port Jervis but subsequently moved away confides, "It was a small town, and we had no choice but to see these people and go to school with their kids, and we knew their names and what their parents and grandparents had done." As late as the 1970s, he recalls, there remained between the new suburban-style high school and the north end of Kingston Avenue a large cornfield, which became for Black students a dreaded gauntlet to run, where bullying white boys lay in wait after class, armed with the most hateful of words.

BIBLIOGRAPHICAL ESSAY

＝───◦◦◦◦◦◦───═

INTRODUCTION

The books of my own to which I refer are *We Are Not Afraid: The Story of Goodman, Schwerner, and Chaney, and the Civil Rights Campaign for Mississippi* (New York: Macmillan, 1988; coauthored with Seth Cagin); *At the Hands of Persons Unknown: The Lynching of Black America* (New York: Random House, 2002); and *Capitol Men: The Epic Story of Reconstruction Through the Lives of the First Black Congressmen* (New York: Houghton Mifflin, 2008). I am also the author of the children's book *Yours for Justice, Ida B. Wells: The Daring Life of a Crusading Journalist* (Atlanta: Peachtree Press, 2009; illustrated by Stephen Alcorn).

1: JUNE 2, 1892

The story this book relates of the lynching of Robert Lewis in Port Jervis, New York, on June 2, 1892, is largely based on coverage of the incident and its aftermath that appeared in local newspapers, regional periodicals including those from New York City, as well as the national press. Most of the events described herein, including the inquest into the lynching, took place during the months of June and July 1892. The local news coverage, consisting of the

Port Jervis Gazette (PJG), the *Evening Gazette (EG)*, the *Tri-States Union (TSU)*, and the *Port Jervis Union (PJU)*, can be viewed on microfilm at the Port Jervis Free Library. See also Kristopher B. Burrell, "Bob Lewis' Encounter with the 'Great Death': Port Jervis' Entrance into the United States of Lyncherdom" (CUNY Hostos Community College, New York, NY, 2003).

For the Sarah Cassidy story see *PJG* 4/29/1891, *PJU* 4/29/1891, and the *New York Times* 4/30/1891.

In New York, Lena McMahon had lived at an orphanage affiliated with St. Stephen's, a Catholic church on the east side of New York City. She was accompanied to Port Jervis in 1874 or 1875 by a priest who was likely from either St. Stephen's or the Society for the Protection of Destitute Roman Catholic Children in the City of New York. The society, known informally as "the Protectory," was founded in 1863 in response to the famous Orphan Train Movement led by the reformer Charles Loring Brace, which had been successful in "placing out" tens of thousands of abandoned city children in small towns across the country. The Protectory's purpose was to ensure that Catholic children were not sent to be raised in Protestant homes.

John McMahon and Theresa Reddy McMahon were not strangers to the unhappy experience of watching someone close to them run afoul of the law, which might explain their initial sympathy for Philip Foley's legal predicament. During a labor dispute at the Pountney glassworks in 1877, Thomas Reddy and a fellow striker had ambushed the owner William Pountney as the latter attempted to escort a scab from his boardinghouse to the factory. Pountney, who was "badly pounded," took out a warrant for Reddy and his accomplice, both of whom hurriedly left town. Of course, George Lea's allegations regarding Foley were far more personal, as they involved a man who had won the devoted affection of the McMahons' daughter. See *EG* 7/5/1877 and 8/14/1877.

2: CITY IN PROGRESS

The D&H Canal was dug between 1825 and 1828 under the supervision of the chief engineer Benjamin Wright, one of the builders of the Erie Canal. His resident engineer (and chief engineer as of 1827) was John Bloomfield Jervis, later known as a designer of locomotives and as chief engineer of the Croton Aqueduct (1842), which bought fresh drinking water to New York City.

An article in the Warwick *Advertiser* on 6/9/1892 shared Interstate Commerce Commission data for 1891. It reported that of the nation's 153,235 trainmen, 1,450 had been killed on the job, and 13,172 injured.

Two good sources for the background history of Orange County, New York, are Samuel Eager, *An Outline History of Orange County* (Newburgh, NY: S. T. Callahan, 1846); and Philip H. Smith, *Legends of the Shawangunk* (Syracuse, NY: Syracuse University Press, 1965).

The history of African American lives in lower New York State can be found in David Levine, "African American History: A Past Rooted in the Hudson Valley," *Hudson Valley Magazine*, January 26, 2017; A. J. Williams-Myers, "The African Presence in the Mid-Hudson Valley Before 1800," *Afro-Americans in New York Life and History* 8, no. 1 (January 31, 1984); and Kevin Barrett, "Orange County's Civil War Colored Troops," *Orange County Historical Society Journal* 26 (November 1997); see also A. J. Williams-Myers, *Long Hammering: Essays on the Forging of an African-American Presence in the Hudson River Valley in the Early Twentieth Century* (Newburgh, NY: Africa World Press, 1994).

Articles dealing with the history of the Kidnapping Club include Jonathan Daniel Wells, "The So-Called Kidnapping Club Featured Cops Selling Free Black New Yorkers into Slavery," *Smithsonian Magazine*, January 14, 2020; Marjorie Waters, "Before Solomon Northrup: Fighting Slave Catchers in New York," *History News Network*, October 18, 2013; and Parul Sehgal, "When a Kidnapping Ring Targeted New York's Black Children," *New York Times*, 10/27/2020. See also Jonathan Daniel Wells, *The Kidnapping Club: Wall Street, Slavery, and Resistance on the Eve of the Civil War* (New York: Bold Type Books, 2020).

The link between the threat of lynching and its terroristic effect on Black families and as a cause of Black migration is treated eloquently in numerous memoirs and histories. Two recommended examples are by Richard Wright: *Uncle Tom's Children* (New York: Harper & Brothers, 1940) and *Black Boy* (New York: Harper & Brothers, 1945). As there was no hope of protection from local white authorities or from the national government, it was this terror, this risk of falling prey to a lynch mob, that inspired much Black migration—to Kansas, to Oklahoma, and to Northern industrial cities. While lynching was more likely to be recorded by coverage in local newspapers or recalled through oral history, almost every African American family has a story of an ancestor who simply disappeared, or had "come up missing," because of an altercation with whites, a dispute over land or wages, or a romantic misadventure. Black-owned newspapers, most famously the *Chicago Defender*, regularly cited lynching in encouraging readers to depart the South; so blatant was the problem that white employment recruiters from Northern industries, who went to Birmingham, Mobile, or Savannah to appeal for Black workers to emigrate for jobs in Northern mills, emphasized the greater safety from lynching in the North.

Stephen Crane's short story "The Knife" is collected in *Whilomville Stories* (1900) and is available at http://www.online-literature.com/crane /whilomville-stories/8/; Jacqueline Goldsby's eye-opening cultural history *A Spectacular Secret: Lynching in American Life and Literature* (Chicago: University of Chicago Press, 2006) contains extensive commentary on the lynching of Robert Lewis and the Stephen Crane novella *The Monster*. Information about the family of Stephen Crane and their lives in Port Jervis is in JoAnn Crane-Coriston, *Crane Chronicles: Over 300 Years of the Crane Family*. Privately compiled genealogical and historical articles created in 2000 are in the "Stephen Crane Folder" at the Minisink Valley Historical Society (MVHS).

The background of Port Jervis is drawn from the shelves of the MVHS; city directories, archival travel and historical brochures; Gerald M. Best, *Minisink Valley Express* (Newburgh, NY: Hungerford Press, 1956); Daniel J. Dwyer and Peter Osborne, *Our Town: Historic Port Jervis, 1907–2007* (Port Jervis, NY: Minisink Press, 2007); and interviews with former and current residents.

An account of the period's baseball craze is James E. Overmyer's "Baseball for the Insane: The Middletown State Homeopathic Hospital and Its 'Asylums,'" *NINE: A Journal of Baseball History and Culture* 19, no. 2 (Spring 2011). Walt Whitman mentions baseball in *Leaves of Grass* and hailed it often as "America's game." His comments cited are from Horace Traubel's *With Walt Whitman in Camden*, volume 4 (1889), available at Project Gutenberg.

3: A SHADOW CAST OVER MY SUNSHADE

Regarding the "Bully Acre," native Ralph Drake remembers Port Jervis generally as "a bully town, where a crowd would gang up on a person."

The descriptions of the movements of Lena McMahon and Philip Foley, the alleged assault at the riverside, and the immediate aftermath are drawn largely from *EG*, *TSU*, and *PJU* for June 3–10, 1892, as well as these same journals' coverage of the inquest (June 6–10).

4: "I AM NOT THE MAN"

The account of the capture and lynching of Robert Lewis is reported extensively in the local Port Jervis press, as well as in regional newspapers including the *Poughkeepsie News*, the *New York Sun*, the *Middletown Argus*, the *Delaware Gazette* (Delhi, NY), the *New-York Tribune*, and the *Honesdale (PA) Citizen*. Additional commentary is in the *Goshen Independent-Republican*, the *New York Times*, the *Middletown Daily Times*, and the *Orange County Press*.

Other details about the lynching and the regional reaction come from the "Robert Lewis Lynching File" at the MVHS; Kristopher B. Burrell, "Bob Lewis's Encounter with the 'Great Death': Port Jervis's Entrance into the United States of Lyncherdom," CUNY Academic Works, MVHS, 2003; and Bruce J. Friedman's "The Day of the Lynching," *SAGA: True Adventure for Men*, April 1955.

Whether African Americans and the Irish shared a belief in premonitions and spirits, or newspaper writers amused themselves by pretending as much, local Orange County papers occasionally mixed straight news with allusions to the supernatural. Several articles appeared over the years alluding to unseen forces using extreme weather as a means of reacting disapprovingly to the Lewis lynching. Many examples, such as the one quoted here, reported actual events while attempting to amuse white readers with what they presumed to be Black people's superstitious nature. Under the headline GHOST OF SI HARRIS, the piece (*PJG* 12/29/1884) reported: "A few days ago Si Harris, a well-known colored man of Middletown, died and since then the colored people of that village have been troubled in their mind by the appearance of his ghost. With no respect for his memory [they] gave a grand ball at the North Street rink on Christmas Eve and the roof fell in, the entire party barely escaping with their lives. Moreover, a ghastly, distorted face with fiery red eyes has been seen peering in at windows."

5: SOUTHERN METHODS OUTDONE

Reactions to the lynching cited are from the *Goshen Independent-Republican*, the *Middletown Argus*, the *New-York Tribune*, the *New York Recorder*, and the *Los Angeles Herald*. Additional regional commentary was cited from the *Monticello Watchman*, the *Honesdale (PA) Herald* and the *Honesdale Citizen*, the *Newburgh Daily Journal*, and the *Susquehanna (PA) Tri-Weekly Journal*. Countless U.S. papers gave an account and/or editorial comment about the Port Jervis lynching during the first and second weeks of June 1892.

The depiction of Robert Lewis's mother comes from the *Paterson (NJ) Daily News* and the *Paterson Morning Call*. The most detailed accounts of the funeral are in the local journals for June 4–6. The town's Black population did decline from 230 in 1880 to 125 in 1900, whether due to fear in the aftermath of the Lewis lynching or economic factors is unknown.

The published admonition to Lena to abide by her parents' advice ran in the *Orange County Press* on 6/14/1892.

Questions about Northern overconfidence in their ability to wield justice are raised in Jason Sokol's *All Eyes Are Upon Us: Race and Politics from Boston to Brooklyn* (New York: Basic Books, 2014); and Michael J. Pfeifer, *Rough Justice: Lynching and American Society, 1874–1947* (Urbana: University of Illinois Press, 2004).

In early August 1892, two months after the lynching of Robert Lewis, one of the most notorious murders in the nation's history occurred in Fall River, Massachusetts, where Lizzie Borden, thirty-two, was accused of killing her father and stepmother with a hatchet. The case—the Irish American small-town family, Lizzie's dislike for and resentment of her stepmother, and the many mysteries that, despite her acquittal, were never resolved—bear some resemblance to the Port Jervis saga.

The Newburgh lynching of Robert Mulliner on June 21, 1863, is reported in the *Newburgh Daily Telegraph* and the *Newburgh Journal*. See also the *Middletown Whig Press* for 7/1/1863. Related accounts of the New York City Draft Riots are in Herbert Asbury's classic *The Gangs of New York* (New York: Alfred A. Knopf, 1927); and James Weldon Johnson's *Black Manhattan*, originally published in New York, 1930 (reprint, New York: Da Capo Press, 1991). The account of Union troops of the 124th New York Regiment tossing a Black man in a blanket appears in the *Newburgh Daily Union* 4/14/1865.

A sensational mob killing of the era was the "Kelsey Outrage," the 1872 murder of a white man named Charles G. Kelsey in Huntington, Long Island, who had sent love poems to a young neighbor, Julia Smith, thus infuriating a competing suitor. A dozen disguised and hooded men seized Kelsey and coated him with layers of hot tar, feathers, and wool so thick he was believed to have succumbed from the torture. His bloody shirt, his necktie, and one of his boots were discovered later on a beach. The alleged leader of the mob soon after married Smith. See the *New York Times* 11/25/1872.

Historians of lynching in the South have noted their contagious potential—one lynching inspiring another, often at a location nearby. It is not unlikely, given the frequent press descriptions and mentions of lynching at the time, that the Port Jervis lynching was at least in part a response to the drumbeat of reports of Southern lynching that ran in the nation's newspapers from

1890 to 1892. It may be instructive to contrast the Robert Lewis lynching of 1892 with an 1885 incident in Port Jervis in which a Black stranger committed five separate assaults on adolescent white girls along North Orange Street in the course of a single afternoon. The girls reported being chased, pushed to the ground, choked, and threatened by "a coffee-colored [man], of burly frame, and a wicked countenance." Their tearful accounts led police to arrest thirty-year-old George Robinson, who said he had come to town a week earlier in search of work. He denied the charges against him but was identified by all five victims. It was thought his motive was robbery, although the *Gazette* ventured that "he may possibly have had a more hellish object in view." Convicted of assault in the third degree, he was sentenced to a year of hard labor. There is no record of the girls' families or anyone else urging extrajudicial punishment. See *PJG* 10/13/1885 and *TSU* 10/15/1885.

6: THE VIGOROUS PEN OF IDA B. WELLS

The Southern myth of Reconstruction—that it was a program of federal overreach that unjustly punished the defeated South—has often tended to obscure key historical aspects of the period, including the effect of the North's ultimate capitulation; Redemption, the South's quasi-religious crusade of resistance; and the eventual institutionalization of Jim Crow segregation, Black disenfranchisement, convict labor, and lynching. Of the vast literature on this sweeping subject, I found particularly helpful Heather Cox Richardson's *The Death of Reconstruction: Race, Labor, and Politics in the Post–Civil War North, 1865–1901* (Cambridge, MA: Harvard University Press, 2001); and Rayford W. Logan's indispensable *The Betrayal of the Negro: From Rutherford B. Hayes to Woodrow Wilson* (New York: Da Capo Press, 1997).

The best introduction to T. Thomas Fortune is his powerful writings in the *Age* from the last decades of the nineteenth century up until the founding of the NAACP. Much of it can be found in *T. Thomas Fortune: The Afro-American Agitator: A Collection of Writings*, edited by Shawn Leigh Alexander (Gainesville: University of Florida Press, 2008); see also Emma Lou Thornbrough, "The National Afro-American League 1887–1908," *Journal of Southern History* 27, no. 4 (November 1961).

Recognition of the life and work of Ida B. Wells has deservedly grown in recent years. A prolific writer, diarist, and public speaker, she has been the subject of several worthy biographies. I have relied on her autobiography, *Crusade for Justice*, edited by her daughter, Alfreda M. Duster (Chicago: University of Chicago Press, 1979); Angela D. Sims, *Ethical Complications of Lynching: Ida B. Wells's Interrogation of American Terror* (New York: Palgrave Macmillan, 2010); Paula J. Giddings, *A Sword Among Lions: Ida B. Wells and the Campaign Against Lynching* (New York: Amistead, 2008); and Linda O. McMurry, *To Keep the Waters Troubled: The Life of Ida B. Wells* (New York: Oxford University Press, 1999). An insightful introduction to her early career is *The Memphis Diary of Ida B. Wells*, edited by Miriam DeCosta-Willis (Boston: Beacon Press 1995).

Several of Wells's own publications are essential sources, including *Southern Horrors: Lynch Law in All Its Phases* (New York: New York Age Printing, 1892), and *A Red Record: Tabulated Statistics and Alleged Causes of Lynching in the United States, 1892–1893–1894* (Chicago: Donohue & Henneberry, 1895). A lesser-known title by Wells, but deeply informative, is *Mob Rule in New Orleans: Robert Charles and His Fight to the Death* (Chicago: self-published, 1900). Finally, a valuable compilation is Ida B. Wells, *The Light of Truth: Writings of an Anti-Lynching Crusader*, edited by Mia Bay (New York: Penguin Books, 2014).

Frances Willard's thoughts about the threat to Southern white families from Black men is in "The Race Problem: Miss Willard on the Political Puzzle of the South," *The Voice*, 10/23/1890.

Bryan Stevenson's remarks about the harmful effects of the "narrative of racial difference" can be found in Joe Helm, "The Author of 'Just Mercy' Says We've Made Talking About Race Political," *Washington Post*, 3/16/2021.

The anti-lynching movement's development and trajectory in the twentieth century is well documented in historical issues of the NAACP's official organ, *The Crisis*, the magazine founded in 1910 with W.E.B. Du Bois as editor. See as well Donald L. Grant's "The Development of the Anti-lynching Reform Movement in the United States, 1883–1932" (Ph.D. dissertation, University of Missouri, 1972). Also useful are books by the executive secretaries of the NAACP during the years of the fight for a federal anti-lynching law: James Weldon Johnson, *Along This Way: The Autobiography of James Weldon Johnson* (New York: Viking Press, 1933); and two titles by Walter White, *Rope and Faggot: A Biography of Judge Lynch* (New York: Alfred A. Knopf, 1929), and *A Man Called White* (New York: Viking Press, 1948). The origins of lynching as nonlethal summary justice during the American Revolution and early years of the Republic are explained in James Cutler's seminal *Lynch-Law: An Investigation into Lynching in the United States* (New York: Longmans, Green, 1905).

7: INQUEST

While there is no official transcript of the inquest extant, it was the custom of the press at the time to transcribe verbatim the arguments presented by lawyers, the statements of witnesses, and the coroner's rulings. For coverage of the coroner's inquest into the lynching of Robert Lewis, see the *PJG*, *EG*, *TSU*, and *PJU* for the period June 6–12, 1892. Another consolidated source for the history surrounding the lynching and the inquest is a series of articles by Peter Osborne, executive director of the MVHS, that appeared in the *Tri-States Gazette* 4/22/1985, 4/29/1985, 5/13/1985, and 6/24/1985.

8: THE AUTHOR OF MY MISFORTUNE

Detective Elwell's mention of John Westfall as someone who, like Robert Lewis, carried messages between Foley and Lena, introduces a man who appears to have been an outsize figure in Port Jervis but whose actual involvement in the McMahon-Foley relationship and the Lewis lynching are unsubstantiated. He was, like Lewis, a Black teamster, and lived with his mother, Emma, and white stepfather, William Franklin, at 6 West Street, directly across the street from the McMahons. John was born in 1861. His biological father, Ira Westfall, had been killed in the Civil War. In his twenties, John Westfall was a player-manager of the Red Stockings, the town's premier Black baseball team, and there are press mentions of someone bearing his name as a participant in a Black musical program at the opera house. Six years after the Lewis lynching, he enlisted and served in the Spanish-American War, but returned only to encounter trouble back home. Local newspapers record his involvement over the years in several altercations, and he died in 1900 after being struck in the head with a rock following a fight in a saloon. See *EG* 3/19/1887 and 6/25/1892, as well as *PJU* 5/6/1892 and *TSU* 11/28/1889, 2/1/1900, and 2/15/1900.

The disapproval of interracial romance was not (and has never been) a white viewpoint exclusively. Wells and T. Thomas Fortune were among the few Black civil rights figures to show their acceptance of Frederick Douglass's second marriage, in 1884, to Helen Pitts, a white educator and suffragist, and to be welcomed as guests at the couple's Washington home. "We are surprised at the amount of gush that intermarriage inspires in this country," Fortune protested. "It is in strict keeping with all the sophistries kept alive by the papers and the people about the colored people. It is the ceaseless but futile effort to show that the human nature of the Black man and the human nature of the white man differ in some indefinable way, when we all know that, essentially, human nature is, in fundamental respects, the same wherever mankind is found."

The discussion of the possibility that Lena McMahon falsely claimed a sexual assault, perhaps with the intent to feature Foley as her rescuer, would be incomplete without a mention of the literary soap opera *Thorns and Roses*, which began appearing in the *Tri-States Union* on Thursday, May 19, 1892, and had an installment on June 2, the day of the lynching, and whose plot and characters paralleled Lena's predicament. The story's young heroine, Agnes, lives with her father and stepmother, who is cold and unkind to the girl. As Agnes grows into a young woman, she begins to resist her stepmother's abuse, especially after she meets Will Hanly, a boy who comes to town to visit his relatives and takes an interest in her.

"At last I had found someone who did not think me wicked or homely, but who saw goodness in my character and beauty in my features," Agnes muses:

> I seemed to have suddenly emerged from a great shadow and to stand in the broad, dazzling light of a new existence. My stepmother was not at all pleased to have the elegant city lad show a preference for me, but she had no means of controlling his tastes, and so her only recourse was to vent her displeasure on my unlucky head, which she did at every opportunity.

Indignant at one of Agnes's displays of independence, the stepmother grabs her by the hair and cruelly holds her face near an open kitchen fire. The girl breaks free of the older woman and denounces her to her father, who is unwilling to take sides, and ultimately Agnes leaves home, vowing not to return. Out on the road alone at dusk—it is her first time away from home—she is assaulted by a drunken man:

> I understood very well that he would not hesitate to deal with me as his fiendish nature might suggest. I continued to struggle for my freedom, but it was useless. I sent up scream after scream, but I had no hope of anyone hearing me.

In the installment published on June 2, a hero on horseback comes along in the nick of time to drive the drunk ravager away, rescuing Agnes and her virtue. See *Thorns and Roses*, syndicated from A. N. Kellogg Newspaper Co., in *TSU* 5/19/1892 and 6/2/1892.

9: THE BLUNDERS OF VIRTUE

An essential source to study of the life and career of Stephen Crane is Stanley Wertheim and Paul Sorrentino, *The Crane Log: A Documentary Life of Stephen Crane* (New York: G. K. Hall, 1994). See also Paul Sorrentino, *Stephen Crane: A Life of Fire* (Cambridge, MA: Harvard University Press, 2014); Thomas Beer, *Stephen Crane: A Life in American Letters* (New York: Alfred A. Knopf, 1923); John Berryman, *Stephen Crane: A Critical Biography* (New York: Cooper Square Press, 2001; edition of original 1950 publication, revised by author 1962); and Linda H. Davis, *Badge of Courage: The Life of Stephen Crane* (Boston: Houghton Mifflin, 1998). I also made use of the Stephen Crane Papers in the Rare Book and Manuscript Library, Butler Library, Columbia University.

Stephen Crane's older sister Agnes, an award-winning scholar and later a teacher at Port Jervis's Mountain House School, died in 1884 of meningitis at age twenty-eight; two years later, in the kind of occupational mishap all too common in Port Jervis, his brother Luther was fatally injured while working as a railroad flagman; he was twenty-three.

The historian Larzer Ziff's quote about the youth who grew up in the wake of the Civil War is from *The American 1890s: Life and Times of a Lost Generation* (New York: Viking, 1966), p. 149. The notion of "flapdoodle" is introduced in Clifton Fadiman's introduction to *The Collected Writings of Ambrose Bierce* (New York: Citadel Press, 1946), p. xvi.

It has long been a mainstay of local lore in Port Jervis that a young Stephen Crane absorbed his preternatural feel for the experience of combat in the Civil War by listening to war stories shared by the veterans who gathered daily at the foot of the Civil War monument in Orange Square. More likely he encountered such men more generally while living in the town—from the fathers of friends and neighbors, in village saloons, and at the Farnum Building, where his brother William had his law office, including the barbershop on the Farnum Building's ground floor (which also makes a cameo appearance in *The Monster*). One individual who has been specifically credited with Stephen's interest in the subject was John B. Van Petten, a distinguished Civil War officer and New York State legislator who served as a history instructor at Claverack College, a military academy Crane attended in 1890. See Robert G. Eurich,

"The Wanderer's Home: How Port Jervis and Its Region Affected the Life and Work of Stephen Crane," 2015, PortJervisNY.com; see also Thomas F. O'Donnell, "John B. Van Petten, Stephen Crane's History Teacher," *American Literature* 27, no. 2 (May 1955).

The Willa Cather quotes that appear in this chapter are from her "When I Knew Stephen Crane," in *Stephen Crane: Bloom's Classic Critical Views* (New York: Infobase Publishing, 2009). A sketch of the financial pressures under which Crane labored is in Joseph Liebling, "The Dollars Damned Him," *New Yorker*, 8/5/1961.

"When Man Falls, a Crowd Gathers" was originally published in the *New York Press*, 12/2/1894.

For scholarly consideration of Crane's *The Monster*, see Jacqueline Goldsby, "The Drift of the Public Mind: Stephen Crane," in Goldsby, *Spectacular Secret*; Ralph Ellison, "Stephen Crane and the Mainstream of American Fiction," in Ellison, *Shadow and Act* (New York: Vintage, 1964); and Elaine Marshall, "Crane's 'The Monster' Seen in the Light of Robert Lewis's Lynching," *Nineteenth Century Literature* 51, no. 2 (September 1996).

Other analyses of *The Monster* cited here include James Nagel, "The Significance of Stephen Crane's 'The Monster,'" *American Literary Realism, 1870–1910* 31, no. 3 (Spring 1999); and David Greven, "Iterated Horrors: 'The Monster' and Manhood," in *Haunting Realities: Naturalist Gothic and American Realism*, edited by Monika Elbert and Wendy Ryden (Tuscaloosa: University of Alabama Press, 2017), p. 55.

Also of interest are Elizabeth Young, *Black Frankenstein: The Making of an American Metaphor* (New York: NYU Press, 2008), p. 105; John Cleman, "Blunders of Virtue: The Problem of Race in Stephen Crane's 'The Monster,'" *American Literary Realism* 34, no. 2 (Winter 2002); Stanley Wertheim, "Unraveling the Humanist: Stephen Crane and Ethnic Minorities," *American Literary Realism, 1870–1910* 30, no. 3 (Spring 1998); and Chester L. Wolford, *Stephen Crane: A Study of the Short Fiction* (Boston: Twayne, 1989).

For an account of the Dora Clark affair, see the *New York Journal* 9/20/1896, 10/11/1896, and 10/17/1896; and the *New York Sun* 10/16/1896 and 10/17/1896. See *The New York City Sketches of Stephen Crane*, edited by R. W. Stallman and E. R. Hagemann (New York: NYU Press, 1966), pp. 217–66; see also Christopher Benfey, "Dora," chapter 8 in *The Double Life of Stephen Crane* (New York: Alfred A. Knopf, 1992). Charles Becker, the corrupt police officer who arrested Clark and was the target of her complaint, was convicted in 1912 of having arranged the murder of a bookie named Herman Rosenthal and died in the electric chair at Sing Sing in 1915.

Several melodramas of the late Victorian era featured plots involving physical or facial mutilation. Possibly the best known was "East Lynne," based on an 1861 novel by Ellen Wood, which became a stage play that toured widely. An audience favorite known as a sure moneymaker at the box office, it was presented at George Lea's opera house in Port Jervis dozens of times. In the drama, a woman leaves her decent, hardworking husband and infant children for an aristocrat. She bears his illegitimate child but soon learns he is a cad who has no intention of marrying her. In a train accident, the child is killed and she is disfigured. She then returns, unrecognizable, to her original husband, who has moved on and has remarried, and who hires her as a nanny to the very children she had abandoned. She reveals her true identity on her deathbed and is forgiven. Americans were also familiar in the late nineteenth century with the story of London's Joseph Merrick, "the Elephant Man," and the P. T. Barnum Museum's forty-year-long-running attraction of "What Is It?" (William Henry Johnson, a Black man with a tapered cranium likely caused by microcephaly, and billed as a missing link). Later, Johnson became a novelty act called Zip the Pinhead at Coney Island and with Ringling Bros., alongside other sideshow stars such as Minnie Woolsey, a.k.a. "Koo-Koo the Bird Girl." The name "Henry Johnson" is that given the Black protagonist in *The Monster*.

Dialogue from *The Monster* is from Stephen Crane, *The Red Badge of Courage and Other Stories* (New York: Oxford University Press, 1998), pp. 168–69.

Stephen Crane's work generally speaks of his humane conviction that all people have inherent dignity and deserve respect, and in *The Monster* his main character is a Black man who behaves heroically and suffers unjust ostracization and disdain. But Crane's writings were not free of the casual racist attitudes of the times in which he lived. In *The Monster* he appears to use racist vocabulary self-consciously, as when he names the place where Henry Johnson's girlfriend Bella Farragut lives "Watermelon Alley," and has a minor white character refer to Johnson as a "coon," yet such allusions and terms were even then offensive and today deserve censure.

In 1959, a half century after the publication of *The Monster*, a film based on the story, *Face of Fire*, directed by Albert Band, was released, starring the actor James Whitmore. *Face of Fire* closely follows the original tale, with a key difference: the film's "Henry" is a white handyman (Whitmore) named

"Monk" Johnson. The fact that despite so essential a change the film works as a powerful allegory of intolerance and small-town claustrophobia is testament to Crane's faith that the tale was timeless and universal. Whitmore in 1951 had narrated the director John Huston's film adaptation of *The Red Badge of Courage*, which starred Audie Murphy. In 1964 Whitmore would play the lead in the movie based on John Howard Griffin's best-selling memoir *Black Like Me* (1961), based on the experiences of a white journalist who disguised himself to live as an unemployed Black man in the 1950s Jim Crow South.

Stephen Crane's letters to William Crane of October 29, 1897, and March 2, 1899, are in *Stephen Crane: Letters*, edited by R. W. Stallman and Lillian Gilkes (London: Peter Owen, 1960), p. 147. See also Helen R. Crane, "My Uncle, Stephen Crane," in *American Mercury* 31 (January 1934).

William Crane, as the executor of Stephen's estate, later sold the copyright to his brother's published and unpublished manuscripts to the publisher Alfred A. Knopf for five thousand dollars.

The phrase "guilty monster," in reference to Robert Lewis, is from *PJG* 6/11/1892: "Had the guilty monster been reserved for regular legal methods," Rector Evans of Grace Episcopal Church in Middletown observed at the time of the Lewis lynching, "he would have escaped with a punishment utterly inadequate to the appalling offense."

For the Harold Frederic incident and Gilder quote see Stephen Crane, *The Works of Stephen Crane*, volume 7 (Charlottesville: University of Virginia Press, 1969), p. xxix.

Julian Hawthorne's review of *The Monster* appears in *Book News*, 2/18/1900, pp. 337–38.

EPILOGUE

The account of Lena McMahon's stillborn child is covered in the *New York Sun* 8/2/1894, *PJU* 8/1/1894, *MDP* 8/2/1894, and *TSU* 8/9/1894. Most regional papers carried a version of the story. The quote from Florence Kadel is in the "Robert Lewis Lynching File" at the MVHS. I was unable to locate a marriage record for Lena McMahon and Will (or William) Dowling in census records or relevant state and city databases.

For background on the Chicago violence of 1919, see William M. Tuttle, Jr., "Contested Neighborhoods and Racial Violence: Prelude to the Chicago Riot of 1919," *Journal of Negro History* 55, no. 4 (October 1970). Descriptions of the lynching incidents in Coatesville and Duluth, the violence in Springfield, Illinois, and the founding of the NAACP may be found in Dray, *At the Hands of Persons Unknown*.

A historic account of the Ku Klux Klan in western Orange County is Chris Farlakas, "An Empire Built on Fear," *Middletown Times-Herald Record*, 3/6/1988. Information was also provided by Ralph Drake.

Sol Carley's difficulties in Goshen are detailed in the *Middletown Daily Press* 4/3/1893. Carley went on to serve as an alderman in the Port Jervis city government.

For later information about Rufus Perry, Jr., see the *Brooklyn Eagle* 5/15/1899. He remained active in local legal and political circles for many years, married Lillian S. Buchacher, and in 1912 converted to Judaism. In 1917 he was accused of having forged his father's name on a house deed shortly before the older man's death; he was cleared of criminal charges but was disbarred for five years. In 1927 he ran unsuccessfully for Kings County judge on the Socialist Party ticket. He died in 1930.

The quote about the possible spread of mobbism is in the *Americus (GA) Times-Recorder* 4/24/1899, cited in Goldsby, *Spectacular Secret*, p. 22.

Information regarding lynching and the death penalty is in Eliza Steelwater, *The Hangman's Knot: Lynching, Legal Execution, and America's Struggle with the Death Penalty* (New York: Basic Books, 2003).

In recent years Duluth has shown itself a singular model of accountability and remembrance for the 1920 lynching. A public memorial was unveiled near the site of the incident in 2003 that features bronze statues of the men who were put to death, and in June 2020, when the one hundredth anniversary of the lynching closely coincided with the Minneapolis police killing of George Floyd, Governor Tim Walz honored the victims by declaring June 15 "Elias Clayton, Elmer Jackson, and Isaac McGhie Commemoration Day." A powerful tribute was spoken at the 2003 opening of the memorial by Warren Read, a great-grandson of one of the leaders of the lynch mob. "It was a long held family secret," he told the gathering, "[until] its deeply buried shame was brought to the surface and unraveled. We will never know the destinies and legacies these men would have chosen for themselves if they had been allowed to make that choice. But I know this: their existence, however brief and cruelly interrupted, is forever woven into the fabric of my own life. My son will continue to be raised in an environment of tolerance, understanding and humility, now with ever more pertinence than before." See "The 1920 Duluth, Minnesota, Lynchings," on the website for America's Black Holocaust Museum (https://ABHMuseum.org/on-this-day-in-history).

On February 26, 1985, Port Jervians awoke to a headline in the *Tri-States Gazette*, O&R CREW RAZES SITE OF LYNCHING. According to the article, "the hanging tree came down Monday." The tree, "cut down by Orange and Rockland Utilities workers from in front of the Baptist Church [on East Main Street], is believed by many residents to be the one from which Bob Lewis was lynched in 1892."

ACKNOWLEDGMENTS

—————⟨∘∘∘⟩—————

Many friends and colleagues in New York City and in Orange County, New York, helped make this book possible. I wish to acknowledge the support and assistance of Ann Roche at the Goshen (NY) Public Library and Historical Society, the Goshen town historian Edward P. Conner, and Michelle P. Fighiomeni of the Orange County Historical Society, as well as the friendship of Sue Scher and Viktor and Alex Prizgintas from the OCHS. I also relied on the generous staff at the Port Jervis Free Library and the Middletown Thrall Library, NY.

A very special thank-you to Nancy Conod, director of the Minisink Valley Historical Society in Port Jervis, who welcomed me to the society's regular Thursday-afternoon roundtables, was a steadfast supporter of my research, and pointed me to numerous contacts and sources. Nancy also made possible the use of images from the society's photograph collection that appear in this book.

The Port Jervis native and chronicler Robert Eurich was an indispensable research companion and authority who guided me through the intricacies of the community's past. Robert's insights and exacting scholarship were shared in countless emails and conversations. From his published writing about Stephen Crane to his leadership in the Friends of Robert Lewis, he has been a valued friend and exemplary colleague.

I'd be remiss in not acknowledging the scholarship of several authors whose work has informed mine. Jacqueline Goldsby has written wisely and extensively on Stephen Crane and *The Monster*; and Daniel J. Dwyer, Betsy Krakowiak, Peter Osborne, and Matthew M. Osterberg have published informative illustrated books about Port Jervis and its people. Of the many good biographies of Stephen Crane available, one source deserving of special mention is *The Crane Log: A Documentary Life of Stephen Crane*, by Stanley Wertheim and Paul Sorrentino (1995). The work of the Hudson Valley historian A. J. Williams-Myers was instrumental in shaping my understanding of Black life in colonial and nineteenth-century New York, particularly *Long Hammering: Essays on the Forging of an African-American Presence in the Hudson River Valley to the Early Twentieth Century* (1994).

Several former and present Port Jervians contributed memories and shared knowledge of the town's history, including the veteran Orange County writer and editor Tom Leek and the journalists Jessica Cohen and Sharon Seigel, as well as Eddie and Mimi Keys, Ralph Drake, Calvin DeMond, Ed Westbrook, and Margaret Spring. A special thanks to the author-historian Mike Worden, formerly of the Port Jervis Police Department, for sharing insights about the history of local law enforcement; and also to Dr. Kristopher Burrell, professor of history at CUNY Hostos Community College (Bronx), whose 2003 paper on the lynching of Robert Lewis remains an invaluable touchstone. I also extend my gratitude to Elizabeth Witherow and her students at Port Jervis High School for welcoming me into their classroom, not once but twice. The partners at Bavoso, Plotsky & Onofry Attorneys at Law in Port Jervis graciously provided a tour of the William Crane House.

Generous financial support for research and travel came from a 2019–2020 faculty research grant from the New School in New York City. For encouragement and letters of support I am immensely grateful to Garnette Cadogan, Jelani Cobb, Jan Gross, Andrew Meier, and Scott Moyers. My Brooklyn friends Daniel Turbow and Jason Dubow answered legal queries and gave editorial advice, respectively. I wish to acknowledge many supportive friends and colleagues at the New York Institute for the Humanities, where I am a fellow, as well as in the Journalism + Design Department at Eugene Lang College, where I am honored to serve on the faculty.

This project would never have seen the light of day without the timely and thoughtful support of my agent, Stephanie Steiker. Thank you also to the artist Heather Drake for design of the map, the copy editor M. P. Klier, the editorial assistant Tara Sharma, the book designer Gretchen Achilles, the cover de-

ACKNOWLEDGMENTS

signer Thomas Colligan, and the talented Mindy Tucker for the author photograph. I can't say enough about the book's two main champions at Farrar, Straus and Giroux: Deborah Ghim, a brilliant collaborator whose contributions to the evolving manuscript were essential; and Eric Chinski, who saw the book's potential early on and whose vision shaped its focus, and whose efforts worked to greatly improve it along the way.

ILLUSTRATION CREDITS

———◦◦◦———

Many of the photographs that appear in the book are from the collection of the Minisink Valley Historical Society (MVHS), located at the Port Jervis Free Library. The several newspaper illustrations from 1892 appear to have been commissioned by the *New York Evening World*. They ran in numerous regional publications in the days and weeks following the lynching of Robert Lewis; the artist(s) are unknown.

Unless otherwise indicated, all images are in the public domain, including those not listed below. Photographer and illustrator names are given when known.

The cover image is from a print that appears on page 474 of *Picturesque America: The Land We Live In*, edited by William Cullen Bryant, and published by Appleton & Co., New York, 1874, volume 2.

Frontispiece map: Copyright © Heather Drake

Page 6   Woman in rowboat, Collection of the Minisink Valley Historical Society

Page 14   Headshot drawing of Miss Lena McMahon, commissioned by the *New York Evening World*

Page 21 Delaware House, Collection of the Minisink Valley Historical Society

Page 23 Headshot drawing of P. J. Foley, commissioned by the *New York Evening World*

Page 25 Erie Depot, Collection of the Minisink Valley Historical Society

Page 26 Headshot drawing of "Bob" Lewis, commissioned by the *New York Evening World*

Page 32 D&H Canal, Collection of the Minisink Valley Historical Society

Page 34 Rail workers, Collection of the Minisink Valley Historical Society

Page 50 Orange Square, Collection of the Minisink Valley Historical Society

Page 69 Headshot drawing of Sol Carley, commissioned by the *New York Evening World*

Page 86 Drawing of the lynching of Lewis, commissioned by the *New York Evening World*

Page 96 Front Street, Collection of the Minisink Valley Historical Society

Page 140 Photograph of Ida B. Wells, 1893, by Mary Garrity, via Wikimedia Commons

Page 155 East Main Street, Collection of the Minisink Valley Historical Society

Page 220 Lynching illustration, 1955, by Brendan Lynch. It accompanied the magazine article "The Day of the Lynching," by Bruce J. Friedman, which appeared in *SAGA: True Adventures for Men*, April 1955.

A Note About the Author

Philip Dray is the author of several books of American cultural and political history, including *At the Hands of Persons Unknown: The Lynching of Black America*, which won the Robert F. Kennedy Book Award and was a finalist for the Pulitzer Prize; *There Is Power in a Union: The Epic Story of Labor in America*; and *Capitol Men: The Epic Story of Reconstruction Through the Lives of the First Black Congressmen*. He is an adjunct professor in the Journalism + Design Department at Eugene Lang College of Liberal Arts. He lives in Brooklyn, New York.